A PORTRAIT OF THE *Auteur* AS FANBOY

A PORTRAIT OF THE *Auteur* AS FANBOY

The Construction of Authorship in Transmedia Franchises

ANASTASIA SALTER and MEL STANFILL

University Press of Mississippi / Jackson

The University Press of Mississippi is the scholarly publishing agency of
the Mississippi Institutions of Higher Learning: Alcorn State University,
Delta State University, Jackson State University, Mississippi State University,
Mississippi University for Women, Mississippi Valley State University,
University of Mississippi, and University of Southern Mississippi.

www.upress.state.ms.us

The University Press of Mississippi is a member
of the Association of University Presses.

Copyright © 2020 by University Press of Mississippi
All rights reserved

First printing 2020
∞

Library of Congress Cataloging-in-Publication Data

Names: Salter, Anastasia, 1984- author. | Stanfill, Mel, 1983- author.
Title: A portrait of the auteur as fanboy : the construction of authorship
   in transmedia franchises / Anastasia Salter, Mel Stanfill.
Description: Jackson: University Press of Mississippi, 2020. | Includes
   bibliographical references and index.
Identifiers: LCCN 2020017011 (print) | LCCN 2020017012 (ebook) | ISBN
9781496830463 (hardback) | ISBN 9781496830470 (trade paperback) | ISBN
9781496830487 (epub) | ISBN 9781496830494 (epub) | ISBN 9781496830500
(pdf) | ISBN 9781496830517 (pdf)
Subjects: LCSH: Moffat, Steven, 1961- | James, E. L. | Rowling, J. K. |
   Smith, Kevin, 1970- | Whedon, Joss, 1964- | Snyder, Zack, 1966- |
   Jenkins, Patty. | Coogler, Ryan, 1986- | Waititi, Taika. | Fans
(Persons) in mass media. | Motion picture producers and directors—Case
   studies.
Classification: LCC P96.F35 S25 2020 (print) | LCC P96.F35 (ebook) | DDC
   306.4/8—dc23
LC record available at https://lccn.loc.gov/2020017011
LC ebook record available at https://lccn.loc.gov/2020017012

British Library Cataloging-in-Publication Data available

Contents

Acknowledgments vii

Introduction: Fanboys to the Rescue! ix

1. Steven Moffat and Fandom's Favorite Troll 3

2. E L James and the Terrible, Horrible, No Good, Very Bad Fangirl 19

3. J. K. Rowling and the Auteur Who Lived 39

4. Kevin Smith and the "Independent" Fanboy 61

5. Joss Whedon and the Allegedly Feminist Fanboy Auteur 87

6. Zack Snyder and the Professional Toxic Fanboy 107

7. Patty Jenkins, Ryan Coogler, Taika Waititi, and the Fan Auteur as L'autre 125

Conclusion: Fanboy Backlash and the Futures of Fan Auteurs 147

Notes 163

Works Cited 167

Index 203

Acknowledgments

We begin these acknowledgments with the admission that they will inevitably be incomplete.

This book would likely not exist without our editor, Katie Keene, who encouraged an idea into a manuscript. We are also profoundly grateful for the thoughtful feedback of our peer reviewer, Suzanne Scott, whose fanboy auteur concept first set us on the path to examine all of these media-makers. We hope we've done it justice.

We have benefited in this work from feedback through our research communities: the Society for Cinema and Media Studies; the Association of Internet Researchers; the Electronic Literature Organization; the Modern Language Association; and the Children's Literature Association. Our friends and colleagues within those spaces who've supported this and other work are too numerous to list.

Thanks to our colleagues at the University of Central Florida, including the Texts & Technology faculty and the Games and Interactive Media faculty, Rudy McDaniel, Amy Giroux, Lynn Hepner, Lindsay Neuberger, Jason Burrell, and Jennifer Sandoval.

Mel would like to thank their fan studies community: Kristina Busse, Alexis Lothian, JSA Lowe, Katie Morrissey, Julie Levin Russo, Suzanne Scott (again), and Mark Stewart, as well as Anastasia's ambitious deadlines, which (though stressful) pushed us to finish this before we were hopelessly buried in new projects from our fan auteur figures.

Anastasia would like to thank the collaborators and friends from media and game studies who have influenced this work: Stuart Moulthrop, Aaron Reed, Matt Kirschenbaum, Bridget Blodgett, Dene Grigar, Amanda Cockrell, Kathi Inman Berens, Leonardo Flores, Carly Kocurek, and Jennifer de Winter, as well as Mel's patience with very rough drafts and constant Twitter updates on horrible things.

And a special thanks to the members of our academia support Twitter group chat, where both good and bad ideas are encouraged. Emily Johnson, John Murray, and Anne Sullivan have all heard far too many fandom rants as a result of this project. Additional thanks are due to Anne Sullivan for being our graphic designer on the fan auteur graph.

Introduction:
Fanboys to the Rescue!

Knowledge is knowing that the Author is dead.
Wisdom is knowing that's just his brand.

The past decade or so has brought a recurring trope of Fanboy to the Rescue—have no fear, it says, this revered franchise is being taken over by a writer, director, or producer who is a "fanboy." In this trope—which, following Suzanne Scott (2011a; 2012; 2013; 2019), we discuss in terms of the "fanboy auteur"—figures like Joss Whedon, Ronald D. Moore, and Eric Kripke are understood as "simultaneously one of 'us' and one of 'them'" (S. Scott 2012, 44). Increasingly, fan credentials on the part of writers, directors, and producers have come to be presented as a guarantee of quality media-making. This is, significantly, a strategy of marketing and branding; it is a claim, from the auteur himself or industry PR machines, that the presence of an auteur who is also a fan means the product is worth consuming.[1] Such claims that fan credentials guarantee quality are often contested, with fans and critics alike rejecting various auteur figures as the true leader of their respective franchises. That split, between assertions of fan and auteur status and acceptance (or not) of that status, is key to unravelling the fan auteur.

In *A Portrait of the Auteur as Fanboy*, we examine the contemporary ascendance of the fan auteur through a series of case studies. We consider both thoroughly mainstream fan auteur figures, such as Zack Snyder and Joss Whedon, as well as more offbeat ones, including Kevin Smith. We examine those who explicitly identify as fans of the source material they engage, like Steven Moffat, E L James, and Patty Jenkins, and those who don't but engage in fannish ways nonetheless, like Taika Waititi and J. K. Rowling. While examples of heirs apparent to transmedia franchises who are framed as fanboys are easy to come by, identification or branding as a "fangirl" is rare for women in similarly prominent roles. Cases of fangirls as auteurs are not only structurally less likely, given women's greater difficulty breaking into the industry in general, but particularly rare within the high-profile franchises that shape geek culture. We therefore particularly analyze how fanboy auteurs occupy a different cultural position than fangirls. Further, we grapple with the ways this narrative is disproportionately available to white creators, with fannish auteurs of color even less prevalent than white fangirl auteurs, both making visible the whiteness undergirding the positioning of figures like Snyder and Jenkins and considering how the position of auteurs of color like Waititi, Ryan Coogler, and Ava DuVernay diverges in key ways. Ultimately, this distinction of visibility and narratives, in which only the fandom of white men creators is easily trusted, reflects the broader challenges white women fans and fans of color face in geek culture.

In this introductory chapter, we first examine the recent rise of (selectively) constructing fans as ideal audiences. Then, we consider the broader "geek turn" in media because it is this industrial context that has given rise to fan auteurs. Ultimately, we argue that, while the rise of the fanboy auteur may be overdetermined by these two forces, the gendered form it takes tell us much about our contemporary understandings of authorship and creativity, geek media, and normative forms of fandom.

Fans as Ideal Audiences

While fans were formerly dismissed and stigmatized by default,[2] "from 1994 to 2009, the word 'fan' and practices traditionally associated with fans were increasingly integrated into media industry logics" (Stanfill 2019, 5). In fact, Scott (2011a, 79) contends that fanboys' "growing status as Hollywood tastemakers has granted them a modicum of mainstream respect." In this way, fans have become "a constituency that media companies both recognize and actively seek to incorporate, encourage, monetize, and manage" (Stanfill 2019, 5). That is, fans are a newly valued audience—and, at times, they're even seen as the ideal one.

However, this incorporation of fans into the norm is highly selective, contingent on complying with the role prescribed to them in the media marketplace: worshipful, not critical; merchandise-buying, not transformative work-making; and certainly of the "proper" demographic. As Scott (2019, 13) notes, "the fanboy's visibility is, in many cases, a byproduct of his compatibility with the more easily marketable or co-optable modes of fannish participation." Put differently, fans have been embraced because (and to the extent that) their forms of participation fit within industry's values. One key value is consumption. Industry's embrace of fandom, Mel Stanfill (2019, 89) argues, rests in part on "normalizing desire for licensed or franchised extensions of an object of fandom." Moreover, even in franchises with interactive transmedia components, "if we look at what these participatory audiences are understood and encouraged to do, it is limited: explore the story world, look for clues, move across platforms, and, above all, consume" (Stanfill 2019, 96). Additionally, Stanfill contends, industry also recruits both promotional labor, spreading the word about the object of fandom, and content labor, producing content that industry can wholesale incorporate into its products. This is another way that it's specifically the fans who are useful to industry that have been welcomed. At the broadest level, Stanfill (2019, 102) argues, the drive is toward "defining the true fan as affirmational rather than transformational—the one who enjoys the story as it is given rather than changing it."

Significantly, this selective normalization is also gendered. "Fanboys have historically been essentialized as desiring incorporation, being heavily invested in canon and authorial intent, and more likely to collect (trivia and merchandise) than create" (S. Scott 2011a, 81); fangirls are known for disinterest in or refusal of monetization, resistance to authorial control, and focus on touchy-feely subject matter. The position of the fanboy thus is compatible with an industry norm that "orients fans toward a vertical relationship between a user and a media product and beyond that the industry" that fangirls often do not have (Stanfill 2019, 179). Normalizing fanboys is also part of broader industry practices; Scott (2019, 51) notes that the contemporary embrace of the fanboy in fact "reinforces Hollywood's ongoing allegiance to sixteen- to thirty-four-year-old straight, white, cisgender men as their default target audience." Additionally, the fanboy is not just a member of a desired age and gender demographic but a participant in a specific, taste-based market: "because journalists and the media industry are actively constructing and courting 'fanboys' as a market segment, with 'fangirls' remaining an invisible (or worse, actively excluded) part of that 'fanboy' demographic, these terms matter" (S. Scott 2011b, 4), because "how fans participate, and whose participation is valued [. . .] is commonly determined by these labels" (S. Scott 2019, 5). This logic, then, is what constructs ComicCon's "male attendees as Hollywood's most prized focus group" (S. Scott 2011a, 60).

On the other hand, industry has not recruited and incorporated other fans and their characteristic practices in the same way. In fact, CW Network president Mark Pedowitz infamously sought to disavow the young women that are his network's bread and butter, saying he wanted to "put the final nail in the coffin (of the perception) that we're a young girls' network" (Berkshire 2015). Not only white women, but fans of color and GLBTQA+-identifying fans who offer readings of characters outside of cisgender heteronormativity, are not welcomed into industry's loving embrace in the same way as their masculine, white, and/or heterosexual counterparts. "Improper" fans are tolerated only when their gaze doesn't challenge (or disrupt) the dominant gaze of the straight, white fanboy; the Other is welcome as an object and silent viewer, but not as commentator and even less as auteur. Thus, as Kristina Busse (2013, 77) notes, "It is often the less explicitly fannish (or, one might argue, the less explicitly *female* fannish) elements that have been accepted by [the] mainstream." Henry Jenkins (2006a) and Busse (2013) have both described the ways that many men in the industry see an unbroken continuum between themselves as fans in their youth and what masculine sorts of fans do now, but feel no such kinship with feminized fandom. This articulation of particularly white men fans with industry goals therefore begins to shed light on the foregrounding of white men as fanboy auteurs.

The Geek Turn in Media

At the same time that (some) fans are being positioned as the new ideal consumer, there has been an upsurge of franchise media centered on geek culture. This has been anchored by the Marvel Cinematic Universe's eleven-year, twenty-three-film (and counting) juggernaut, but also includes reinvigorated DC, *Star Wars*, *Star Trek*, and more franchises. This geek turn has complex causes. First, in an era of rising production costs and greater demand for return on investment, drawing on familiar intellectual property is less risky than trying out untested concepts. As Derek Johnson (2013, 5) notes, "control of intellectual property resources became increasingly central to corporate strategy, both in their potential to be protected as proprietary and their potential to be widely shared and flexibly multiplied on a production level." This points to the next benefit; once an existing intellectual property is reinvigorated once, franchising further—including in transmedia ways—is safer still.

Within the drive to franchising, fannish intellectual properties have notable benefits. As greater availability of broadband made peer-to-peer transfer of even film-sized files increasingly easy by the end of the first decade of the twenty-first century, there was a move toward going big, including extensive use of 3D, to create an in-theatre experience that couldn't be replicated with a downloaded bootleg. This drove tentpole movies ever more toward spectacle, making speculative media's flying and explosions and alien landscapes all the more attractive. Moreover, "fantasy and science-fiction are world-dominant," and "the more richly imagined a storyworld is from the beginning, the more stories can be told about it, and the more discoveries it offers to the user. This is why world-dominated narratives present much better material for transmedia" (M.-L. Ryan 2015, 5)—and spinoffs and sequels and more.

Another key feature driving franchising of geeky, fannish properties is, tautologically enough, the fans. Benjamin Derhy Kurtz (2014, 1) argues that "efforts made by the industry to create these authentic universes in order to target involved audiences demonstrate how transmedia practices have impacted not only on storytelling processes, but the text—and the *brand*." That is, we get texts with a higher degree of the speculative world-building that creates a sense of "more" behind a story because that's what drives the engagement industry seeks. Thus, Johnson (2013, 6) argues that franchising "has developed as a logic of multiplied cultural production alongside an increasing industrial focus on niche groups and their social capacity for participation" such as the intensive consumption and promotional and content labor described by Stanfill (2019). Labor questions are key here—"it is the meaning-making activity of consumers that forms the basis of brand value" (Arvidsson 2005, 237), often side-by-side with "only minimally acknowledging the implicatedness of the activities of consumers" (Lury 2004, 12). Through the intersection of these industrial trends, then, geek franchise media have become ever more central to industry business models.

Enter the Fanboy Auteur

The fan auteur may be the inevitable outcome of the convergence of normalizing fandom with the geek turn in industry; certainly, as an emergent (and maybe ascendant) concept, it very much speaks to its moment. This is unsurprising given that, as Michel Foucault (1980) reminds us, authorship is a technology, a way to assign texts to an entity constructed by the laws and institutions of its context. That is, the fanboy auteur, while tied to a set of real people, is most interesting as a construct. We therefore need to ask "how authorship is contested, granted, claimed, denied, fought over, and/or shared" in this specific context (Gray 2013, 89). In particular, in Foucault's model, the author is a definable quality, coherence, style, and time period. Thus, for example, Gene Roddenberry is the "author" of *Star Trek*, and deviating from his particular quality, coherence, or style is "often described as a 'betrayal' of Roddenberry's personal vision, thereby displacing discomfort with the series content onto some other aspect of the production process (Paramount, the networks, other members of the production team)" (H. Jenkins 1995, 187); the belief in Roddenberry's quality, coherence, and style requires that divergences be someone else's doing.

As the Roddenberry example begins to suggest, what we have traditionally believed about the author is borderline mystical. As Derek Johnson and Jonathan Gray (2013, 3) note, authors are "imagined to stand at the gateway and threshold between creativity, innovation, wonder, and magic, and us—all of those experiencing and taking pleasure in media culture in the mundane space of everyday life." This liminality speaks to a quasi-supernatural status, similar to the slippage John Hartley (2013, 24) identifies, where authorship connects "mortal people to the divine attribute of immortality and the ability of nature to create anew." There is an "Author-God" (Barthes 1978, 146)—we make sense of authors in terms strikingly like those of religious or superhuman figures. With the rise of Romanticism from the late eighteenth through the mid-nineteenth centuries, the author came to be seen as the singular origin of artistic production from nothing more than his genius, and this singular creation from nothing is often used to authorize almost infinite power.[3] This produces a situation in which "the author as figure is often posited as the individual who created the product, he or she who can variously be thanked or blamed, and he or she who then 'gave' it to us" (D. Johnson and Gray 2013, 3), signaling this kind of belief in creation in a vacuum. Such reverence is why the author needed to die in Roland Barthes's (1978) poststructuralist formulation: to get out of the way so that power could be relocated in interpretation. However, like other forms of category membership, authorship is performative, created through repeated enactment.[4] Gray (2013, 105) notes that this authorial involvement is powered by their interactions: "authors can exert power over texts while writing them, but they can also exert as much if not more power when they interact with marketing teams, licensees, fans, and other clusters of authorship." Ultimately, "authorship is therefore about control, power, and the management of meaning and of people as much as it is about creativity and innovation" (D. Johnson and Gray 2013, 4).

If authorship is a construct, the author is especially constructed in film and television, where a singular author is inherently specious given the army of workers required to produce such texts. What media authors do, are, and mean is a question that has an important history of study.[5] With film and television in particular, "to credit the director with authorial status requires an odd and indefensible amnesia towards the scriptwriter, the cinematographer, the actors, the editor, and countless other individuals and teams" (Gray 2013, 93). The fiction of singularity, however, is powerful. We tend to, as *Star Trek* fans do, "acknowledge the collaborative aspects of the production process while ascribing primary inspiration to a single author, [such as] Roddenberry, and his 'very personal' philosophy" (H. Jenkins 1995, 186). The degree to which the processes of media-making have to be ignored to invent the author figure underscores how deep-seated the belief in authors is. The inherent contradictions of media authorship are intensified in the transmedia franchise, which is beyond the scope of any one controlling force many times over. As Scott (2012, 43) notes, "Transmedia stories disintegrate the author figure, as artists in different media collaboratively create the transmedia text, but, in order to assure audiences that someone is overseeing the transmedia text's expansion and creating meaningful connections between texts, the author must ultimately be restored and their significance reaffirmed." The quality, coherence, and style of such transmediated texts require positing an author.

Through this projection of qualities, it becomes clear how media authors are brands (Gray 2010). As Johnson and Gray (2013, 2) argue, "to see press or marketing for almost any item of media today without seeing the invocation of at least one author figure is rare," and it's specifically this marketing angle that reveals the brand status. The use of authors is a "promotional factor" (S. Scott 2012, 44). However, it's not only economically that authors are "constructed by the industry, creative personnel, and viewers alike as signifiers of value" (Gray 2010, 136)—rather, it includes "affective value" (S. Scott 2012, 45). Auteurs who achieve this type of brand "become paratexts in their own right" (Gray 2010, 136), often eclipsing the contributions of others involved in the media product and drawing fans into the metanarrative of their body of work. These auteurs thus become "an inter- or paratextual framing device, a matrix of other (inter)texts that served as a paratextual role in directing interpretation" (Gray 2010, 127). This, of course, is precisely why it is "film and television, which much more visibly depend on collaborative authorship," which are "overall less invested in killing their auteurs even as poststructuralism affected the conceptualization of filmic creators" (Busse 2017, 26). Media branding both relies on and reinforces the idea that fragmented, multiauthored, corporate productions are somehow unified and coherent: it needs "the construction of a unified author figure to serve as a creative and textual coordinator. There are practical and promotional factors motivating this consolidation, but concerns arise when a unified author figure results in an attempt to unify and regulate the audience's interpretations of the text" (S. Scott 2012, 44). Although those who, like Scott, champion fan interpretive freedom might be concerned, as Barthes argued, unifying and regulating interpretation is precisely what authors do. Certainly, the meaning the author can provide the text is valuable: franchises with a connected, invested auteur can secure the legitimacy of spinoffs and build that affective value of the auteur's "stamp of approval" (S. Scott 2012, 45).

If the fan auteur as a social position is a product of the centering of fans as ideal audiences and the geek turn, then, the basic contours of the concept reflect this. Fan status becomes a valuable self-branding tool for some media production staff. Here we think about the fan auteur as particularly positioned along two axes: their position as transformational or affirmational (obsession_inc 2009) and the extent to which they are primarily known for being fans of the media they author. The transformative/affirmative divide, which we might think of as the *fan* auteur axis, is deeply gendered (obsession_inc 2009). Affirmational fans are disproportionately men and affirm the source text: collecting both objects and knowledge and prioritizing textual fidelity and authorial intent. Transformational fans are disproportionately women, and they rework a source text—often so that it serves perspectives originally marginalized, which makes transformation also a tactic of fans of color (Seymour 2018; Warner 2015b). Thus, E L James is highly transformative, but so is Ryan Coogler, and the white men tend to cluster together as affirmational (see Figure 1). On the other axis—which we might think of the fan *auteur* axis—is the extent to which the figure's creative work is tied to their own personal fandom. J. K. Rowling is not a fan of Harry Potter and Taika Waititi is not a fan of Thor, but Zack Snyder and Steven Moffat are legendarily fannish of precisely the properties they make.

Understanding the fan auteur as having both a fan axis and an auteur axis helps make sense of the tension in the concept between thinking of authors as the origin of texts, as creative geniuses operating in isolation, as sometimes-godlike authority figures, and/or as the final determinant of a text's meaning and the apparent leveling of the hierarchy in the narrative of the fanboy auteur as "just like you." Accordingly, these are figures "whose status as 'visionaries' is alternately tempered and bolstered by their self-identification as fans" (S. Scott 2013, 440). They are liminal (S. Scott 2012; 2013), both "one of 'us' and one of 'them,' consumer and producer" (S. Scott 2012, 44). In particular, the fanboy auteur is inherently bilingual, exalted for "his perceived ability to speak the promotional language of both visionary auteur and faithful fanboy" (S. Scott 2013, 440).

This fan/auteur translation runs both ways. On the one hand, fan auteurs bring fan knowledge to their work. There is, in particular, something gendered about this: the fannish auteur can

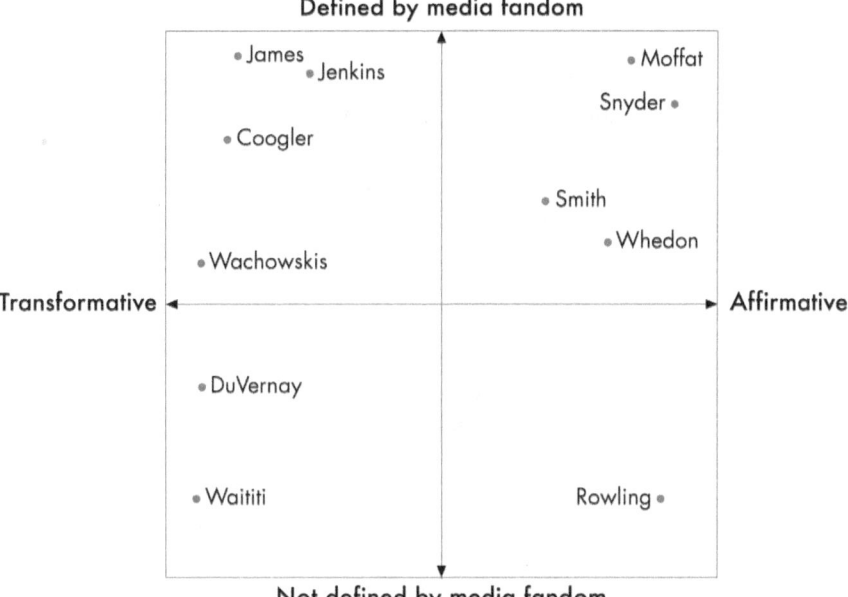

Figure 1. Our proposed taxonomy of fanboy authorship.

evade the feminizing stigma of fandom and paternalistic arrogance of the auteur simultaneously. Accordingly, while the fanboy auteur's reverential approach to genre or source text could be viewed as an inherently more "passive" (or, in essentialist terms, "feminine") creative approach than auteur theory has previously afforded, it is precisely this reverential quality that makes them ideal contemporary auteurs to mobilize an active fan base. (S. Scott 2013, 441)

That is, the fanboy auteur's subservience to the canon is what enables him to become its new master and get buy-in from fandom writ large. In this way, the fanboy auteur can be "nostalgic for the object of his youth and fannishly invested in protecting the core qualities of the property" (S. Scott 2013, 444) at the same time that he, unlike the fans complaining about Viacom betraying Roddenberry, is positioned to do just that. The fanboy auteur can thus be the perfect solution to the transmedia franchise that outlives (whether chronologically or contractually) the auteur, as he promises both fidelity and vision, recruiting fan trust.

On the other hand, fan auteurs bring auteurship back to fandom through cultivating relationships with fans, particularly on social media. Having "knowledge of niche and cult properties, and the ability to cultivate relationships with the fan communities that surround those properties" (S. Scott 2013, 456), is a key part of fan auteur engagement, as we'll see in the coming chapters. Social media and the web have played a strong role in amplifying the voices of these auteur figures even as they are often otherwise invisible outside the credits of their products themselves: social platforms allow auteurs "to add their voice to the audience's understanding of their products, and thus [they] are increasingly able to construct themselves as authors" (Gray 2010, 108). This assertion of control is particularly interesting alongside the fact that one key characteristic of the fanboy auteur is that he is "more 'approachable'" (S. Scott 2013, 440), more like the (ideal) audience. If, as Busse (2017, 37) argues, "when we look at fans, we get a glimpse at the current state of the author, encompassing the question of ownership of texts; authorial control over ideas; shared world building; and readerly collaboration," the converse is also true; as fans tell us about the author, so too the author also tells us about fans. Ultimately, the fan auteur sits at the intersection of a variety of shifts in media production and fandom, and can tell us much about both.

About this Book

This book is organized as a series of interrelated case studies about fan auteur figures. To make sense of how they are culturally understood, we turned to press coverage as a source that both reflects mainstream ideas and helps shape cultural common sense. For each of our cases, we searched online newspaper database LexisNexis for the auteur's name and the word "fan." These searches returned between 950 and 1,000 stories for each figure; the data was then cleaned by removing duplicate stories and those that did not address the auteurs' fannishness. This body of text about each figure was then read in its entirety, noting emergent common themes both in how others describe them and in how they describe themselves. This foundation of systematic collection was supplemented with internet news sources, tweets, and, in some cases, analyses of the auteurs' works—though, as we are interested in the auteurs as figures, this was minimal. Our analytic approach was discourse analysis. This is an interpretive strategy that pays careful attention to what people say about the object of analysis, how they say it, and the ways that language is an exercise of power. In this way, we investigate what the proliferating cultural concept of the fan auteur means in the contemporary era through tracing its discursive contours.

Chapter 1, "Steven Moffat and Fandom's Favorite Troll," interrogates how Moffat both avows and disavows fandom. On the one hand, Moffat-as-fanboy is both the author of his shows and his own ideal audience as he performs and expects broad and deep knowledge of the text's history. On the other, there is tension with actual fans—as opposed to the imagined fans who are just like himself—and he rejects those he thinks are not being fans the right way. We then explore Moffat's auteur side, which we argue is characterized by insistence on doing things his way, with his past as a continuity- and detail-obsessed curatorial fanboy showing through in sometimes overly complex stories and a dictatorial approach that both leverages knowing all of *Doctor Who* and Arthur Conan Doyle and abides by it only when it suits him. Indeed, we contend that the most standout characteristic of Moffat's brand may well be being abrasive to anyone and everyone. We finish the chapter by considering the substantial concerns his work raises around inclusion—or lack thereof.

In the second chapter, "E L James and the Terrible, Horrible, No Good, Very Bad Fangirl," we examine the double standard between fanboys and fangirls: fanboys redeem fandom and fangirls are contaminated by it; fanboys take the obvious step to professionalize while fangirls are sellouts; fanboys make bold choices with their uncompromising creative visions while fangirls are control freaks who break all the rules. Fangirl auteurs never quite get to be auteurs. Moreover, we argue that not only is James not really allowed to be an auteur, but she's something of a punching bag, routinely targeted with gleeful vitriol for every decision, including by large groups of people piling on via Twitter. A substantial part of James's position, we contend, comes because *Fifty Shades* sits at the intersection of fanfiction, romance, and erotica, all of which are marginalized both as low-quality and because they deal with sex; this leads to its success being either explained away by or blamed on technology, under the assumption that neither the sex nor the writing can possibly be appealing. Ultimately, we argue, *Fifty Shades* disrupts norms in some ways and upholds them in other, possibly more dangerous ones.

In Chapter 3, "J. K. Rowling and The Auteur Who Lived," we begin with a history of Rowling's interactions with fandom; not only was Harry Potter one of the first truly massive internet-based fandoms, but Rowling has been famously open to engaging with her fans on the internet, from JKRowling.com to Pottermore to Twitter. We argue that Rowling's auteur persona demonstrates a drive to be at the center of the fan experience, between providing a never-ending drip-feed of canon, moving fans into her proprietary Pottermore space, and actively seeking fan attention. In fact, by telling her fans how to interpret and continually re-centering herself, we contend, Rowling models proper fandom as obedient to the author, one vital sense in which she is a fangirl auteur. We then address the ways Rowling's auteur status has proved flexible, expanded to *The Cursed Child* and *Fantastic Beasts and Where to Find Them*, despite her relatively minor involvement. However, we argue, controversy around racism and homophobia in these texts has perhaps once and for all dispelled the illusion of her authorship as progressive. We conclude by examining the ways that Rowling's recent Twitter usage crystallizes her overall auteur persona: a need to be at the center of her fan base's attention and the arbiter of all meaning in her texts.

Chapter 4, "Kevin Smith and the 'Independent' Fanboy," begins by discussing Smith's "View Askewniverse," which we view as a series of films both by a fanboy and featuring fanboy characters. We then examine the ways Smith has leveraged his fandom to build his career, both in the sense of the body of people who follow him, especially on his website discussion board, and in the sense of parlaying his geek credibility into a transmedia career as a professional fanboy through projects such as reality show *Comic Book Men*, the *SModcast* podcast, and authoring comic books. However, while Smith's fannishness is unimpeachable, his auteurishness is less well established, and he has not often been given the reins of film franchises, largely because he lacks the necessary reverence. The chapter also explores the ways Smith can never quite escape the conservatism of mainstream fanboy identity even as he expands his reach as an auteur. We end with the argument that it is the presence of Smith himself—whether visual, audio, or physical—that serves as the guarantor of Smithian quality.

In the fifth chapter, "Joss Whedon and the Allegedly Feminist Fanboy," we first interrogate the role of being a feminist in Whedon's branding, arguing that, while he successfully branded himself as feminist for two decades, closer analysis and subsequent revelations demonstrate this to be far more style than substance. Whedon's branding as a fanboy, by contrast, is more robust and permeates his public persona, from his casual fashion to his texts to actively participating in his own and other fandoms—though we note that it is in tension with his auteur status. Finally, we argue that Whedon actively leverages the illusion of intimacy enabled by Twitter and fan site Whedonesque to extract the unpaid fan labor that has powered his career.

In Chapter 6, "Zack Snyder and the Professional Toxic Fanboy," we begin by interrogating Snyder's aspirations to auteur status, arguing that they are in tension with his one-note style that always goes darker, grittier, and more violent, no matter what. Next, we contend that Snyder's self-aggrandizement and unwillingness to move beyond his comfort zone join with his strong attachment to a toxic masculinity rooted in extreme violence and his routine misogyny to make him the archetypical toxic fanboy. Despite, or perhaps because of, these characteristics, Snyder has a powerfully invested following, which he engages and cultivates through social media, rendering him a highly polarizing figure who remains at the center of discourse even years after leaving a franchise behind.

Chapter 7, "Patty Jenkins, Ryan Coogler, Taika Waititi, and the Fan Auteur as L'autre," first considers how these auteurs are similar to the norm, deploying the origin story of being fans since their youth. Next, we interrogate how Jenkins and Coogler, in particular, are the subject of a mountain of superlatives, nearly always framed as being the most, the best, or the first at something. The chapter then explores the ways the auteur as Other tends to be held responsible for the continued success of their entire category. Fourth, we parse out the uneven availability of auteurist opportunity for such figures, despite their successes. Finally, we investigate how representation in these films is presented as tightly interwoven with the identities of the auteurs.

In the conclusion, we contrast two cases of fangirl auteurs—the Wachowski sisters and Ava DuVernay—with the rise of fan backlash. On the one hand, we argue, media-makers can no longer opt out of the spaces and patterns of fan engagement. This brings a great deal of risk as campaigns for hiring and firing—sincere or otherwise—are an increasingly prevalent tactic in fandoms and the culture wars alike. On the other hand, DuVernay and the Wachowski sisters are interesting cases whose established auteur status enabled them to move into fandom. The Wachowskis have historically avoided the spotlight and have embraced outsiderhood only recently. DuVernay takes an overtly political approach to being a public figure, directly naming systems of inequality and the media industry's issues as well as making a strong use of Twitter as a platform. We end with a consideration of some other possible futures: proliferating fannish media can allow a wider variety of auteurs, but tentpole properties continue to be haunted by the specter of mainstream fan rage.

A PORTRAIT OF THE *Auteur* AS FANBOY

1

Steven Moffat and Fandom's Favorite Troll

> I'm going to be honest and fans may hate me for it but they have to remember that I am a fan myself. A proper list-making-borderline-autistic fan. I am head mingmong. I'm King Ming. But I don't do anything for the fans. I honestly don't think that the fans want me to do anything for them. Except maybe for the odd little line now and then. Some little thing somewhere. Russell does that. I do that. We all do that. And only you will get it. But we don't do anything for the fans. There aren't enough fans. There's the whole audience. There are fans but there's millions of an audience. (Soon 2008)

Steven Moffat is, at first glance, very different from some of the other auteurs profiled here. His work is primarily located in Britain and less integrated in the US media landscape, but is nonetheless decidedly influential. The properties he leads are centered in television, and unlike Joss Whedon, he hasn't made the leap to film with its correspondingly larger potential audiences and budgets. However, he is perhaps the quintessential example of a fanboy auteur, having a high degree of both making media of which he's specifically a fan and taking a textual-fidelity affirmational approach. Moffat is also an inheritor of *Doctor Who*, a franchise that has been increasingly centered on its devoted audience since its return in 2005. In fact, Matt Hills (2006, 103, 107) argues that Moffat shows "how fans can become celebrities by virtue of moving across into the category of media professionals/producers working on the very text which they are fans of," as one of "an elite group of fans who have written for and produced the 2005 BBC Wales-produced" *Doctor Who*. Hills (2006, 111) further notes that the existence of this group "is partly a product of *Doctor Who* fans having grown up with the show they love, being inspired by it to work in the media industry," and subsequently being in a position to work on Doctor Who when it was reinvigorated. While Moffat is part of a larger group of fans-turned-media-makers, he in particular has emerged as an auteur figure. Hills (2010) argues that Moffat's auteurization started in the Russell T. Davies era of *Doctor Who*, when common fannish practices of finding out everything about production led them to learn about the other figures involved with the show, including Moffat, and their distinctive creative characteristics. However, it has also been reinforced by Moffat himself through practices of self-praise, tight control, and insistence on his vision at all costs. Moreover, Moffat functions particularly clearly as a brand; as Louisa Stein and Kristina Busse (2014) argue, his involvement with *Doctor Who* brought that cult audience to *Sherlock* out of the gate. In this way, Moffat crystallizes the fan auteur in particularly clear form.

In this chapter, through an analysis of more than 950 news stories, we interrogate how Moffat both avows and disavows fandom. On the one hand, Moffat-as-fanboy is both the author of the show and his own ideal audience, both performing and expecting broad and deep knowledge of the text's history. On the other hand, he has tension with actual fans—as opposed to the imagined fans who are just like himself—and rejects those he thinks are being fans the wrong way. We then explore Moffat's auteur side, characterized by insistence on doing things his way; his past as a continuity- and detail-obsessed curatorial fanboy shows through in sometimes overly complex stories and a dictatorial approach that at once leverages knowing all of Who and Doyle and abides by it only when it suits him. Indeed, we contend that the most salient characteristic of Moffat's brand may well be being abrasive to anyone and everyone. We finish the chapter by considering the substantial concerns his work raises around inclusion—or lack thereof.

Is He or Isn't He? Avowing and Disavowing Fandom

Moffat's status as someone whose media-making is bound up in his own fandom is well known. Notably, he turned down a three-movie deal with Steven Spielberg to make films based on the comic book character Tintin—considerably higher profile—to focus on *Doctor Who* instead. In an article describing Moffat as "fandom's evil overlord," a fan and critic notes that he "writes fanfiction for a living":

> While *Doctor Who* is something of a cult favorite in the U.S. and overseas, it's mainstream family viewing in the U.K. Three generations have grown up with the show, and *Doctor Who* has now reached the point where most of its cast and crew are lifelong fans of the show. Basically, its writers are filming fanfic of a TV series they watched as kids. And what's *Sherlock* if not a modern-era fanfic of the Sherlock Holmes stories? (Baker-Whitelaw 2013)

However, despite this diagnosis, scholarly analysis differs on whether Moffat is more fan or auteur—perhaps because he himself both avows and disavows fandom. Ellen Harrington (2014, 79) argues of Moffat and his *Sherlock* collaborator Mark Gatiss that "their status as fans legitimizes their connection with these characters, allowing them to pursue Sherlock Holmes and reinvent him, all the while unabashedly following Conan Doyle's detective formula and including the sort of nostalgic details that reward fans of the original series." That is, because they are fans, they can stick quite closely to the "formula" without shame. Hills (2014, 35), by contrast, contends that there is no such full-force embrace of fannishness, as "distinctions of media professionalism need to be conserved and defended, such that showrunners are always positioned as more than just fans." Hills (2014) calls this approach "heretical fidelity": Moffat and Gatiss emphasize how faithful they are, but also play up their authorial agency to make different choices. Breaking with faithfulness is key because "if production discourse was one-dimensionally about faithfulness to Sherlockians and the Canon then *Sherlock* would move too close to the realm of fanfiction, lacking markers of professionalized and valorized official authorship" (Hills 2014, 35–36). Indeed, this need to both embrace and distance himself from fandom is visible across Moffat's career.

On the one hand, Moffat performs the quintessential fanboy. Echoing the common fannish approach of authority through length of tenure, he stakes a claim to have consumed the media text from its inception: "A dedicated 'Whovian,' he claims to remember watching the first Doctor, William Hartnell, who quit the Tardis when Moffat was four" (Burrell 2011). Moreover, he compounds this hipsterism with an insistence on how much harder he had it back in the day: "That form of fandom was much more active than it is now. . . . You only had what you could create yourself. There was no Who on TV. We had nothing" (Colgan 2014). This, too, is a bid for authority through authenticity. Further, he makes a point to stake out his broad and deep knowledge of the text's history. He certainly does so with *Doctor Who*:

"Steven Moffat has joked he would triumph over [*Who* actor and fan] Peter Capaldi in a battle of who is most knowledgeable about the hit show," saying, "His love, we can compete on that, just let it be understood. But in a face-off, in a head-tohead [*sic*], he's nowhere bloody close.... I'm ahead on knowledge. I am. Honestly" (*Liverpool Echo* 2015). Moffat similarly frames himself as even more knowledgeable than Arthur Conan Doyle himself:

> We were also trying to work out an obscure point of continuity that Doyle gets wrong.... In his first story Watson has a wound in his shoulder and in this second story it's transferred to his leg. So we came up with the idea it was actually psychosomatic. Therefore he was in therapy. We were just to trying to fix an incredibly obscure continuity error. That's how it started. We get paid for this. (Burgess 2013)

Moffat's fannishness is particularly clear here in his excitement that they can be obsessed for a living, but also in his deployment of encyclopedic knowledge.

Moffat brings his fandom perspective to bear repeatedly, as when, in an interview following the leaking of unfinished episodes, he admitted that he too would have looked when he was a fan:

> To be honest, I don't blame the guys who went and looked, cos I would've. I would've as a fan. It would have ruined it for me but a new Doctor? I'd have had to go and have a look. They have at least learned something, which is what episodes look like when we sign off on them, like *Into The Dalek*, it just looks ridiculous! It's some people running around some rooms that have an extraordinary fixation with green curtains. It's nothing at all! (Mellor 2014)

This fannishness also spills into production. Sometimes, the collapse of the self as fan auteur and "the fans" is overt, as when Moffat says, "You're writing what you would want to watch. You are writing your personal obsessions and hoping that people will share them" (S. Heyman 2014). At other times, it is more indirect. As Hills (2014, 34) notes, the discussion in commentary tracks centers on "Moffat and Gatiss' own status as 'Sherlock Holmes fanboys,' with this gendered identity being (problematically) extended to those assumed to be listening to the DVD commentary." Many incidents thus demonstrate that Moffat-as-fanboy both is the author of the show and serves as his own target audience.

At the same time, however, Moffat disavows fandom. In one interview about *Sherlock*, he said, "Once we decided to make it modern day it all fell into place. I am a total *Sherlock* fan but I do think on some adaptations the attention to period detail gets in way of the action" (Batley 2010). This "I'm a fan, but" is exactly the intersection of claiming and disavowing that Moffat occupies. He also projects it onto others: "Showrunner Steven Moffat said he is not worried about signing up self-confessed fan of the show Capaldi to the starring role. 'He can absolutely separate the two things. I mean, he can separate the job he's doing from the fact he's a fan of it'" (Leigh 2013). Although the comment is overtly about Capaldi, one cannot help feeling that Moffat is also talking about himself here.

There is even greater tension between Moffat and actual fans as opposed to the imagined fans who are just like himself. Joss Whedon's and Kevin Smith's engagement in fan forums over the course of many years created a stronger bond with their audiences; Moffat, by contrast, used his forum and Twitter posts not only to share with his fans but to criticize them. While the original posts are no longer available, fans have archived quotes and screen captures from some of Moffat's more memorable engagements on the Gallifrey One forums. For example, in response to discussions of whether Rose and the Doctor had sex raised by "The Doctor Dances," Moffat wrote:

> I say, no I didn't! The whole scene was about the fact they WEREN'T at it—indeed, it was the Doctor being slightly hurt that Rose hadn't even considered him in that light.
>
> There's precious little evidence they ever got up to anything, I'd have said—that it doesn't stop it being a love story, of course (it clearly was) but unrequited surely? Oh, it's all sex with you lot, isn't it? And when the writer of Coupling says you're banging on about sex too much, it's time to start listening. (lolcoholic 2008)

This response exemplifies Moffat's refusal to listen to fans when they disagree with him—it's total and does not entertain the possibility that the fan interpretation has any basis in his text. The tendency was even more dramatically displayed when he deleted his Twitter account: "Fans first noticed that the account had gone missing in the wee hours last night when they attempted to reference Moffat's account in their tweets about the latest episode, 'Dinosaurs on a Spaceship.' Speculation abounded that Moffat deleted the account because of heaps of negative commentary from fans" (Byrne-Cristiano 2012). While often such deletions are framed as resulting from fans who harass someone off the platform, Moffat's brand is such that what makes sense to this journalist is that he was fleeing from criticism.

When speaking about fans rather than engaging, the contours of Moffat's disavowal emerge even more clearly. His unwillingness to engage with fans, on display with the Twitter deletion, is a recurring theme. In a mild version, he simply denies a role for engagement. Thus, while he acknowledged the fan fiction and fan video explaining *Sherlock*'s survival of a fall at the end of Series 2, he denied that his own work was in dialogue with them: "We don't look. We can't look. I'm running two shows that have got very large and very vocal fandoms. I wouldn't admit it to myself if I had to look at it. No, the meta feel comes from the original Sherlock Holmes, the original stories" (Cornet 2014). His refusal to look here is overdetermined—he's too busy, but also it would be shameful. His response seems almost inherently contradictory to his performed identity as a previous respondent to fanboys on forums, but does help re-secure the lone genius model of the author. More dramatically, he has actually argued against engaging fans as opposed to the broad audience:

> How do you tell really? You only hear from the die-hard fans, and they form a tiny untypical fraction of the audience. Far as I can tell, it's [*Coupling*] been pretty good. Some very good stuff in the press. A lot of Richard Coyle fans frothing away [after he left the show], of course, like I assassinated him or something, which is fantastically funny and reason enough alone for the internet to have been invented. But leaving aside that inevitable portion of the audience who should only watch television with a handy rag to chew, we generally seem to win people over by the end. The general audience—the vast majority who watch it if it's on and forget about it afterwards—barely seem to have noticed the change. (Author 2005)

While undeniably fans are only a tiny fraction of any mass media audience, they are a particularly active and loyal one that provide a great deal of free labor (Stanfill 2019). Disavowing them entirely was relatively common in 2005, but Moffat held much the same attitude nearly a decade later: "I love *Doctor Who* fans . . . and I am a *Doctor Who* fan, but the show is not targeted at them" (A. Harrison 2013). This statement of "it's not for you" is at odds with the demand implicit in his writing to watch like an affirmational, detail-obsessed fan, which we will discuss more in the next section, and his DVD commentaries' explicit invocation of fanboys, again showing the structuring tension of avowal and disavowal.

At other times, though, Moffat frames fan desires as something to heed. As one journalist reported, "co-creator Steven Moffat has admitted that he felt the pressure of expectation from fans and their many speculative theories about how Sherlock survived" (Owen 2014). He even directly contends, "I've been a fan all by my [sic] life and I know we have to deliver" (*Western Mail*

2013), and it's likely not coincidental that this embrace of fandom bolsters himself. Moffat has also acknowledged taking inspiration directly from a fan film for the Series 8 credits:

> Billy Hanshaw just decided to make a *Doctor Who* title sequence.... He put it up on YouTube. And I happened across it and I thought it was the only new idea for a *Doctor Who* title scene since 1963. And we got in touch and we said, "OK, we're going to do that one." So, I suppose when we talk about *Doctor Who* fandom online, that's what we should be talking about. Not all the random madness and hate-filled nonsense that goes on, but we should be talking about the extraordinary creative response that there is to *Doctor Who*. That we give them a show and they give us our show back, sometimes better. (K. Butler 2014)

Moffat's framing of the new credits sequence suggests the relationship with fandom he is looking for—a give and take, but one where fandom is receptive to and productive for his idea of the canon. However, he also doesn't miss a chance to reject those he thinks of as not being fans the right way, the ones who are not so useful to him.

The Abrasive Auteur

As this begins to suggest, Moffat's auteur side is characterized by insistence on doing things his way. Some might view this positively as being an iconoclast, but he is also eligible for some less flattering words. His writing is complex—or overly complicated; referential—or self-indulgent; he guides franchises with a firm hand—or is a control freak. If we think of the auteur as having a distinctive style, Moffat definitely fits the bill. His writing is notoriously labyrinthine, and has variously been called "convoluted and alienating" (Kelly 2017), "too complicated" (Todd 2011), "confusing" (Burgess 2015), and even "baffling" (*Wells Journal* 2015). As one critic noted of his run on *Doctor Who*, "Sadly, today most of the talk surrounds the over-complexity of the storylines and the fact that script-editor and showrunner Steven Moffat doesn't end stories, instead providing yet more twists and turns, before triggering another story-strand entirely" (PR Script Managers 2017). That is, while sometimes narrative complexity is valued as compelling storytelling, Moffat's critics suspect him of complexity for complexity's sake.

In addition to being complex, Moffat's stories are often very insider, assuming a lot of familiarity with the text's history; in one colorful phrase, a critic suggests that *Doctor Who* is at risk of "disappearing up its own space-time vortex" (A. Harrison 2013). As one broader comment on Moffat's work noted, this tendency can be off-putting for those who aren't hardcore followers:

> Even shows as successful as *Doctor Who* and *Sherlock* should be aiming—especially given the accumulating publicity they receive—to introduce new viewers, and there were stretches of "The Time of the Doctor" and "The Empty Hearse" that must have been almost incomprehensible to new or casual consumers. The sections involving the number of Doctorly regenerations and the way in which Sherlock cheated death sometimes felt like a chatroom for aficionados rather than a programme for a general audience. (M. Lawson 2014)

By making such choices, that is, Moffat often closes the doors to viewers not willing to follow him in his obsessions, despite his frequent refusal of the idea that fans are his target audience.

One way to interpret these plot acrobatics is that Moffat is focused on being clever, even at the expense of being substantive. One journalist noted that a particular plot "is no doubt ingenious, and *Doctor Who* under Moffat is a stylish, madcap fantasy. But I wonder whether I really know Amy Pond. Beneath the sass and the sauce and the wit and (there's no getting away from this) the skirts, I've yet to completely empathise with her, or work out what makes her tick" (Martin 2010). One shortcut taken by Moffat's writing, then, is character development. Another journalist recounts: "'A story is an ending,' Moffat said at Comic-Con, 'and how you get there.' This implies that he landed on his dramatic twists first ('What if River Song is Amy Pond's daughter? What if Danny Pink becomes a Cyberman? What if Missy is secretly the Master?') and worked backwards from there" (Robinson 2015). Taking such an approach would account for the twist-driven, thin-on-connective-tissue writing described by others.

These kinds of excesses of cleverness may have something to do with Moffat's high opinion of himself. After all, "He calls himself 'The Moff'" (Burrell 2011). He also defends self-centeredness as a writing strategy: "I always pour myself into my characters. . . . Otherwise, I'd have to research and meet other people—and I can't be bothered with all that" (Rampton 2004). While "write what you know" is an old and valuable dictum, expressing such profound disinterest in others is uncommon. Moreover, Moffat tends toward self-aggrandizement when speaking about his work. One journalist commented that "Moffat's usually accused—rightly so—of exaggeration when it comes to the contents of Who. Everything is 'the worst threat,' every plot a 'game-changer'" (Macdonald 2013). If other auteurs like Patty Jenkins and

Ryan Coogler are often loaded down with superlatives by journalists, then, Moffat's superlatives are coming from inside the house. He's not at all shy about it, saying of his plans for one actor: "Once you see what she's up to on the show, you'll appreciate what a clever idea it was" (Greenwood 2015). This tendency was described at length by a reviewer of *Sherlock* who noted that one episode "felt like it had an appropriately spooky twist for both audiences and the show's creators, Steven Moffat and Mark Gatiss—the spectral hand that had been patting you on the back for so long turned out to be your very own"; the episode, he said, was "90 minutes of self-congratulation, first for the creators who made the show, and then for the audience for tuning into it" (Berry 2016). This kind of exaltation of fans for being smart enough to appreciate Moffat's genius goes hand in hand with frustration with those who apparently aren't: he complains that "sometimes fans of the show overlook what he considers to be important points in the plot" (*The Sun* 2015). Moffat's investment in himself as auteur thus has many entailments.

As Moffat's career has evolved, his past as a continuity- and detail-obsessed curatorial fanboy shows through in an approach that might be described as "my way or the highway." In response to those concerned about what his becoming executive producer might mean, he directly said: "If people are worried that because I'm taking over *Doctor Who* it's going to be really, really frightening, well then . . . tough" (*South Wales Echo* 2008). His desire for total control leads to habits of intense secrecy about upcoming episodes and lashing out when it's violated: "Steven Moffat has attacked fans who leak details about the show's plot on the internet. The 49-year-old Bafta winner said: 'You can imagine how much I hate them. It's only fans who do this, or they call themselves fans. I wish they could go and be fans of something else'" (Foster 2011)—even though, years later, he would admit he would have been among those looking at spoilers (Mellor 2014). Another journalist described the extreme measures taken to secure this secrecy: "Cast changes are kept as quiet as possible until the big reveal. Code words are used, actors don't even know what they're auditioning for, and not even the cast knows where the storylines are going" (Laws 2014). Treating his show like an MI-6 asset often goes hand in hand with Moffat making self-satisfied announcements of his own knowledge, which in turn are recirculated by frustrated fans on social media, as with this one, hashtagged "#steven moffat is a troll":

> Moffat: He never gets his name. The show's called *Doctor Who*, clearly the question is important. And only I know why.
> Interviewer: Is that just an idea that you'll never tell anyone, or is it something that you've never decided?

> Moffat: No, I actually found out the truth and I'm . . . I'm not going to tell anyone.
> Matt Smith: Welcome to our lives. A succession of Moffat knowing information, having the power to withold it, and smiling at us. (per-mare-ad-astra 2012)

That is, mirroring Whitney Phillips's (2015) definition of trolling, Moffat is someone who deliberately acts to upset other people in a way congruent with dominance-centered forms of masculinity that value power over others. Overall, Moffat tends to frame himself as the absolute ruler of his shows—the keeper of all knowledge and the arbiter of all truth.

Moffat no doubt feels justified in asserting such control, because he apparently perceives himself to know best. As Hills (2015b, 367) notes, he is ever-ready to rewrite canon to serve his current story: "The 'Continuity Nightmare Child' represents a situation where Moffat, as a producer fan, asserts his control over the show's canonical narratives by repeatedly retro-modifying the programme's narrative universe, effectively making over the show's narrative in the images of his own specific creations." That is, Moffat may leverage knowing all of *Who* (and Arthur Conan Doyle) inside out to elevate his status and secure authority, but he abides by it only when it suits him. The sense of all-knowing-ness even extends to being quite sure what fans want—or, at least, what the fans he wants want, as when he proclaimed: "The Doctor Who Experience is a fan's dream come true—a fully interactive adventure that will allow viewers of the show to get as close as possible to some of the scariest monsters from the series" (*Western Mail* 2010). Is that really what fans dream of? Maybe not, but Moffat would if he were them. Elsewhere, he ventriloquized fans to support his own creative decisions, saying: "And to be fair most of them say: 'For God's sake don't make it for us.' They want it to be successful. They don't want it to be a niche thing, because then it would die" (A. Harrison 2013). This, too, is hard to square with his penchant for plot twists and stories that require encyclopedic background knowledge.

In addition to his direct conflicts with fans discussed above, Moffat seems to enjoy showing off to third parties about his hostility to them. His announcement in one public appearance is typical in this respect: "We have three new words—which may be misleading, are not titles, are only teases or possibly clues, but might be deliberately designed to get you into a lather. Who knows?" (Frost 2012). Rather than upsetting fans being an unfortunate side effect to preserve surprise, it's "deliberately designed." He specifically refuses any responsibility or concern over this: "Moffat confesses he doesn't feel at all guilty about leaving fans hanging. 'Do I look like I've got feelings? No! It's brilliant. I love it.'" (*New Zealand Herald* 2011). As this starts to suggest, many think he actively enjoys upsetting his fans, as when one journalist said he was "clearly reveling in wrongfooting the show's millions of fans" (Jeffries 2012). In all of these ways, then, Moffat's most standout characteristic is being abrasive to anyone and everyone in the service of his own authorial status and storytelling goals.

Women are Sexy Companions, not the Doctor: Failures of Inclusion

Moffat's politics are not as ostentatiously bad as Whedon's abuses of his actors or Snyder's love letters to toxic masculinity and rape culture, but his work still raises substantial concerns around inclusion (or lack thereof). As one journalist quipped: "Psychotic women as villains? Check? Psychotic women who can escape from hi-tech prisons but inexplicably always go back? Check. Little girls who, in a 'twist,' turn out to be the main female adult in the story? Check. Mr Moffat's issues with women are a matter for his psychiatrist" (Hewitt 2017). The reference to therapy is disparaging, but perhaps not entirely off-base given that accounts of Moffat's pre-*Doctor Who* work, such as *Coupling*, emphasize how rooted it is in his obsessive willingness to chronicle his own sexual desires and mishaps:

> Judging from the breasts-and-panties preoccupations of "Coupling," Moffat has been harvesting material for this show from every naughty thought and locker-room conversation he has had since he was 13. Now a man in his 40s—he'll cop to 41—with a Scottish brogue and a head of kinky black curls, Moffat is not shy about sharing his thoughts on all matters sexual, whether it is his extreme fondness for girl-on-girl action or his opinion that if Jessica Rabbit is a bit cartoony, then "more women could be a bit more cartoony." He says that the most embarrassing personal experience he has included in the show is Susan finding Steve's girl-spanks-girl tape. "When I wrote it, that had only just happened to us," he says. "Sue found a similar tape in our VCR. I did add the spanking element, though. I didn't think the real tape was quite pervy enough." (Sternbergh 2003)

Moffat admitted he based the characters in *Coupling* on himself and his wife, claiming in interviews that the series constitutes "my life as told by a drunk" ("Coupling Steven Moffat" 2004). This practice of making his own sexual desires front and center in his TV work is more dramatically uncomfortable than something like E L James's interest in BDSM showing through in *Fifty Shades of Grey* because of his level of insistence that everyone must know that it's really his desires, often in vivid detail.

This tendency continued into *Doctor Who*, particularly with the figure of Amy Pond, who he overtly understood in sexual terms, saying: "I had an ultimate goal in mind for [actor] Karen [Gillan] and that was to add some sexual tension in the famous blue police box" (Docherty 2010b). This was perhaps a foregone conclusion from "her first appearance in a stripper outfit" (Dowell 2010). Moffat didn't take any criticism about this any more than he does about anything else: "One article said 'when did *Doctor Who* assistants have to be sexy?' I thought: 'Since the beginning of the show!' We have had assistants in a bikini in the past. We are in the nursery now compared with that" (Ferguson 2010). This is a fascinating concatenation of an insistence that *Doctor Who*'s companions have always been sex objects with self-congratulation over allegedly having better gender politics than decades-old TV.

Moffat's disrespect of women loomed largest, of course, with the question of a woman as Doctor Who. Of all suggestions for changes to his work, Moffat proved particularly hostile to fan campaigns to cast a woman. As one journalist recounted, "Physicist Stephen Hawking revealed he d [*sic*] like to see a female Doctor, with a male assistant. But the show s [*sic*] chief producer and writer, Steven Moffat, appeared to dismiss that idea, with his scathing comment that there was as much chance of Dame Helen Mirren playing the Doctor as there was of a male actor playing the Queen" (Stevens 2013). At other times, he was more measured while nevertheless refusing to change the gender of the Doctor: "The key thing about the Doctor's regeneration is that you must convince the audience it is not a new man or a different man, it's the same one. . . . It is a bigger ask for him to turn into a woman. But maybe one day that will happen" (Docherty 2010a). In a later interview, Moffat argued that regeneration as a woman would only work for an iteration that was "more sexless":

> The Scottish writer said he considered changing Matt Smith with a woman after believing that casting a woman after David Tennant's spell may have been too early. "We could have replaced Matt Smith with a woman, given that his Doctor was more sexless and less of a lad, but then I got obsessed with seeing Peter [Capaldi—the actor whom he ultimately cast] in the Tardis." (Walter 2017)

This belief in a strong gender binary would indeed have been an impediment to casting a woman. However, Moffat's decision to cast a woman as the villain the Master (which he acknowledged second-guessing in interviews) did open the door for a change with the next regeneration. Thus, just three months after the clapback to Hawking discussed above, he was taking credit for something he had been actively hostile toward previously: "There is absolutely no reason why a woman can't play Doctor Who and I am the person who has made that possible (walesonline Administrator 2013). In fact, he eventually became so invested in a woman Doctor—despite refusing to do it himself—that when Jodie Whittaker was eventually cast to be the thirteenth Doctor by his successor Chris Chibnall, "*Doctor Who* boss Steven Moffat has told critics to 'shut the hell up' and stop claiming there is a backlash from fans against the casting of the first female Time Lord" (Howarth 2017). While critiques of sensationalist journalism's tendency to magnify polarization are well taken, there definitely was at least some degree of backlash (Quine 2018).

For all of Moffat's obsessive sexualization elsewhere and apparent love of lesbian pornography, he's reluctant to countenance the potential gay love story between Sherlock and Watson—known as Johnlock—which is perhaps unsurprising given the homophobia baked into hegemonic masculinity on both sides of the Atlantic, but nevertheless interesting.

> Moffat and [Benedict] Cumberbatch have denied from before the first episode any possibility that Sherlock could be gay, with Cumberbatch adding the odd assertion that he is also "very male" [both quoted in Connolly 2010, as though perhaps to assert an essential category, as opposed to a performed one. Yet the modifier itself is disruptive, suggesting that there exist degrees of maleness that the character could theoretically inhabit]. But authors do not determine the meaning of the text, and Sherlock's queer hauntology remained productively open. (Fathallah 2015, 496)

There was an element akin to gay panic in refusing gayness before the show even aired, as if Moffat and Cumberbatch were aware that—much as Mel Stanfill (2017) argues about fan advocacy of relationships between women—shows in which the relationship between men is central attract such fan attention. Interestingly, Moffat's defense is not that Sherlock is heterosexual, but rather closer to arguing for asexuality: "Series writer Steven Moffat admits he cannot understand why people got so caught up looking for a romantic link between the detective and Watson. Steven said: 'Everyone should have their own interpretation. But if you focus on sex with Sherlock, you have to understand that it, for him, is brainwork. The other part is actually uninteresting to him'" (*The Sun* 2011). While asexual representation would be greatly advanced with such a high-profile character, this version is more Cartesian dualism separating body and mind, verging on disgust for embodied materiality, than anything of the sort.

Troubling gender politics also come in when considering the role of Moffat's wife Sue Vertue, who, much like Deborah Snyder, is both vital to his work and ignored by many in favor of her husband. Like Snyder, Vertue is framed as the superego to her husband's otherwise unbridled id.

> I'm not saying this for any other reason than it is absolutely true. She is the person who runs all of Sherlock. She's the person who either kicks us up the arse or restrains us. . . . She's the person that made us write it in the first place. It has has [sic] been HER project from the very beginning, she manages the estate of Sherlock every single day. She is the general. She is the Chief Executive Officer. She is the absolute, ultimate boss of this show. . . . If you love Sherlock, if you have adored everything about it, the one person you have to thank the most isn't Benedict, Martin, Mark, or me or any of those people, it's my wife, Sue Vertue. (McEwan 2017)

Though this praise is effusive, it's notable that, while Moffat identifies her vital role as a continual collaborator and credited producer, she is given minimal attention in the discourse of their shared creations. Vertue is a producer and never a writer, despite making important contributions to the storylines: "When I wrote the first series [of *Coupling*] I did it mainly from a man's point of view—until Sue began to chip in with simple facts. She told me that a woman would never go and have a facial just before a first date as it would make her face go blotchy and red, for example!" (Office 2004) Though she apparently plays an essential role, Vertue is not very high profile; her Wikipedia page is extremely sparse, and she is almost never interviewed alone. When she is, "the shadow of her mother [longtime TV executive Beryl Vertue] and husband loom large," in the words of one journalist (Barrett 2016).

While many critics have noted the misogyny of Moffat's characters, some people have jumped to his defense. This includes two of his women actors. Alex Kingston, who plays River Song, for example, "credits Moffatt for writing such strong female characters" (Griffin 2015). Similarly, *Sherlock* actor Amanda Abbington said that, in addition to her own character Mary, "I think [writers] Steven [Moffat] and Mark [Gatiss] are very good at establishing strong, quite flawed characters. I think Mrs Hudson is just beautiful, and so is Molly. We need more female characters like this on TV" (Cox 2017). Moffat has also been defended by a number of fans. For example, one fan points to Rory as the ideal man and husband:

> Ah yes, Rory. The figure that critiques of misogyny in Moffat's *Doctor Who* love to simply ignore. Because, of course, he is the Moffat era's actual vision of idealized masculinity—a figure at relative peace with what he has in the

world who retains his own identity and saves the day, but is nevertheless wholly devoted to the needs of the woman he loves. At every turn he's the ideal husband. He's always willing to do what needs to be done, even when it's unpleasant and scary. He's actually older than the Doctor—another fact that nobody bothers to remark upon. (Sandifer 2014)

This, of course, is hard to square with the man who plastered not only his own sexual mishaps all over the screen but also his wife's, but it does indicate that interpretations of Moffat's gender politics are conflicting.

Readers may have noticed the absence of race in this discussion of representation so far. Indeed, discussions of race and/or characters of colo(u)r are almost entirely absent from the press coverage of Moffat's work, much as people of color are few and far between in the work itself. In fact, the only companion of color in Moffat's era was emphasized instead as "the programme's first openly gay permanent companion" and "the first clearly defined gay character in the programme's history" (*Belfast Telegraph* 2017)—and the fact that she is also Black was not mentioned in the press data we collected. Although this is in part because there had been another Black woman companion—Martha Jones, played by Freema Agyeman from 2007 to 2010—and the queerness of Moffat's character Bill was her novelty, it does have the effect of disappearing her Blackness.

Interestingly, Moffat talks a much better game on race than he does on gender—despite what the show looks like. In a 2016 article, Moffat claimed to have offered the role of Doctor Who to an actor of color before Capaldi (which, the journalist pointed out, was corroborated by Neil Gaiman saying in 2013 that an actor of color who was a friend of his had been asked). Moffat indicated enthusiasm for the prospect; after Pearl Mackie's casting as Bill, "Moffat said it would be 'amazing' to have two non-white leads" (Plunkett 2016). However, in a rather spectacular display of colorblind casting (Warner 2015a), he added, "In fact, a lot of people would barely notice. . . . I certainly don't think there's ever been a problem with making the Doctor black, which is why it should happen one day" (Plunkett 2016). The idea that no one would notice the casting of a Black Doctor is also at odds with his proclamations of the importance of representation. Moreover, Moffat's comments on the matter walk a strange line between commitment to improving a poor job of representation and his usual self-aggrandizement: "We decided that the new companion was going to be non-white, and that was an absolute decision, because we need to do better on that. We just have to. I don't mean that we've done terribly—our guest casts are among the most diverse on television—but I feel as though I could have done better overall" (Plunkett 2016).

Despite his own patchy history of representation, Moffat has demonstrated a commitment to the show's new direction after his stint ended. He answered fans criticizing the new Doctor on social media with a reply centering on the need for fandom to move forward: "You know, it's always easier to miss the things you love than learn to love new things—but not nearly as much fun. Get with #teamjodie" (E. Harrison 2019). His own next projects, however, seem to center more of the same type of men who have made his career thus far: Moffat's pending adaptation, a collaboration with Mark Gatiss on a new Dracula series, promises to take a similar twist to a literary inspiration by making Dracula, a villain defined by abuse of women, "the hero of his own story" (Fullerton 2019). He plans to follow the project with a crime thriller, *Inside Man*, which centers on a prisoner on death row.

Conclusion

Overall, Steven Moffat is something resembling the Platonic ideal of the fanboy auteur. He reinforces many stereotypes of the fanboy: he knows his objects of fandom inside out and backward; he is more than a little misogynist and he's kind of creepy about sex. As an auteur, he's also a fairly pure instance: he has a distinctive style, refuses to let anyone shape his creative choices, and is enamored of his own cleverness. However, Moffat does come down more on the side of auteur than fan, contending in an interview: "Fans always look back, but shows have to look forward" (Monetti 2008). While this may not be very accurate—Moffat revels in dredging up every detail and complexity ever associated with *Doctor Who* or *Sherlock Holmes*—it is his strong self-branding as an independent creator. It is therefore particularly interesting that, according to big data expert Barnard Marr, at least some of the creative decisions on *Sherlock* weren't Moffat's (or Gatiss's) at all. Marr reports that a BBC testing program "using cameras designed to monitor audience members' faces and interpret the emotions being displayed" was used on a *Sherlock* trailer and found that "viewers who went on to rate the show highly showed a greater reaction to events on the screen that were tagged as 'surprising' or 'sad' rather than 'funny'. This led the programme's producers to include more dark, thriller elements in the show in favour of less comedy" (Marr 2016, 145).[1] This is rather directly antithetical to the "Moffat knows best" approach the man himself touts. In the end, Moffat not only exemplifies the fan auteur, then, but also shows the position to be hopelessly fictitious—a product of branding much more than a description of reality.

2

E L James and the Terrible, Horrible, No Good, Very Bad Fangirl

> The doors open and I hurry in . . . desperate to escape . . . I really need to get out of here. I turn to look at him and he's leaning against the doorway beside the lift, one hand on the wall . . . he really is very, very good looking . . . it's distracting. His burning green eyes gaze at me . . ." Isabella . . ." he says as a farewell. "Edward . . ." I reply and mercifully the doors close.
> "Master of the Universe" by Snowqueens Icedragon (Eakin 2015)

It is difficult to find a franchise more popular as a target for hatred than *Twilight*—unless, of course, it is the *Twilight* fan fiction-derived *Fifty Shades of Grey*. *Twilight*'s fangirls have taken the blame for a number of sins: ruining ComicCon, destroying vampires, and promoting "bad" films. The editors of *Bitten By Twilight* use their acafan status to reclaim the perception of the fandom, noting that "as academics, and fans, we see the *Twilight* fandom as diverse, reflective, and insightful" (Click, Aubrey, and Behm-Morawitz 2010, x). However, this view is far from mainstream. That *Twilight*'s popularity was primarily with women, and particularly young women, was a major element in the hatred the series inspired. However, it was also part of what made the franchise a powerful starting point for many women emboldened by Meyer's success and drawn to the fusion of romance and supernatural—including one fangirl whose own success would come to rival Meyer's. The story of E L James is in part a story about *Twilight* fan fiction, and indeed became a force that would propel fan fiction's visibility in mainstream discourse.

From the ranks of fan fiction-authoring *Twilight* fangirls emerged E L James as the creator of her own franchise. The origin story of her success has become the stuff of fan fiction legend: James's most significant and popular work started as an erotic work of *Twilight* fan fiction entitled "Master of the Universe" (excerpted at the opening of this chapter). The fanfic grew in popularity, and eventually James published it as an e-book with a "small press . . . that had grown out of *Twilight* fanfiction archives" (Jamison 2013a, 212). The e-book spread through communities of readers and attracted the attention of Random House for a major deal. E L James's work has become the ubiquitous exemplar of fan fiction-turned-mass-audience text: "E. L. James famously converted her online 'Twilight' novel, 'Master of the Universe,' into the 2011 blockbuster 'Fifty Shades of Grey' by removing names, vampires, and anything else that might infringe a 'Twilight' copyright, a move known in fanfic circles as 'filing off the serial numbers.' (She also removed the earlier text from the Web)" (Burt 2017). But as much as *Fifty* is famous, it is infamous: the origin story attracted such suspicion (both within and outside the fan fiction community) that comparisons of the novel and its fan fiction precursor became a major topic of speculation. "One fan analyzed chapter one of FSoG against chapter one of MOTU and found an 89 percent similarity between the text of both; essentially, only the names of the characters had been changed. Furthermore, as the *Fifty Shades* wiki notes, there is a direct correlation between almost all of the characters in *Twilight* and almost all of the characters in *Fifty Shades of Grey*, right down to Christian's exes" (E. G. Ryan 2015).

James may not be Meyer's no. 1 fan, but she is certainly a fangirl, and one so successful that her name has become forever entangled with Meyer's: it is impossible now to measure the impact of *Twilight* without reference to the publishing influence and success of the *Fifty Shades* franchise. And that is ultimately what makes James such a powerful example of the fangirl auteur. If fangirls are known for unauthorized texts that reject the authority of the source (Busse 2013; S. Scott 2019), then a fangirl auteur would be someone who does so in order to install herself as the new authority. James did just that, wresting away the popular perception of the franchise from the originating author, as well as the reputation, even though she was far from the anointed heir. Ultimately, James is an exemplar of the fangirl zone of our taxonomy—highly transformative and highly known for making media out of her own fandom. In this chapter, we'll first discuss how James demonstrates the double standard between fanboys and fangirls—fanboys redeem fandom and fangirls are contaminated by it; fanboys take the obvious step to professionalize while fangirls are sellouts; fanboys make bold choices with their uncompromising creative visions while fangirls are control freaks who do everything wrong anyway—fangirl auteurs never quite get to be auteurs. We'll then interrogate the ways that James can never shed the stigma of her fannish origin any more than she can cease being defined by the explicit sexuality of her work, and she is constructed as both threatening and utterly mockable. This is perhaps unsurprising, as we'll explain towards the end of the chapter, given that her work is both transgressive and deeply normative.

Fangirl Auteurs: Double Standards

E L James is rarely mentioned alongside the figures who dominate discussions of the fan auteur. Upon closer examination, it becomes clear that the position of the fan auteur is shot through with double standards between fanboys and fangirls, highly visible with James as nearly the Platonic ideal of the fangirl auteur. Fanboy auteurs elevate their fan base by association: on the one hand, they lend credibility to their pursuits and interests; on the other, they frequently mention in interviews how their success is thanks to those many hours of obsessive tracking of the exploits of superheroes or similar curatorial pursuits. By contrast, the narrative of the transformative fangirl-turned-auteur is not so friendly to the community of practice from which she arises; if anything, James is somehow looked at as a cautionary tale, and both her fan base and other fan fiction authors are degraded by association in news coverage. There is frequently slippage between criticisms of James's writing in particular and of fan fiction in general. One journalist notes that "James's work no longer contains overt references to *Twilight*. But no wonder she wasn't on the major publishers' radar: Fan fiction never makes its way into print, partly because of the copyright issues and partly because the writing is so unoriginal and generally bad" (R. Smith 2012), making a blanket statement about the low quality of fan fiction as if it flows naturally from criticism of James. Another journalist actively links the two, blaming her work on her fan origins: "But James really can't write at all. She began as a writer of fan fiction inspired by the *Twilight* books and, unfortunately, it shows" (Cremen 2012). While the fanboy auteurs in our case studies are frequently disparaged as part of mainstream popular culture by some critics, they also have far better received work and fan bases that are never dismissed along quite these (gendered) lines.

It is therefore perhaps unsurprising that James attempts to escape some of the "fangirl" labeling, a departure from the fanboy-proud approaches of many of the auteurs analyzed in this book. In particular, unlike others profiled here, James does not frequently engage directly with her audience now that she is successful. Instead, her efforts have been more cautious and limited, and in particular they are dramatically different from the communal practices that characterized her as a fangirl writing fan fiction within a community of authors and commenters. As fan studies have shown, fan creation is often communitarian in scope, circulating between and among people contributing in different ways to that larger cultural formation (B. Jones 2014; Turk and Johnson 2011). Specifically, fan production and circulation is often described as a gift economy. Karen Hellekson (2009, 114–15) argues that "fan communities[,] as they are currently comprised, *require* exchanges of gifts" as "the gift of artwork or text is repetitively exchanged for the gift of reaction" (emphasis added). Fandom social norms mean that the gift of creative production obligates feedback, and this is why the "lurker," who reads but doesn't write, can be seen as a "leecher" (H. Jenkins, Ford, and Green 2013, 63), though "reciprocation isn't direct quid pro quo but a fuzzy exchange where authors are understood to deserve feedback from the community but not every single member" (Stanfill 2019, 164). This directly contravenes expectations of the lone author-genius.

While James does still engage her audience, and her appearances at ComicCon have been particularly successful, there is also backlash against any success she has or outreach she makes, usually one disproportionate to the act itself. That is, James's dissociation from her fannishness may come in part because, while the fanboy auteur is allowed to profit from his fanboy credentials—whether directly, as is the case of professional independent fanboy Kevin Smith, or indirectly, as with Steven Moffat and other auteurs helming the franchises of their childhood fandom—the profitability of fangirls is viewed with deep suspicion. Headlines describing James's success will often belittle her in the same breath: for instance, the *Los Angeles Times* reported that "'Fifty Shades' author E L James worth $58 million, despite being spanked by critics" (Schaub 2015).

Significantly, as this begins to suggest, James's now considerable wealth does not buy her legitimacy. Even when she appeared at the top of the *Forbes* list of top-earning authors, the accolade came alloyed with criticism because she "didn't follow any of the rules for getting to the top, but she's there all the same, debuting on the 2013 top-earning authors list with an estimated $95 million in earnings. (FORBES [*sic*] bases its estimates on sales data, published figures and information from industry sources between June 2012 and June 2013)" (Bercovici 2013). We can imagine that a fanboy auteur in a similar rule-breaking position might be viewed as an iconoclast, and indeed when Steven Moffat "granted the Time Lord another dozen physical regenerations, thus resolving (at least in the minds of the producers) the problem, much discussed on fan sites, that according to the rules originally set down, the Doctor was permitted only 12 embodiments," the press treated this as "a plot twist" and not randomly making something up to allow him to write what he wanted (M. Lawson 2014). Similarly, Zack Snyder foregrounded his own defiance of rules in an interview: "We were talking about how there are rules. They say you can only make a 3D movie in certain ways and you can only make certain shots, and I felt like what we did is we really made this 3D movie in a cinematic way" (After Hrs Correspondent 2010). Thus, it becomes all the more striking when for James, the "rule-breaking" that is admired in a fanboy auteur is a source of mockery, suspicion, and negative judgement, a reason to marginalize her even within discussions of successful authors.

The double standard also becomes visible with questions of creative control. When a fanboy auteur keeps control of adaptations of his characters or work, he is perceived as looking out for his fans or serving his vision; when a fangirl auteur does the same, she is not granted the same legitimation framing. When E L James was asked why she was becoming a producer on the film adaptation of her novel, she responded: "Because I could. (Christian Grey would appreciate that comment.) I didn't want to take the money and run—I wanted the movie to be one the readership would love" (Luscombe, Tsai, and Laub n.d.). Although James mentions fans here, she leads with asserting her own ability to take control. Whatever might have been lauded about this action from a fanboy was perceived as controlling behavior from James.

This is consistent with a substantial volume of stories about conflict with director Sam Taylor-Johnson on the set of the first *Fifty Shades* film. For the second film, it was announced that another director "has taken over the reins from Sam Taylor-Johnson, who clashed with James. Whereas the author wanted slavish adherence to her, ahem, prose, Taylor-Johnson had the gall to try to improve it. She partly succeeded: The ably directed 'Fifty Shades of Grey' was better than you'd expect" (Coyle 2017). This story emphasizes both the low quality of James's "ahem, prose" and that she resisted attempts to help her such as Taylor-Johnson's. In one colorful example, "Hollywood sources say that the director and author even rowed about the final word in the film, with Taylor-Johnson favouring 'red,' a 'safe word' used in the bedroom by the protagonists, and James insisting on 'stop.' It was, says one, 'the most petty and ridiculous argument in the world' and the climax of months of tension between the pair" (B. Davies 2015). Taylor-Johnson's recounting of these conflicts was relatively diplomatic: "'Everything throughout the process was debated,' Ms. Taylor-Johnson said. Speaking of Ms. James, she added: 'When you have someone who has incredible passion about and understanding of their material, it's quite hard to hand over the reins. I understand and appreciate that, because I'm the same'" (Lyall 2015). James, by contrast, "never once refers to director Sam Taylor-Johnson by name" in one interview (Roach 2015). Similar accusations of over-controlling behavior are leveled at other women, including J. K. Rowling, but in the case of fanboy luminaries such as George RR Martin the same behavior is received as integrity and authorial defense of a vision.[1]

Being a fan is a liability for James: she gets little credit for her accomplishments, and critics look askance at her for seeking creative control. All of this adds up to James not really having auteur status, as became particularly clear at the point at which she theoretically *became* a franchise auteur—that is, when the films were made. The films' success, despite critical derision, is, like the books, the subject of speculation and clear resentment: "*Fifty Shades of Grey* pulled in $166 million in 2015, and though the sequel, *Darker*, slipped last year, it still managed to haul in an impressive $114 million. Freed is looking like it will seduce audiences out of $90 million to $100 million. Should it hit expected targets, *Fifty* is about to become a billion-dollar franchise worldwide" (Mandell 2018). These numbers place the series on par with the transmedia franchises helmed by other auteurs in this book, yet the reverence for the achievement available even to potentially similarly marginalized auteurs like Patty Jenkins, Ryan Coogler, or Ava DuVernay—whose accomplishments are breathlessly recounted as "the first this" and "the highest grossing film for a that"—never accompanies discussions of the profitability of *Fifty Shades*. Another reviewer noted the importance of women as an audience in an almost begrudging admission of the success of the films:

> It feels like beating the same old drum to say—once again—that women buy movie tickets and that studios would be wise to cater to them more often, but here we are. "Fifty Shades of Grey" was yet another example of the female demographic boosting box office. When the movie came out in February 2015, it made $85 million in its opening weekend, more than double what the heavily marketed, more dude-centric action flick "Kingsman: The Secret Service" earned. "Fifty Shades" went on to pull in $571 million worldwide, which is quite something for a movie with a $40 million budget. (Merry 2018)

In these ways, then, we see the contours of what fangirl auteurs are allowed to be, and it's not all that much.

Flogging Erika: James as Acceptable Target of Abuse

Moreover, not only is James not really allowed to be an auteur, but she's something of a punching bag. While all fan auteurs have their detractors, James is routinely targeted with gleeful vitriol for every decision she has made, and her fans are often guilty by association. Certainly, there is much to criticize about *Fifty*, but the ways that criticism makes James apparently fair game for anything people wish to say or do is startling. First, an examination of headlines about the series demonstrates a tendency to extravagant and even cruel mockery. Here are a few samples:

> "Stop donating *Fifty Shades of Grey*, pleads Oxfam shop" (*Belfast Telegraph* 2016)
> "Sexy or sick?; *Twilight* fan scores huge with *Fifty Shades* trilogy" (Osterheldt 2012)
> "All pain, no pleasure in new 'Fifty Shades'" (A. Alexander 2018)
> "If only there were shades of nuance in 'Fifty Shades of Grey'" (Weist 2015)
> "Grey Without Matter" (Kanjilal 2012)
> "'Mummy porn' book hits spot for women" (*New Zealand Herald* 2012)

Fifty, the story goes, is sick, painful, unwanted, unnuanced, unintelligent, and deeply gendered.

This snarking habit took on more disturbing contours in a Twitter chat hosted in 2015, in which E L James received significant abuse centered on the hatred of her work (Hale-Stern 2015). As Bethan Jones (2018, 417–18) recounts, "James's Q&A hashtag was quickly taken over by users who commandeered the hashtag and used it as an opportunity to highlight the ways in which both [follow-up novel] *Grey* and the *Fifty Shades . . .* series perpetuate the notion of abuse as romance." Many of the tweets echoed the type of mockery that mainstream media coverage had already perfected. A journalist contended that "*Fifty Shades Of Grey* author E L James' Twitter Q&A majorly backfires as it's taken over by haters" and that "the author was left red-faced when Twitter trolls took the opportunity to throw hate at her raunchy novels during the live Q&A" (Pocklington 2015). Whatever one might think of James's prose or gender politics, the pattern of large groups of people piling on via Twitter to a woman who is perceived to be out of line raises some concerning parallels to both the #Gamergate abuse campaign around women in video games and the harassment of actor Leslie Jones over the all-woman reboot of *Ghostbusters*—in short, the means are suspect.

Moreover, there is slippage between verbal confrontation and language of physical violence that ties disapproval of James's writing back to her body. The aforementioned Twitter chat was described as "E L James gets a Twitter spanking" (*Toronto Star* 2015), and the language of negative responses to James as "spanking" is relatively common (as seen above in describing James as having been spanked by critics). This is, in part, due to the BDSM content of the novels, and there's nothing inherently wrong with spanking, but the ways that James's body imaginatively becomes fair game for hitting—without her consent—is troubling. Indeed, this tendency is akin to the habit of interviewers of asking intrusive questions about the extent to which *Fifty Shades of Grey* relates to James's own sex life:

> There is also the question of the research for the S&M games her characters indulge in. "Well, yes, they are my fantasies lived out and explored," she tells *GQ* magazine. "But I don't know how much detail I want to go into! Um, well, let's just say I had a very nice time researching the book. That's all I'm going to say! I'm actually now blushing!" (Steger 2012)

Again, although James did write a sexually explicit novel series, that does not automatically make her own practices open for discussion, and she expresses discomfort with the question. This differs from, say, Moffat proudly proclaiming, of his own volition, that he used his own sexual mishaps in his writing. The fact that people treat James's writing as though it entitles them to her personal life is a reminder that the erotic narratives of women authors are continually dissected in terms of the author's expected desires. White men are imagined to be able to neutrally tell stories about any experience, and so their writing is not thought of as reflecting their real lives (a courtesy not usually extended to white women or people of color).

Fifty Shades of Shame: Sex, Prose, and Moral Panics

There's a reason James is seen as fair game and not granted auteur status, of course—because her work is seen as shameful. *Fifty* sits at the intersection of fan fiction, romance, and erotica, all of which are marginalized both as low quality and because they deal in sex. It is also no coincidence that three genres primarily produced and consumed by women are lumped together in this discourse. As Anne Jamison (2013b, 313) describes the hierarchy of fiction devaluation,

> such attitudes, even in geek culture, are remarkably entrenched. If genre fiction is something like literature's ugly cousin (from literature's point or view), and romance is sci-fi, fantasy, and detective fiction's annoying girl cousin, a tagalong picked last for the team, then fanfiction has long been the ugly cousin's stepfamily's misshapen mixed-breed dog, the one everyone is too ashamed to let out in public but unable to quite put down or even neuter.

When a story like *Fifty* is both fan fiction *and* romance, with more than a splash of erotica thrown in, it may well reach euthanasia level. That such a thing should have sold millions of copies (not to mention movie tickets and sex toys), then, requires an explanation:

> Why is James so successful? Perhaps the headline plot about how Anastasia can reconcile herself to Christian's need to inflict pain is only a particularly lurid metaphor for the more mundane compromises of any relationship. These novels are less about spanking and sex toys than about the unspoken pacts women find themselves making with possessive partners. As an explanation, it isn't exactly more reassuring than thinking her fans enjoy the prose. (Cummins 2017)

As this demonstrates, reviewers can never dismiss the work without questioning the readership, and in particular there is a clear assumption that it must obviously be neither the story's quality nor the sex that appeals. It also echoes moral panic from *Twilight* reviewers concerned that teenage girls would be caught up in the fantasy of an abusive, controlling, stalking Edward to the extent that they would seek to recreate those dynamics in their own relationships. In both instances, the lack of respect for the readership is clear. This, too, reflects Jamison's literary hierarchy: where's the similar performative handwringing about men who assign their literature students *Lolita* as a great American novel?

The mix of fan fiction, romance, and erotica may be particular to *Fifty*, but these genres also themselves have overlap. The parallels between the fangirl and romance community are numerous. The Romance Writers Association was formed in part due to the lack of respect for writers in the genre in other spaces, and the community became known for inclusive practices: "They welcome newcomers, they share competitive information and they ask advice from newbies" (Larson 2018). This is very different from the practices of most professional writers' associations, in which publishing a book with a gatekeeper-approved publisher is a necessary rite of passage before membership is even granted, but parallels the norm in fandom that anyone can write (Green, Jenkins, and Jenkins 1998; H. Jenkins 2006b; Yang and Bao 2012). On the other side of the overlap, contempt for James and *Fifty* comes from the ways fan fiction is associated with not only fangirls but sexual desire. In particular, fan fiction is often conceptualized as adding unneeded or unwanted sex to mass media texts that were fine without it. This is, of course, compounded by the reality of James's work, which in its original fan fiction form added sexual fulfillment and fantasy to a narrative where the deferral of sexuality is a structuring absence rooted in Stephenie Meyer's conservative Mormon beliefs. While the erotic nature of James's work certainly plays a role in its reception, the idea that this is erotica appealing to people who are not supposed to be erotic—an assumption embedded in the derisive term "mommy porn" itself—adds to the suspicious, disgusted lens through which *Fifty Shades* has been received in critical discourse, and this is a pattern of refusing the legitimacy of women's sexual desire also found with fan fiction and romance.

These intertwined genres, long successfully marginalized, burst into the mainstream with *Fifty*'s juggernaut sales. This apparently required an explanation, and the blame fell on that other perennial scapegoat (alongside sex and popular culture): technology. James's success is often attributed to platforms rather than her work's quality or viability: it's not her story's appeal but the rise of the Kindle that gets credited with *Fifty Shades* becoming a mainstream work. The relationship of the series to the growing popularity of e-readers could also be viewed as symbiotic: "*Fifty Shades of Grey* was one of those decade-defining books that made the genre of romance palatable to the masses. It also opened up the use of Kindles and e-readers to a new audience, and according to an Amazon source, the Kindle edition sold four times as many copies as the print version" (Donnelly 2015). The Kindle made *Fifty* happen, but so too did *Fifty* make the Kindle happen.

Technology did two things for James's books. First, it mitigated the sex problem. One reporter went so far as to claim "the *Fifty Shades* phenomenon would never have happened without the privacy afforded by e-readers" (Richards 2015). What frequently goes unsaid in these reviews is that women should want to read *Fifty Shades* in secrecy: that is, they should be ashamed to read the books at all. The emphasis on discreet consumption became the go-to explanation for the purchasing of these novels and their generic kin: "Retail analysts said that sales of erotic novels for women were booming because electronic devices such as Kindles allow discreet downloading and reading" (Hough 2012). This echoes an assumption that discretion, and by extension shame, should accompany the reading of fan fiction. Even James's agent credits the role of secrecy: "One of the things about this is that in the 21st century, women have the ability to read this kind of material without anybody knowing what they're reading, because they can read them on their iPads and Kindles" (Bosman 2012). This is a bit of an overstatement—one's Amazon shopping record and recommendations are certainly a reminder of how known one's reading choices really are—but there is certainly a difference between the public consumption of a *Fifty Shades* novel and the relative anonymity of the e-reader, iPad, or cell phone. Moreover, before *Fifty* rose to fame, its black covers with coded imagery were relatively nondescript—especially when compared to the kinds of covers one might find on an equivalently bodice-ripping romance novel.

Second, technology bypassed the gatekeeping of traditional publishing. Positively, this disruption was seen as enabling different voices, especially women, to be heard. As fandom journalist Aja Romano (2012) puts it:

> The breakout success of *Fifty Shades* debunks sexist stereotypes about women and technology . . . the removal of the gatekeepers of publishing has huge implications for publishing; but it also has huge implications for gender equality. The women in *Twilight* fandom who formed their own publishing houses followed in the footsteps of pioneering female-run digital publishers like Samhain, Ellora's Cave, and Torquere Press, who founded their businesses as romance writers and fans. The success of each of these digital publishers proves that women can not only be their own gatekeepers, but that they have the technical skills to thrive in the process.

The relationship between romance and fan fiction became visible again here with this overt paralleling of their digital publishing ventures. Moreover, James's experience with fan fiction, where serial installments often play a major role in sustaining interest in readership, also lent itself to e-books in a way that traditional publishing wasn't yet prepared for. As editor Scott Pack noted about the series' role in redefining the publishing model: "The publisher was also very smart to publish the three books rapidly, because what we've learned now is that the digital world likes things that come at them thick and fast. But up to that point, they would leave up to 18 months between each release of a series, so this kind of rapid publishing was very new in 2012. . . . Regardless what you think of the writing, it is the book that redefined that digital to print publishing of books" (Ellis-Petersen 2015). Pack is among the few to give James credit for this type of influence instead of attributing her success to a group of shameful, discretion-requiring, "mommy-porn" fans with no discernable taste.

As this suggests, the belief that electronic publishing meant losing quality control was a much more common perspective. While James is the most visible of the fangirls-turned-publishing powerhouses, she is far from the only success story of this kind, but the assumption of lower-quality work goes hand in hand with any of those publishers' names. Even Amazon rarely amplifies these publishers (and frequently undermines them with programs like Prime Reading, which allows for unlimited consumption of particular e-books), despite the reliance on the Kindle by their readership. Moreover, these types of publishers and writers are segregated in the market. E-book sales are not weighted in most major rankings, and self-published or indie digital publishing houses are not afforded the same respect or name recognition as branded print publishers—even when they vastly outsell those counterparts. In this way, not only do trends in these markets tend to be less of an influence on mainstream publishing, but in fact these publishers are effectively cast out of mainstream publishing altogether.

Ultimately, the intense, almost panicked need to explain *Fifty* through something other than women enjoying reading about sex turns into a panic of another kind—what Alice Marwick (2008, n.p.) calls a technopanic, a form of "moral panic as a response to fear of modernity as represented by new technologies." Moral panics in general are often "acting on behalf of the dominant social order," and in particular they "often entail looking back to a 'golden age' where social stability and strong moral discipline acted as a deterrent to delinquency and disorder" (McRobbie and Thornton 1995, 562, 561). In this case, there is a pair of imagined pasts—Victorianism as inflected by Puritanism is the past where women didn't read "this kind of material," and the good old days of publishing is the past where only the approved could be heard. As with most moral panics (Cohen 1972; Marwick 2008), the perception of danger here is disproportionate to the actual threat. Nevertheless, it is apparently more palatable to be able to push off changing sexual norms onto nefarious technology that made them do it.

Forever a Fangirl

Given the shame swirling around James's positionality, then, it may be unsurprising that she would disavow the one aspect she could, her fannishness. As Jamison (2013a, 212) notes, although she has not hidden it, James has tended to downplay her role in fandom—a role that was initially revealed to the general public on *The Today Show* in March 2012, when viewers wrote in on the show's website to suggest "the book everyone was talking about" had been plagiarized from a well-known fanfiction. James clarified—the fanfiction was hers. As the *Fifty Shades* story grew, James increasingly acknowledged her debt to Stephenie Meyer, and eventually praises the interaction and response she got from the "smart, warm, witty" women she met in fandom. But overall, she does not dwell on the fanfiction community as a source of inspiration.

This is despite the fact that E L James also worked with other fangirls more formally in building the presence that would power *Fifty Shades* to mainstream success. Her editor, Amanda Hayward, has similarly been described as a fangirl in articles that emphasize how the success propelled her from "housewife" status: "Until *Fifty Shades* came along, each was a middle-aged housewife, with kids and husbands and tedious jobs they hated who led online lives as writers or reviewers of risqué stories set in their favourite fictional universes. Hayward, 36, a mother of two daughters, was a writer of Harry Potter and *Twilight* fan fiction" (Morris 2012). This is very different from the types of profiles we see ascribed to other editors, and places the emphasis on how much Hayward (and, for that matter, James) resembles the fans who would later propel *Fifty Shades* to the top of the sales charts.

At the same time that this has become widely known, E L James has done her best to separate herself from the fangirl persona. The author's "About Me" page makes no reference to the trilogy's origin story, instead referring to her childhood dreams of becoming a writer:

> I'm a former TV executive, wife and mother-of-two based in the leafy suburbs of West London. Since January 2012 my life has taken an extraordinary turn with the runaway success of the *Fifty Shades* Trilogy. From an early age I had always dreamt of writing stories that readers would fall in love with—and my dreams have come true, thanks to you guys. Now that life seems to have settled down a little, I want to crack on and write my next novel—another adult, provocative romance. I do hope you will enjoy that too. (E L James 2018)

While James regularly updates her website, the bio has not been updated since November 2012, not long after the "runaway success" to which James refers. James has also separated herself not just from fan fiction but from self-publishing with her decision to continue with Random House: "E L James has said she intends to stick with traditional publishing, and Random

House, reveling in a 75 percent jump in operating profits, is more than happy to oblige. Post-*Fifty Shades*, the new publishing paradigm is clear: do it well yourself, and then have a traditional publisher do it better" (Sales 2013).

Possibly as part of this strategic mainstreaming, James has been accused of not being as welcoming to fans building on her foundations as she expected Meyer to be of her success. When her French publisher sent warning letters saying, "Some of these titles, which pick up on elements of the book, are clearly parasitical.... We would like those planning new releases next year to know that we are watching very closely to ensure they are not parasitical," critics pulled from the remaining evidence of the online life of the series to comment on the hypocrisy (Boog 2012). In such ways, James straddles a divide: she drew on someone else's work, and her work has in turn been the subject of parody and imitation, which her publishers have tried to quash. Her perceived affront to fans is particularly poorly viewed given James's apparent unwillingness to credit fandom in her origin story, a reminder that the fangirl ascendant may never be viewed as having sufficiently repaid her debt. On the one hand, James could be seen as pulling up the ladder behind herself, refusing to allow the next E L James to emerge from her own fandom and stopping the cycle of transformative works. On the other hand, there is not an expectation of other fan auteurs that they give the next person a leg up; that Ava DuVernay does so is something that stands out about her rather than being standard. It is difficult to disentangle how much the expectation applied to James is gendered—women are expected to nurture the next generation in a way that men are not—and how much of it is again about the particular fan traditions from which she arose.

The unwillingness of James to acknowledge her connection with fandom and resistance to transformative works that build on her transformative works has attracted critique, particularly given the clear debt of her work to the fan community. Indeed, the community has at times turned on her. In part, this is due to the consequences of James's visibility for their own work and perception. A frequent frustration was that James was "bringing fandom into disrepute" (B. Jones 2014, 3.1): "Of course the one area [of the community] that rises to big public attention is pornographic.... Now people think we're all a bunch of—to use the term people always use—'bored lonely housewives' or just 'women writing mommy porn'" (Miller 2015). Aligned with this concern, many detractors pointed to the superior quality of other fan fiction, suggesting that paying for *Fifty Shades* is in fact being cheated: "Literary fiction in this genre lives on the net, not snuggled between the covers of copycat mainstream publishing. The *Fifty Shades* phenomenon is not only coopting readers into publishers' risk-averse search for the quick but safe buck, it is also cheating them by exacting a price for what they could always read for free" (Kanjilal 2012). It is, of course, problematic to assume that a fangirl's desire to profit in itself makes a work unworthy. This is not unlike the suggestion that fans of romance novels should look only to the Brontës or Austen for satisfaction, not the profit-seeking work of current authors. However, it is consistent with the ways fandom, as a gift economy, has historically had a value system distinct from that of capitalism. Fans have often explicitly distanced their creations from the market because noncommercial use is perceived to be safer from legal action over intellectual property infringement (Hellekson 2009; S. Scott 2019).[2] "Fandom's separation from the market also appears in the norm that it is inappropriate to monetize work done on a fan object for one's own benefit" (Stanfill 2019, 165). In particular, "resistance to monetization often arises from the belief that, like other forms of love or intimacy, being 'sullied' with money demeans fan love," but "the outcome is that fan work cannot be financially rewarded and is therefore devalued anyway" (Stanfill 2019, 165–66).

The other key objection from fans to James is also about valuing fan work, though from the other direction. Fan communities have a tradition of giving feedback on works in progress, which both acts to help writers hone their craft and forms communal bonds. However, the counterpart to constructive criticism is that as fan producers incorporate it to improve, their work ceases to be solely authored by them. Jones (2014, 3.4) notes that this erasure of the fan community's role in creating *Fifty* plays a part in the resentment the work has engendered in some fan fiction authors and community members: "the central issue in relation to fan exploitation and labor is that fan fic readers and reviewers did some of the work in creating *Master of the Universe*, but James took sole credit for its success." It's not uncommon for the auteur to be the visible face of collective effort—Kevin Smith is perhaps most successful in putting his fanboy collaborators in front of the camera, but other auteurs frequently rely upon collaborators that go unmarked and even unmentioned. However, as suggested above with pulling up the ladder behind herself, this behavior is perceived differently from James—the same double standard emerges, compounded by the norms of transformative fandom. Jones (2014, 3.8) describes James in similar terms to the fanboy auteur, but tellingly categorizes her as a thief where the fanboy auteur might be credited with amplification: "James thus straddles the line between producer and fan, stealing from commodified culture to create *Master of the Universe* while stealing from fandom to make a success of *Fifty Shades*." This draws on the awareness of fans as a resource used by successful auteurs (B. Jones 2014; Lothian 2009; Stanfill 2019).

In this separation of her work from the community of its production and their "feedback, encouragement, interaction, and publicity" (Jamison 2013a, 213), James tries to assert herself as a lone author in the Romantic tradition. However, on another level *Fifty* can never be de-ficced, because, as Jamison (2013b, 316) notes, to do so removes much of the context that gave the initial fanfic meaning.

> I'm not arguing that *Fifty Shades* somehow can't stand on its own (20 million+ readers say otherwise), but rather that the same work was more literary (read: more complex, discursive, critical, stylistically motived) when it didn't. "Master of the Universe" was more engaging intellectually as part of a complex system of interwoven, mutually commenting fictions and character studies than it could ever be on its own.

Jamison (2013b, 316), who has used the story in her literature courses, contends that one key factor in its teachability was its enmeshment in the broader body of text: "'Master of the Universe' read like a pastiche" of common tropes in the fandom like "The 'Office' genre: 'Mogul' Edward. The BDSM fic. The more-assertive Bella (submissive Bellas were always depicted as more assertive than Meyer's original characterization). The dial-a-childhood trauma game"; she notes that "This isn't cheating. Drawing obviously and explicitly from other fics is standard practice in fan writing communities." This is to say that James didn't write in a vacuum or only in relation to *Twilight*, but rather was creating within a rich set of community practice and tropes which, comparable to form restrictions in poetry, formed the conditions against which she made a specific contribution to the body of text. Additionally, *Master of the Universe* acted as a commentary on *Twilight*, as well as its own work of erotic romance. Jamison's literary perspective enhances her appreciation of intertextuality more than might be the case for the average reader, but it is nevertheless the case that clever cultural references are the hallmark of auteurs like Whedon and Smith—the number of tropes in Whedon's *Cabin in the Woods* alone gives James a run for her money—but this is not seen as derivative or unoriginal when done by fanboys.

Fulfilling Whose Fantasies?
Fifty Shades as Transgressive and Normative

Fifty Shades was a mainstay of pop culture week in one of our courses in 2014 and 2015. Students, disproportionately women in the media studies and gender studies classrooms in question, would on average start out with a positive orientation toward the books, which was then destabilized by having them read Meg Barker's (2013) analysis of how the framework of consent in the books is a heteronormative one of pursuing man and resisting woman. Then, partway through class, the second reversal: Yes, but it enabled millions of women to read and enjoy sexually explicit fiction relatively openly. This, ultimately, is the space *Fifty* inhabits: it disrupts norms in some ways and upholds them in other, possibly more dangerous ones.

Fifty Shades of Grey was particularly remarkable for James's introduction of sexuality to a text and fandom that had previously been associated with religious conservatism, as Deborah Whitehead analyzed through examining the intersection of "mommy bloggers" and other fans of *Twilight* in discourse surrounding the series (Whitehead 2013). In particular, as "mommy blogger" suggests, these were women who occupy a culturally desexualized role. Similarly, older women reading *Fifty Shades of Grey* were the subject of the recent *Book Club* movie:

> The women in this movie read "Fifty Shades of Grey" with a healthy range of reactions. [Mary] Steenburgen's character, trapped in a loving but sexless marriage, says, "This book has got me in a total tizzy." [Diane] Keaton rolls her eyes and mutters, "Give me a break," before deciding, "Best book ever!" and later, "I hate this book!" [Candice] Bergen, who brilliantly deconstructs the old crone stereotype, says, "I'm learning things no one my age should know about." [Jane] Fonda marks the good passages with a yellow highlighter and announces, "This book is a wake-up call!" (At 80, Fonda's appearance is more fantastical than anything E L James has ever created.) (Charles 2018)

The fangirl fantasy writ large—dismissed as "mommy porn"—made visible something that was more easily ignored before James's success put it in the spotlight of every bookstore, airport newsstand, and movie studio: women's, especially older women's, desire. This is part of the series' transgression, and indeed "her work's appeal may also derive from the fact that it is not culturally sanctioned. Readers, as their buying patterns have suggested for some years, do not need a critical imprimatur to select their next read. That *Fifty Shades* reads far more as a fantasy about money and power than extreme sex may not be coincidental" (Alex Clark 2015). However, as this suggests, even the reviews that acknowledge the rebellion manage to deride the fan base for those same desires (as if fantasies about money and power are somehow uncommon, or uniquely worthy of derision when presented as women's wish fulfillment; as if Batman and James Bond are not fantasies about money and power). Nevertheless, at least part of the rejection of *Fifty* is a response to its genuine challenges to the status quo. James noted this potential for change in an interview on the best parts of her success: "There are two things about all this whole experience that I have found incredibly rewarding.... The one that it brings women together, to discuss it, to have fun, to debate it. The other thing is... people who haven't read books for years are reading it" (Gregory 2012).

However, *Fifty* upholds norms as well. The *Twilight* series on which it draws has been critiqued for its association with dated gender roles, and particularly with a Mormon-derived dominant white masculinity, as Danielle Borgia argues: "*Twilight* series' subtexts of white supremacy interact with its conservative gender ideologies to promote women's subordination to white men, described as protection and romantic love" (Borgia 2011). *Fifty Shades* does not fall far from this tree, upholding "wider gendered sexual assumptions. Generally Christian initiates something and, if Ana doesn't explicitly say 'no' or use her safeword to stop play, they end up doing it. Thus the heteronormative dynamic of the active man and passive woman is reproduced" (Barker 2013, 898). Moreover, "Ana rarely communicates any desires of her own, but rather Christian orchestrates their scenes completely. This reproduces common myths around men's natural sexual needs and women's lack of them" (Barker 2013, 898). In such ways, *Fifty* upholds troubling beliefs about women and desire even as it destabilizes other beliefs about women and desire. Similarly, Nakagawa (2011) identifies *Twilight* as casting sex as a way to connect psychologically with the otherwise dangerous vampiric man, arguing that in doing so the book manages to turn paranormal romance into an expression of "family values." Barker (2013) identifies a corresponding logic in *Fifty Shades* that men need to be tamed by being tricked into or coerced into marriage. Either way, men are a harmful force, and it is the job of women to manage or repair them.

These notions are normative, but when taken to the degree of *Fifty* the usual assessment is that "James's work is not BDSM, but is rather an abusive relationship" (B. Jones 2018, 417). While the story is framed as an instance of the consensual power exchange of BDSM, Christian's "behavior within the rest of the relationship is often far from consensual. He frequently violates their arrangements and does things that Ana has explicitly asked him not to do" (Barker 2013, 899). It is this that has led to "the BDSM community's vocal rejection" of "the portrayal of BDSM as abusive and dangerous" (Harman and Jones 2013, 962). These formations are both entirely congruent with the framework of heteronormative models of gender and sexuality and become clearly visible as abusive when stripped to their bare power relations. This was not universally noticed when the story was from Anastasia's point of view, but the second trilogy retelling the story the from Christian Grey's point of view rendered it much more apparent. An independent bookseller, interviewed about an apparent decline in interest, suggested a shift in cultural climate post-#MeToo was partially responsible, arguing that

> it would be morally uncomfortable and indeed questionable for women who posted about #MeToo on social media to then walk into a shop and buy a book about how being beaten up by a man has a place in a sexual relationship. We've always felt that if the focus of the book had been reversed, and that it was written by a man, and it was written from Christian Grey's point of view from the outset—with explicit passages about how much he enjoyed physically distressing a woman—no publisher in the country would have considered publishing it in the first place. (Flood 2017)

Despite that, the novel was still the "fastest selling mass-market fiction title since *Grey*," thanks in part to the same e-book sales that powered previous titles (including 660,000 copies in the first month of e-books) (Flood 2017).

Conclusion

In the end, while there are legitimate things to criticize about James's work, upon closer analysis it's clear that's rarely why people criticize her. James herself has acknowledged that she is aware of the lack of enthusiasm from critics, and the hatred on Twitter, but doesn't dwell on it: "It's very simple, I just don't look at this stuff. I know it's there. People can be vicious and nasty, but I think hate is the new opiate of the masses, and it's amplified on all these tech platforms that profit from it" (Lengel 2019). Her "crime" is the violation of fandom norms, BDSM rules, and normative taste all in one go. She's also at fault for her work's explicit sexuality by and for the "wrong" people. And, most significantly, James is critiqued because of the double standard that marks her fannishness as a liability rather than an asset. A review of James's first novel outside of the *Fifty Shades* universe, *The Mister* (2019), criticized her perceived fangirl adherence to the way the genre used to be:

> James is clearly—and self-confessedly—a fan of romance novels, and *The Mister* seems to evoke the formula of historical romances of yore, when men were strong and complicated (and rich), and women were delicate and soothing (and helpless). But the genre itself moved on a long time ago. Nora Roberts

is writing books about female firefighters and hostage negotiators. The pervasive whiteness of romance is finally being challenged. Stories like *The Mister*, which seem to want to wrench female sexuality and status back into the realm of feudalism, have a long distance to go to catch up. (Gilbert 2019)

Criticism piled up for the book even as it moved to number one on the charts, selling fifty-two thousand copies in a single week (Flood 2019). One bookseller credited the fan base with the success, noting that "it's one of those big momentous books which comes into stores and causes excitement" (Flood 2019). James herself continues to place the emphasis on writing for herself, noting in an interview following the book's release that "I write what I want, about what I want to read" (Mallenbaum 2019). James is thus in many ways the purest example of the fangirl auteur, and a helpful example in tracing the limits of the fan auteur.

3

J. K. Rowling and The Auteur Who Lived

This is the age of social media. You think I don't get told in no uncertain terms that I've done the thing they didn't want to happen to a character, or why on Earth am I taking it into theatre? No, believe you, in the age of social media, one is never deluded about the fact that some people aren't happy, expect not to be happy. That's the way it goes. (M. Phillips 2017)

J. K. Rowling is perhaps the best-known exemplar of a woman as transmedia franchise auteur today. Originating from the ranks of children's authors, where women are common but have historically not seen great profit or literary respect from their work, Rowling has maintained control of her franchise empire with rare finesse. Her seven-novel saga of Harry Potter's battles against Lord Voldemort launched a transmedia franchise that would grow to include ten films and counting, a theatrical production, multiple theme parks around the world, and an endless array of clothing, games, Lego sets, and so forth—and with no end in sight. As one of the most visible and powerful auteurs in the past century, Rowling makes for a compelling case study in the challenge of navigating auteurship as a visible woman.

In terms of our model of fan auteurs, Rowling is on one axis an outlier and on the other thoroughly in the core of the category. The narrative of Rowling's work is not the narrative of a fangirl; she does not self-identify as such. Nor is she, strictly speaking, a fan of the media she makes. However, she in many ways acts as her own "Big Name Fan"—a fannish term for those well known in a fandom who often act as leaders or a center of gravity. She definitely has a deep and longstanding relationship to fandom. Even among young-adult franchise authors, she is noteworthy for encouraging and connecting with the fandom as one of the first authors to welcome fan fiction, engage fans, and fuel the community with direct communication even before social media. Although Rowling might not seem like a fan, Dion McLeod and Travis Holland (2017) argue that she is modeling what she sees as correct fandom and is the "ur-fan" of her own franchise.

Rowling has also nearly continuously released new canon materials throughout the lifecycle of her franchise, adding to the stories in ways that have been both provocative and controversial—what Suzanne Scott (2007) has called "Moore-ing," after Ron Moore's similar practice of tying down interpretation through filling in all of the gaps with official material. In this way, Rowling is speaking to widespread fan desire for more of a beloved story world, but also potentially talking over them by closing down interstices to explore. Her habit of Moore-ing combines with being her own most affirmational fan to resemble what Mel Stanfill (2019) calls the domestication of fandom—attempts to render fans docile and useful rather than risky. In such ways, Rowling wraps around the edge to show the fan auteur at the boundary: the auteur as highly affirmational model fan. The other side of the Harry Potter story is how these practices of fannish inclusion and canon-addition have spiraled out beyond Rowling herself, as Jack Thorne and John Tiffany have written a formal, authorized extension of canon as *Harry Potter and the Cursed Child*. Here, analyzing both news stories and a number of Rowling's tweets, we interrogate these crossings of official and unofficial, the crevices in canon and spackling them over, and the franchise's legitimate(d) and queer fictional offspring. Ultimately, Rowling's failure to successfully navigate the changing expectations of progressive authorship have been particularly telling, and her franchise's final fate is still uncertain even more than a decade after the epilogue was seemingly complete.

In this chapter, we begin with a history of Rowling's interactions with fandom; not only was Harry Potter one of the first very large internet-based fandoms, but Rowling is famously open to engaging with her fans on the internet, from JKRowling.com to Pottermore to Twitter. We argue that Rowling's auteur persona demonstrates a drive to be at the center of the fan experience, between providing a never-ending drip-feed of canon, moving fans into her proprietary Pottermore space, and actively seeking fan attention. In fact, by telling her fans how to interpret and continually re-centering herself, we contend, Rowling models "proper" fandom as obedient to the author, one vital sense in which she is a fangirl auteur. We then address how Rowling's auteur status has proved flexible, expanding to *The Cursed Child* and *Fantastic Beasts* despite her relatively minor involvement in those properties. However, we argue, controversy around racism and homophobia in these texts has perhaps once and for all dispelled the illusion of her authorship as progressive. We conclude by examining the ways that Rowling's recent Twitter usage crystallizes her overall auteur persona—a need to be at the center of her own fan base's attention and the arbiter of all meaning in her texts.

Fan's Best Friend?

J. K. Rowling's first novel, *Harry Potter and the Philosopher's Stone*, was released by Bloomsbury Press on June 26, 1997, after an infamous string of rejections and in the midst of Rowling's own financial struggles. In some ways, a fairly standard British boarding-school fantasy, and a debut middle grade-young-adult novel before those categories were even well established, the book was not, at first glance, the type of work to launch a transmedia franchise. Nevertheless, *Philosopher's Stone* and its sequels would skyrocket past initial sales expectations. The seven-novel cycle inspired such intense fandom that it would bring about midnight book-release parties, the intense fear of spoilers, and an online rumor mill that would grow to take advantage of emerging platforms on the web. Released at a time when fan fiction websites were on the rise and single-fandom blogs devoted to news and rumors were still widespread (pre-Tumblr), the franchise would inspire many to join fandom, becoming an exemplar of early online fandom and particularly a hub of fan fiction writing and engagement with transformative work.

Moreover, not only was Harry Potter one of the first truly massive internet-based fandoms, but Rowling is famously open to engaging with her fans, especially on the internet. From early on in her franchise, Rowling took advantage of the opportunity to connect with these online communities. This included giving out a "fan site award" (M. Rich 2008); sitting for interviews with fan sites (Annelli 2007); giving fan sites "a sneak preview" of her Pottermore site before its launch (Reuters 2011); and responding to fan sites' postings, as when, "in response to an April 28 editorial by a leading Potter fan site, www.the-leaky-cauldron.org, which noted that it had been receiving 'spoiler' e-mails—and expected many more—alleging advance knowledge of ['Harry Potter and the Deathly Hallows'] contents," she posted a plea on her own website to keep any such information secret (*Monterey County Herald* 2007).

In addition to engaging with fans, Rowling is famous for having not only tolerated but embraced fan fiction. As the BBC reported in 2004, "J. K. Rowling has given her blessing to fans who write their own Potter stories online"; "A spokesman for Rowling's literary agent said she was 'flattered people wanted to write their own stories'" (Waters 2004). While this did come with some restrictions, they were relatively reasonable: "Her concern would be to make sure that it remains a non-commercial activity to ensure fans are not exploited and it is not being published in the strict sense of traditional print." There was also concern about Rowling's brand value; the spokesman further said that "writers had to ensure that the stories were not obscene and were credited to the author and not to J. K. Rowling" (Waters 2004). While it's quite likely that the permissiveness was a direct result of understanding Harry Potter fan fiction as a way specifically for children to practice writing, the welcome was nonetheless extended to all. As Henry Jenkins (2006a, 172) reports, the now-defunct children's fan newspaper the *Daily Prophet* described itself in lofty terms: "By creating an online 'newspaper' with articles that lead the readers to believe this fanciful world of Harry Potter to be real, this opens the mind to exploring books, diving into the characters, and analyzing great literature." Jenkins (2006a, 183) took a similar stance on fanfic's social benefit for youth: "through online discussions of fan writing, the teen writers develop a vocabulary for talking about writing and learn strategies for rewriting and improving their own work." Overall, there has been a general perception that "the emergence of the vast online Harry Potter fandom was an important sociocultural event showcasing the ways in which youths are able to circumvent the restrictions to content adults aim to put in place"; moreover, given the prevalence of queer content in the fandom, "we can certainly consider youth participation in the Harry Potter fandom and their clear interest, through the cycle of production and consumption they created and enjoyed within that digital space, in non-heteronormative narratives as transformative" (Duggan 2017).

Eventually, Rowling created her own website, JKRowling.com, at a time when author webpages were relatively rare. Launched on May 15, 2004, the interactivity of the site was unprecedented for an author page and reflected a substantial technical investment for the time. Seasonal changes and ongoing updates allowed it to remain a major source of fandom speculation through to the launch of the final novel in the series. Sections of the site (such as the bulletin board) would be dissected on websites such as the HP Lexicon for clues and answers to burning questions (Hoobs 2006). Fans noted details ranging from shopping lists and potion recipes to events and phone numbers, and interacting with the site could trigger animated events and changes throughout (such as visits from Peeves the Poltergeist). As one fan wrote nostalgically of the interactivity Rowling's site offered her fandom early on: "The most crucial page of all on JKRowling.com contained nothing except a locked door with a 'Do Not Disturb' sign hanging from it. At first, no one could make sense of it, and then one day, the sign came off" (Khosla, 2017). The site's modality rewarded the repeat visitor and the attentiveness of devoted fans, who circulated the news and unraveled the puzzles behind it: "In the coming years, this would become a rallying cry to the fandom: 'The sign is gone,' or 'The door is open' meant 'GET TO YOUR COMPUTER RIGHT THIS SECOND WE HAVE NEW BOOK INFORMATION!!!!1!' This is how news broke pre-Twitter, and it was glorious" (Khosla 2017). In these ways, Rowling built a relationship with her fans. This was expanded with Pottermore, which launched seven years later. It promised a collaborative reading experience, suggesting that fans who joined would be sorted into houses, compete, and able to access new parts of the "canon" through their reading experience. Cassie Brummitt (2016, 112) describes Pottermore as "a unique digital franchise text that can be updated and rearranged according to shifting brand strategies."

As Khosla's mention of Twitter suggests, Rowling later moved to platforms that would become increasingly significant for shaping her connection with fans after the novels themselves were completed. One of the most important of the platforms for Rowling, as with many of our other case studies, would prove to be Twitter, where the intimacy she'd crafted with personalized messages and stories of fan connections could easily continue and be amplified. These interactions frequently involve answering questions posed by fans, ranging from large to small details about the universe. For instance, one interaction on Twitter in 2015 centered on Harry's (and presumably Ginny's, although she goes unmentioned) choice of their son's name:

> Rowling attempted to explain her decision after a fan asked: "Why did you pick Snape to name Harry's kid after? I'm genuinely curious as he was nothing but abusive towards everyone." In a series of tweets she replied: "Snape died for Harry out of love for Lily. Harry paid him tribute in forgiveness and gratitude." Some ardent fans were unhappy with the response, with one replying: "Kind of strange you'd say 'in forgiveness,' I mean Snape held no malice against Harry (which Harry came to knew, [sic] eventually)." (Powell 2015)

Such Twitter interactions with fans—contentious and not—are routine: "Rowling conducts Q&A sessions with fans, answering questions like why Hagrid the Groundskeeper can't produce a Patronus charm or why Viktor

Krum said Hermione's name a certain way in *Harry Potter and the Goblet of Fire*" (J. Alexander 2018b). Significantly, Rowling's first tweet, on September 17, 2009, suggested that one of her goals in joining the platform was to speak for herself rather than be an object of discussion: "I am told that people have been twittering on my behalf, so I thought a brief visit was in order just to prevent any more confusion!" (Rowling 2009). While she wouldn't pick up the pace immediately, Twitter would later become the site of some of Rowling's most contested announcements and interaction.

Authorship and/as Authority

The announcements mentioned above were to become integral to Rowling's auteur persona. As Julia Alexander (2018b) puts it, "J. K. Rowling never stopped writing Harry Potter." Rowling has continually provided additional information about the characters and the world of the series long after the final book's publication in 2007; post-*Deathly Hallows*, "Rowling didn't stop. On her Twitter account, on the encyclopedia-like Pottermore website, in a new play called *Harry Potter and the Cursed Child* and in the upcoming movie *Fantastic Beasts and Where to Find Them*, the official magical world of Harry Potter keeps expanding" (Ohlheiser 2016). The tidbits added in this way include "the full name of the character 'Moaning Myrtle'" (Blackwell 2015) and confirming "the long-rumored existence of an American school of wizardry" (Rahman 2015). Rowling also "picks specific dates to talk about Harry Potter's offspring" (J. Alexander 2018b), such as "I'm in Edinburgh, so could somebody at King's Cross wish James S Potter good luck for me? He's starting at Hogwarts today. #BackToHogwarts" on September 1, 2015 (Rowling 2015).

In some ways, additional material about a favorite story world is a dream come true for fans. After all, it's the desire that supports sequels, prequels, and the release of behind-the-scenes information. However, Rowling's additions include details no one had asked for, like the décor of the Hufflepuff common room. One fan and critic summarizes the problem with such additional content, revealing just how little the fandom wants this type of canon:

> The problem is that as much as the fandom thought it wanted more information about the Wizarding World, it didn't really. The past 10 years have perfectly demonstrated what an oversaturation of contextless canon looks like. Between Pottermore, Rowling's own tweets, and *Cursed Child*, many fans now purposefully ignore any information provided after *Deathly Hallows* was

published. Limitless canon, in the form Pottermore offers it, is not what we want. While we loved finding out information about wand cores in the beginning, subsequent years began to feel more strained as we were presented with more information that was revealed outside the books. Even though it was written by Rowling, it felt oddly transgressive. The books and movies were finished. (Mansuri 2018)

Thus, what seems fan-friendly in this continual release of new canon isn't, in fact, responsive to their desires at all.

This adding-on after the fact was particularly contentious when Rowling sought to increase the diversity of the wizarding world through extratextual pronouncements. This included "creating a deeper backstory for one character after one reader questioned why there are no Jewish characters in the series" (J. Alexander 2018b). Rowling also added non-European international wizard schools to her world, except that all of them were in specific countries except one school in generic "Africa" (McGeorge 2016), reproducing the troubling and racist reduction of a large and diverse continent to an undifferentiated mass. Moreover, Rowling infamously "revealed" Dumbledore's sexuality in a Q&A with fans at Carnegie Hall. This last has been particularly controversial, perhaps indicating the whiteness and queerness of the fandom. Certainly, it reproduced problematic tropes of gayness as harmful to suggest that Dumbledore's same-sex love caused him to play a role in the first dark lord's success: "I always thought of Dumbledore as gay [ovation].... Dumbledore fell in love with Grindelwald, and that that added to his horror when Grindelwald showed himself to be what he was. To an extent, do we say it excused Dumbledore a little more because falling in love can blind us to an extent?" (EdwardTLC 2007). In an oft-quoted 2007 interview with fan site the *Leaky Cauldron*, Rowling addressed the question of whether revealing Dumbledore's sexuality was relevant:

> That's how I think—in fact, that I know—that some, perhaps, sensitive adult readers had already seen that. I don't think that came as a big surprise to some adult readers. I think a child would see a friendship and a very devoted friendship. But these things also occur. So I—how relevant is it? Well, to me it was only relevant in as much as Dumbledore, who was the great defender of love, and who sincerely believed that love was the greatest, most powerful force in the universe, was himself made a fool of by love. (Anelli 2007)

Framing the issue as that she had always thought of him that way, and that some sensitive (queer?) readers had already noticed, seeks to absolve

Rowling of the actual absence of LGBTQ+ representation in her text while getting credit for it regardless.

Ultimately, the full cowardice of Rowling's declaration would not fully be realized until more than a decade later, when the opportunity to place Dumbledore and Grindelwald's relationship on-screen would come and go in the sequel to *Fantastic Beasts and Where to Find Them*, which we will discuss later. However, fans both appreciated the apparently progressive intent behind these revelations and found the execution to be a cop-out: "Though there are plenty of unquestioning fans celebrating Rowling's embrace of the concept of black Hermione, there are many more fans challenging her for what they view as a mix of hypocrisy and failed intentions. Again and again, HP fans aggressively reject Rowling's attempts to position herself and her view of the HP world as a progressive one" (A. Romano 2016). In this way, too, Rowling's gestures toward fan desires don't always connect.

In addition to these valid criticisms about Rowling apparently wanting credit for things she failed to actually do in her books, her textual additions had another problem. Other than the obvious differential association with canon, the basic structure of Pottermore was all too familiar to any fan who'd used fan websites, wikis, LiveJournal groups, or fan fiction or roleplaying forums for a shared reading experience outside of Rowling's control. That is, fans had long had spaces for these kinds of activities, but now they were officially provided in a space controlled by the author herself. On the one hand, "in its launch video, Rowling positioned the website as a conversation between herself and the fans" (Brummitt 2016, 112), seeming to promise open and egalitarian dialogue. However, as Brummitt (2016, 113) notes, ultimately "the website seeks to make its increasingly promotional role more palatable through its continued association with author (and authority) figure J. K. Rowling." That is, Rowling's involvement helps paper over the ways Pottermore is just one of many outposts in the franchise. This kind of adoption of fan practices laced with control is what Stanfill (2019, 177) refers to as trying to implement fan sharecropping: "Fans are given access to a place to grow fandom under the assumption that doing this officially is better, but if they take the deal, they not only have to abandon fan traditions of critique and gift economies but are also asked to put themselves under industry control and work on perpetually disadvantageous terms."

Rowling's co-opting of fan practices may be most sharply demonstrated by the *Harry Potter Lexicon*, a fan project that morphed into an attempted commercial publication that was the subject of a 2008 lawsuit. Both Rowling and the holder of the films rights, Warner Brothers, were fine with the Lexicon when it was a noncommercial website. "Rowling has openly praised the

Web site on which the Lexicon is based, giving it a 'fan site award' in 2004 and commenting in interviews that she even relied on the site—which provides an annotated catalog of characters, spells, magic potions, locations and events in her books—while writing" (M. Rich 2008). Lexicon author Steve Vander Ark's "expertise was so sought after that Warner Bros. flew him to the set of the fifth Harry Potter movie and used his lexicon every day during production" (Kearney 2008). Turning the website into a for-profit book, however, provoked a lawsuit, despite the fact that "the [publishing] company and Vander Ark have said the book would only promote the sale of Rowling's work and that Vander Ark's website, used by 25 million visitors, had been called 'a great site' by Rowling herself" (Kearney 2008). Even fellow fans were unimpressed by Vander Ark's decision to profit off community labor that informed the Lexicon, with several former collaborators separating themselves from his work during the trial: collaborator Melissa Anelli even came to the trial "to support Jo" (Wu 2008). In pursuing the suit, Viktor Mayer-Schonberger and Lena Wong (2013, 2) argue, "Rowling and Warner Bros. not only went after a huge fan of Rowling's, who had helped her and her book sales, but did so by arguing that authors should maintain near complete control over their fictional characters," which they describe as "essentially negating the very idea of fan fiction." That is, "Rowling's is an important voice in a growing chorus of authors whose main worry with regards to fan fiction seems to be not about economics, but about control" (Mayer-Schonberger and Wong 2013, 4).

It is this emphasis on control that appears to drive Rowling, who in her moves to put herself at the center of the fan experience models affirmational fandom. She has made a number of choices to ensure her own centrality that border on outright manipulation of her fans. The reveal of Pottermore, for example, led fans on a chase across the internet: "The project was unveiled when Rowling set fans a series of clues, asking them to enter 10 sets of coordinates into a site called secretstreetview.com. A letter could be found at each location, spelling out the Pottermore name. The website bears Rowling's signature and the message: 'Coming soon . . .'" (Singh 2011). Rowling has at times even explicitly confessed her own trollishness: "After a fan tweeted 'Everytime @jk_rowling tweets I stop what ever I'm doing and analyze it for an hour,' Rowling started to tease: 'See, now I'm tempted to post a riddle or an anagram. Must resist temptation . . . must work . . .'" (Steele 2014). Ultimately, the never-ending drip-feed of canon, moving fans into her proprietary space, and active seeking of fan attention all demonstrate the tight interconnection of authorship and authority for Rowling.

Indeed, some of the stranger incidents in Rowling's career make considerably more sense through the lens of trying to assert such authority.

Throughout her career, J. K. Rowling has had a particularly contentious relationship with the press, and has taken steps to control her own message and narrative dissemination where possible. Her frustration with the press even inspired a character in the Harry Potter universe, Rita Skeeter, whom J. K. Rowling acknowledged was shaped by the feeling of being continually hounded and misquoted by the press: "When I got to the point in the writing where I had to introduce Rita, I did hesitate, because I thought, People will think this is my response to what's happened to me. But I had a lot more fun writing Rita then [sic] I think I would have done if it hadn't happened to me. Rita will be back" (Jeff Jensen 2000). Rowling's characterization here seems to reference the challenges she's faced with the British press and particularly tabloid reporters, as she described in an interview: "'If you lock horns with certain sections of the British press you can expect retribution pretty quickly,' she said, claiming that the attitude on tabloid newspapers was 'utterly cavalier, indifference, what does it matter? You're famous; you're asking for it'" (Halliday and O'Carroll 2011). That ongoing problem of the consequences of fame has played a major role in Rowling's navigation of her auteur status, even pushing her at one point to switch to publishing under a pseudonym to avoid scrutiny for a new novel.

The creation of that pseudonym was perhaps startlingly intensive. Rowling described crafting the character and even the cover story she used when submitting the novel to her editor under the false name:

> But he's a kind of craggy guy. I had a whole biography—very detailed biography worked out for him. There are certain individuals who helped me in this, and we, together, concocted a CV for Robert Galbraith, who is ex-military and who is working in the private security industry. And that's why when he produces this novel, he doesn't want to have his face plastered all over his books because he has a day job. And I have to say that the whole cover worked really remarkably well. (Montagne 2015)

In fact, Rowling seems to have had trouble letting Galbraith go after going to all the trouble to invent him, tweeting about him as if he were a real person separate from her as late as 2017 (Rowling 2017b) and giving an interview in character well into 2018 (Jordan 2018). The deception has shades of her earlier authorial identity choices (including the very use of initials rather than a visibly feminine name on Harry Potter) while also suggesting a need for a different type of authorial validation: the book was submitted without the benefit of her auteur status to sell it. When Rowling's authorship was revealed, she indicated that her initial desire was to have the experience of authorship without her auteur status governing the reception: "I had hoped to keep this secret a little longer because being Robert Galbraith has been such a liberating experience.... It has been wonderful to publish without hype or expectation, and pure pleasure to get feedback under a different name" (Siddique 2013).

As if concocting an entire fake identity was not enough drama, the case also became a sensational example for computer-determined authorship:

> England's *Sunday Times*, responding to an anonymous tip that Rowling was the book's real author, hired Duquesne University's Patrick Juola to analyze the text of [*The Cuckoo's Calling*], using software that he had spent over a decade refining. One of Juola's tests examined sequences of adjacent words, while another zoomed in on sequences of characters; a third test tallied the most common words, while a fourth examined the author's preference for long or short words. Juola wound up with a linguistic fingerprint—hard data on the author's stylistic quirks. (Zax 2014)

The use of computer analysis to fingerprint Rowling is particularly interesting given that it assumes an author's style is unchanging and definitive—even when, in this case, Rowling is writing very far from her defining genre and audience.

Though the Galbraith example is colorful, Rowling's more mundane actions show the same desire to assert control over her authorship. While she has shown a continual willingness to personally engage her audience through technology, the digitization of Harry Potter as a franchise was a slower process: for years, Rowling resisted the release of e-book editions. When electronic editions were finally announced, it was on her terms and under her control as part of her proprietary Pottermore platform. Pottermore is indeed tightly controlled to keep its focus on Rowling. As Brummitt (2016, 124) points out, "'The Pottermore Correspondent' or 'PMC,' an anonymous journalist . . . is a regular figure throughout the website, and aside from Rowling, is the only writer attributed by name"—though "by name" is a bit of a stretch given what is surely a communal staff pseudonym. Although PMC is "tasked with delivering 'insider information' and 'news, interviews and behind-the-scenes secrets' (Brummitt 2016, 124), one ex-writer noted that "reporting from inside a franchise that so values its secrecy has been limiting because there's so much [Pottermore] can't say that other outlets can" (Di Stefano 2018). That is, non-Rowling writers for Pottermore were enjoined from being too revelatory.

In fact, Rowling's annual undermining of the stories as originally written on the anniversary of the Battle of Hogwarts by apologizing for killing characters—for example, in May 2017, she apologized on Twitter for killing Snape with a note suggesting she recognized the controversy of that particular character in fandom: "OK, here it is. Please don't start flame wars over it, but this year I'd like to apologise for killing (whispers) . . . Snape" (Rowling 2017a)—are also about asserting her authority. As McLeod and Holland (2017, 4) point out, regarding Rowling's habit of extratextual addition, after each new pronouncement, "fans who wish to read the texts through the dominant authorial lens established by Rowling must then reinterpret the meanings they had previously found in the texts." In this yanking of reader strings, "Rowling's actions attempt to disallow the reader's interpretive space by continually reaffirming hers' [sic] as the legitimate authorial voice for meaning-making" (McLeod and Holland 2017, 5), and for some unknown number of readers, it works. Rowling thus "rejects authorial death and re-asserts the role/influence of authorial intent" (McLeod and Holland 2017, 5); she refuses to die in the sense of Roland Barthes's (1978) death of the author and recognize that she cannot control all meaning. Ultimately, "the question of how much influence an author has, or should have, over the interpretation of her text is of obvious relevance to fandom, and fans were divided in their perceptions of Rowling's motives; some saw her as benignly supplying more information upon direct fan request, while others saw a more sinister desire to control the interpretation of her books" (Tosenberger 2008). The role of fandom is significant here: McLeod and Holland (2017, 6, 7) identify Rowling as the "ur-fan" of her own franchise, "a role that combines authorial agency with fannish behavior" like "arguing about and contesting certain viewpoints actively inside fan communities." We argue a slightly different point here: In telling her fans how to interpret and continually re-centering herself, Rowling is modeling a form of proper fandom as obedient to the author. This is one vital sense in which she is a fan auteur.

The Cursed Child, or Delaying Sunset on Rowling's Empire

It was *Harry Potter and the Cursed Child* that showed Rowling did in fact have staying power as a franchise auteur beyond the original scope of Harry Potter. That the play's authenticity relied on Rowling's involvement was clear when it was successful despite changes that in other franchises have caused fan uproar, like being cast with new actors who "bear little resemblance to the actors—Daniel Radcliffe, Emma Watson and Rupert Grint—who played the characters in the popular Hollywood movies" (Kestler-D'Amours 2015). The most controversial casting, of course, was selecting a Black woman, Noma Dumezweni, as Hermione. Response was decidedly mixed:

While there has been much praise for casting a black actress, the decision has some fans arguing over what skin colour Hermione was described as having in the books. Rowling put some of that to rest when she publicly welcomed the award-winning, Swaziland-born actress to the role. "Brown eyes, frizzy hair and very clever. White skin was never specified. Rowling loves black Hermione," Rowling wrote on Twitter. (Kestler-D'Amours 2015)[1]

In addition to Rowling's public support, it was also pointed out that "the casting isn't a huge leap for some die-hard Potter fans, who have depicted Hermione as black for years in illustrations and other fan art" (Kestler-D'Amours, 2015). Indeed, as another journalist noted:

> That Hermione, one of the most talented characters in the books, is dismissed for her birth as an inferior "'mudblood" is not just a sidelight. It's arguably the aspect of the saga that makes it more than the personal quest of one chosen boy to fulfill his destiny. And her personal experience is reflected in her character's activism, as when she founds a group to push for the labor rights of house elves. If anyone would argue for diversity of representation in casting Hermione, it would be Hermione herself, the original, and proud, SJW [Social-Justice Witch]. (Poniewozik 2015)

That is, because Hermione was a key target for the in-universe prejudice that gave the good vs. evil battle of Harry Potter moral weight, the casting was actually more thematically appropriate than that of Emma Watson in the films. Thus, despite such apparently dramatic change, many saw *Cursed Child* as contiguous with the novels.

Significantly, Rowling's auteur status was enough to ensure *Child*'s canonicity despite her relatively minor involvement. As many noted, "the play was not written by Rowling herself. English playwright Jack Thorne wrote the script based on 'an original new story' Rowling wrote with Thorne and theatre director John Tiffany" (thespec.com 2016). This did not seem to matter a great deal, with the focus remaining primarily on Rowling. Indeed, one theatre critic suggests that Thorne's lack of visibility as an auteur was a draw for Rowling for the collaboration:

> While Thorne maintains a modest presence on Twitter, he can be relied on to say as little about the plays as Rowling wants. Shy and self-effacing, prone to the awkwardness of many very tall people, he rarely and reluctantly gives interviews, in which he usually includes a warning about being better at dialogue on the page than in person: "I don't have that skill." (M. Lawson 2016)

Thorne, though the literal author, is positioned as more of a ghostwriter, which was reinforced by "how the name J. K. Rowling is so much bigger on the cover of the printed play" (Schwartz 2016).

It's clearly Rowling's auteur status, then, that gave *Cursed Child* its huge success—and it was indeed huge: "The announcement predictably sent Twitter into a frenzy, with thousands of fans retweeting the announcement and many saying they would be making the trip to London especially" (D. Ellis 2015). "When the tickets first became available, the play broke West End records by selling 175,000 tickets in just 24 hours" (*AFP—Relaxnews* 2016). Another journalist noted that "the show, which must be viewed in two parts with two tickets, is sold out for a year in London" (Oleksinski 2016). Kristy Sedgman (2018) observes that the high prices and limited access to the play created a division between fan audiences who could experience it directly and those left with the (frequently mocked) book version of the script. Such inaccessibility doesn't always hinder affection (as is evident from the intense fandom around Broadway musical *Hamilton*), but in the case of a work that was originally much more broadly available, it creates a definite disconnect. Nevertheless, the book was spectacularly successful as well: "within the first day of pre-orders, the 'Special Rehearsal Edition script' had topped Amazon and Waterstones best-seller charts" (*AFP—Relaxnews* 2016). Indeed, the book had "a global print run in the millions" (Lawless 2016). It also attracted all the same frenzy as had accompanied earlier Potter releases: "costumed Harry Potter fans awaited the midnight release of the new installment of J. K. Rowling's saga" (Slattery and Alcorn 2016).

Certainly, Rowling's drive for auteurial control put in an appearance with *Child* too: "In a recorded message, Rowling encouraged theatregoers to 'let audiences enjoy *Cursed Child* with all the surprises that we've built into the story'" (*Daily Observer* 2016). Accused by some followers of creating the video to ensure ticket sales, Rowling responded, "This isn't about ticket sales: we've been sold out for ages" (Moon 2016). Rowling framed her concern for spoilers very much in terms of fan engagement, asking preview "theatergoers to be careful not to spoil the play for those who . . . will see it during the regular season, using the hashtags #KeeptheSecrets and #DontBeWormtail, alluding to a double-crossing villain from the books" (McCarthy 2016). However, given her broader tendencies to assert her own control, this may not be the only (or even primary) reason.

Cursed Child's success came despite the play's detractors. One popular criticism was to dismiss it as fan fiction. Sometimes the reasons for this were fairly literal: "*Cursed Child* is fan fiction, in the sense that the text wasn't written by J. K. Rowling" (Schwartz 2016). However, more structurally, one reviewer pointed out that *Cursed Child* resolves nothing; as a narrative, it stands apart and irrelevant from the central drive of the series previously:

> the usual next step, feverish picking apart of new canon, birthing new theories, has been muted, mostly devoted to critiquing the book's perceived failings. The organic excitement at seeing another piece of the Potter puzzle snap into place had disappeared. We already have that puzzle finished, mounted and framed above our mantlepieces. Simply put, *Cursed Child* was doomed to feel like fan fiction rather than canon because the series was resolved. Anything more seems trivial, extraneous—a fun hobby for fans, but not a vital new dimension to the Harry Potter we know. (Fallon 2016)

Similarly, Michal Shick (2016) suggests that the problem with *Child* is one of a narrative that seems to be continually asking the question "what if?":

> I think this is more than the growing pains of change, the mild discomfort we all felt while digesting the latest Harry Potter novel. I believe That Fanfiction Feeling represents a fundamental difference between Rowling's approach in her novels, and the tact taken by John Tiffany and Jack Thorne. Rowling's series was constantly inventive and powerfully imaginative, but also deeply consistent. It was not self-aware; it was loyal to the pulse of themes and characters pounding through a remarkable body of work.
>
> *The Cursed Child*, however, beats to the drum of "What if?" questions, spinning off into a kaleidoscope of surprising (and to be honest, bizarre) answers. To that end, the story feels like fanfiction; this is not a measure of quality, but a measure of intent. Author-approved or not, *The Cursed Child* shares the fundamental sensibilities of fanfiction—not of canon.

Existing outside of, and being unable to influence, the main trajectory of a story and raising alternate realities are certainly markers of fan fiction. Yet a more apt comparison may well be exactly the sort of fictitious franchise authorship Rowling actually inhabits. As one journalist notes, *Child* is "as much fan-fiction as any episode of television—it might be written by someone else, but if the original showrunner is still on board, it's most definitely cannon [*sic*]" (Schwartz 2016). In this way, *Child* is perhaps more similar to Rebecca Tushnet's (2007, 160) example of "an authorized 'Tom Clancy's Op Center' novel written by a ghostwriter, for which Clancy's name serves as a brand," where the brand value (with greater or lesser success) relies on "a consumer's belief that a good or service is authorized by a particular source" more than authorship proper.

Fans also resisted the fan fiction label. A survey of fans conducted by the hosts of fan podcast *Fansplaining* found that most did not view the work as fan fiction despite the popularity of drawing comparisons (Klink and Minkel 2017). Reasons cited by fans on either side included questions of authorship, professional publication, and existing as a for-profit and endorsed part of the canon (Klink and Minkel 2017). However, another key reason to reject external application of the label "fan fiction" is that it's ultimately pejorative and fans are unlikely to be receptive to using "fanfic" toward dismissal of validity. In fact, some argue that fan fiction is better than *Cursed Child*. As one Tumblr post pointed out, the notoriously worst fanfic of all time, "My Immortal," did many things better than *Child*, including its treatment of bad parenting and a more canon-consistent treatment of time travel (Duran 2016).

While fans did not join in on the "fan fiction" criticism, they did have critiques. In particular, they pointed out that despite the inclusion of Dumezweni as Hermione, the play raised many of the same representational concerns as the novels. Queer representation especially has been a continual site of concern among fans:

> This whole situation is built on a bedrock of heteronormative assumptions. Ginny's childhood crush on Harry was awkward and relatable at age 11, and it later blossomed into true love. Scorpius's pursuit of Rose is a charming quirk, and Ron's teen relationship with Lavender Brown was played for laughs. But Albus and Scorpius, who already love each other and are presented as an inseparable partnership, apparently cannot be put in the same category as these straight teen romances. (Baker-Whitelaw 2016)

Youth aged 11–14, as Albus and Scorpius are in the play, often have their first crushes and even relationships, but like the first seven books, *Child* implies that only some kinds of relationship are eligible for inclusion. A sarcastic post from Tumblr noted the extent to which same-sex love is forbidden by imagining "*Cursed Child* writers"—notably, not J. K. Rowling—showing up at Albus and Scorpius's wedding to shout "no homo" (*A Potter Head* 2016).

Mainstream Beasts: *Fantastic Beasts* and the End of Rowling as Progressive

The Harry Potter universe returned to the big screen in the *Fantastic Beasts* series, which bears a tenuous link to Rowling's previously published Hogwarts "textbook" *Fantastic Beasts and Where to Find Them*. Acting as a prequel to the main series, the *Fantastic Beasts* arc marked the first turn from Rowling's traditional approach to transmedia authorship, in which her words had always before preceded any adaptation. In this case, while Rowling is credited on the scripts, like *Cursed Child* her authorship, though not her authority, is tenuous at best. However, her status as writer and producer on the project does make her the most visible person when the works in question are sources of dispute and controversy, which has particularly surrounded *Fantastic Beasts 2* and has perhaps once and for all deflated the illusion of her authorship as progressive.

One of the controversies in *Fantastic Beasts* has been the casting—and retention—of Johnny Depp as the villain at the same time that his abuse of women has been a high-profile topic of discussion. Rowling's post addressing Depp's casting did little to assuage the controversy:

> For me personally, the inability to speak openly to fans about this issue has been difficult, frustrating and at times painful. However, the agreements that have been put in place to protect the privacy of two people, both of whom have expressed a desire to get on with their lives, must be respected. Based on our understanding of the circumstances, the filmmakers and I are not only comfortable sticking with our original casting, but genuinely happy to have Johnny playing a major character in the movies. (Rowling 2017c)

Rowling essentially dismisses Depp's spousal abuse as a personal matter, but also implies that she knows things about the "circumstances" that somehow negate the violence. In so doing, Rowling implicitly asks her fans to trust that unspoken knowledge, but while this is an authorial relationship she has relied upon in the past, this is a case (particularly in the era of #MeToo, as we will discuss in the Whedon chapter) that strains it considerably, especially when she caps it off with strong support of Depp's current and future involvement in the franchise.

But this is not the only *Fantastic Beasts* problem. The most recent controversy as of this writing is the revelation that Voldemort's snake Nagini is actually an Asian woman. "That doesn't sound too offensive until you realise [the character, played by actress Claudia Kim] is one of the only women of colour in the franchise and that Nagini's main role in the series is to sustain Voldemort with milk and act as a vessel for his soul. Kim's role is reduced to playing a character who will become a white man's pet—literally" (Mitra 2018). This reproduction of racist tropes is "entirely in keeping with Rowling's own track record on representation and inclusion" (Mitra 2018). Although Rowling (2018b) insisted this was not, as one might assume, an innovation in response to years of criticism of that track record, but rather something she had known "for around twenty years," it feels as tacked on as outing Dumbledore given that, of the series' characters of color, "not one is central to the plot or fleshed out in any way. They are often inaccurate stereotypes or tokens that act as halfhearted nods to diversity. Cho Chang, for instance, is a mash-up of two Asian last names that shouldn't really go together" (Mitra 2018). Another journalist noted that "the casting is particularly problematic given that Asian actresses in Hollywood have historically been relegated to roles as two-dimensional, hypersexualized and subservient props, or as deceitful, sly dragon ladies" (Yam 2018)—and a subservient snake woman nearly fills every square on the Bingo card. Rowling's (2018c) Twitter clapback only made matters worse: "The Naga are snake-like mythical creatures of Indonesian mythology, hence the name 'Nagini.' They are sometimes depicted as winged, sometimes as half-human, half-snake. Indonesia comprises a few hundred ethnic groups, including Javanese, Chinese and Betawi"—but not, as Kim is, Korean. Thus, Rowling also reproduces the "interchangeable Asian" trope as well.

Third, the new film series brought the apparent reversal of Rowling's post-canon declaration surrounding Dumbledore's sexuality. Scholars and fans at the time of the announcement speculated on the impact of Rowling's Dumbledore pronouncement on future interpretation (Pugh and Wallace, 2008), but did not perhaps realize how little it would impact actual production. As one editorial summarizes:

> David Yates finds himself making *Fantastic Beasts 2*, the entire point of which is that it's about Gellert Grindelwald, whom Rowling had said (but not written) that Dumbledore was in love with. So the film-makers of this Potter-adjacent franchise that nobody had foreseen are in a spot of bother, since for obvious reasons it would be politically and financially savvy if the new films could also somehow get away with him being gay while never stating it, like the seven books and eight films we've already had. That's the thing with coming out, or being an ally: you might actually have to run the risk of taking some sort of personal hit, or having to stand up for yourself. (Salmon 2018)

As one understandably cynical critic notes:

> due to the very overseas grosses that [film studio] WB is counting on, they must play coy even as the first *Fantastic Beasts* was arguably a metaphor for the self-destruction that occurs when folks are forced to hide who they are in terms of sexual orientation. Metaphorically gay is safe, but explicitly gay

is not. We all know what they should do, but we can't always expect the folks who produce superhero movies to act like superheroes. (Mendelson 2018a)

Mendelson further suggests that Rowling would never have declared Dumbledore gay knowing the future of the film franchise, and indeed her pronouncement is all too familiar to fans used to statements like "Lando is pansexual" (*Star Wars*) or "Valkyrie is bisexual" (*Thor: Ragnarok*) without textual support. This seems to place Rowling's initial announcement in the realm of queerbaiting, or "situations where those officially associated with a media text court viewers interested in LGBT narratives—or become aware of such viewers—and encourage their interest in the media text without the text ever definitively confirming the nonheterosexuality of the relevant characters" (Ng 2017, sec. 1.2).

Upon garnering backlash over the absence of Dumbledore's gayness from the film, Rowling tweeted: "Being sent abuse about an interview that didn't involve me, about a screenplay I wrote but which none of the angry people have read, which is part of a five-movie series that's only one instalment in, is obviously tons of fun, but you know what's even *more* fun?" (Rowling 2018d). The text was followed by a gif of pressing the mute button and smiling, suggesting Rowling's desire to silence the negative feedback and her confidence that her fans would trust in her eventual vision being revealed. However, the fandom has not proven so willing to follow, with one writer noting that rather than facing up to the absence of the gay identity she had previously proclaimed, "she's taken to Twitter to share new information, and also vent her frustration with *us*. If that's what she needs to do, then she can do it, no one is going to stop her. But now, she's turned the safe space she created to share new information about characters into a desolate area—all within ~~140~~ 240 characters or less" (Paige 2018). The same medium in which Rowling's personal approachability served as an invitation for questioning and feedback from fans has now lost its shine as *Fantastic Beasts* turns out to be chock-full of entirely mundane relations of domination.

Conclusion: The Author Who Tweeted

As these incidents suggest, if Rowling initially gained a positive reputation for her internet interactivity with her fans, it has more recently taken a turn for the worse. Many auteurs have recently suffered the consequences of visibility on Twitter. Most notoriously, James Gunn's removal from the *Guardians of the Galaxy* franchise director's chair (subsequently rescinded, but still haunting the social media use of auteurs) stands as a reminder of the risks of this type of direct engagement, particularly when it is politically charged. Rowling has demonstrated a willingness to use Twitter as a highly personal platform, with mixed results. One reviewer notes a potential connection between Rowling's own approach and how she depicts social media in *A Casual Vacancy*:

> And a powerful and protected writer risks getting things wrong. One teenager bullies another on Facebook, anonymously and repeatedly, which could happen only if the victim refused to make use of the network's privacy settings. . . . And, in a tellingly odd turn, three characters read unwelcome, but essentially accurate, judgments about themselves on a tiny local Web site, and all three disintegrate into fear and fury. The novel seems to treat extreme touchiness as a default psychological setting. (Parker 2012)

It does seem quite plausible to map this back onto Rowling's own (lack of) understanding of social media.

One of Rowling's more notorious social media episodes involved a reply to a Donald Trump tweet in which he bragged about "having written many best selling [*sic*] books, and somewhat priding myself on my ability to write," complaining that "Fake News constantly likes to pour over my tweets looking for a mistake. I capitalize certain words only for emphasis, not because they should be capitalized!" (Shapiro 2018). When the tweet was quickly deleted and replaced with a corrected spelling of "pore," Rowling's (2018a) reply—

> hahahahahahahahahahahahahahahahahahahahahahahahahahahahahaha-hahahahahahahahahahahahahahahahahahahahahahahahahahahahaha
>
> someone told him how to spell "pore"
>
> hahahahahahahahahahahahahahahahahahahahahahahahahahahahahaha-hahahahahahahahahahahahahahahahahahahahahahahahahahahahaha

—was screenshotted and widely circulated. This is only one of several widely documented incidents involving Trump: in another, she replied to a tweet in which he claimed "collusion is not a crime" with a quote from Tweedledee from *Through the Looking Glass* (Moran 2018). Her engagement has even involved other celebrities, such as a conversation with Stephen King following Trump's blocking of the horror novelist on Twitter (Gibson 2017).

However, Rowling's own tweets have been occasionally subject to scrutiny, along with her Twitter likes and choices to follow transphobic accounts

(Fairchild 2019). As we have seen in this chapter, her initial rationale for joining the platform was to speak for herself, and her frustration with the tabloids bears more than a passing resemblance to Trump's complaints about Fake News. She has also, as we've discussed, used the platform to be deliberately manipulative, powerfully defensive, and routinely supercilious. In one particularly questionable incident, she declared that "this country needs to be freed of fascists on both right and left" (Rowling 2016). As one fan commented, "wow can't believe the woman who wrote a children's book with hook nosed banking goblins is bad at recognizing fascism in real life" (תרצה 2017). Meanwhile, Rowling's public profile as an activist has risen: she was honored with the Robert F. Kennedy Human Rights award in 2019 (Lejeune 2019). Nevertheless, there is a certain narcissism to Rowling's use of Twitter, and in some ways it crystallizes her overall auteur persona: she has a need to be at the center of her own fan base's attention and to be the arbiter of all meaning when it comes to her texts.

4

Kevin Smith and the "Independent" Fanboy

Randal: All right, look. . . . There's only one Return, okay? And it ain't of the King, it's of the Jedi.
Hobbit fan: Oh . . . *Star Wars* geek.
Randal: Oh, I'm the geek? Look at you two whipping out your "preciouses."
Elias: You'll have to excuse him. He's not down with the trilogy.
Randal: Oh, what the fuck happened to this world? There's only one trilogy, you fucking morons. (*Clerks II*)

Kevin Smith occupies a distinct position in our taxonomy: his work is fairly strongly affirmational, but he's equally known for making media of his own fandoms and not. Unlike Zack Snyder or Joss Whedon, his name has not been emblazoned on a popular film franchise. He has not been proclaimed heir apparent to the likes of George Lucas or Gene Roddenberry, and while Stan Lee appeared in one of his films, it was not a classic Marvel cameo but instead a surprising role and done in tribute to Smith's own fanboy status. When Smith has authored a work of central significance to fandom, it has typically not been located in the Hollywood center of gravity. On the one hand, he has at times been in the not-quite-auteurist position of a guest director for television, working on productions ranging from *Flash* and *Supergirl* to Canada's much-loved, hard-hitting teen soap opera *Degrassi*. On the other hand, Smith's transmedia franchise authorship has primarily been in the space of comic books rather than other comics media. Like Joss Whedon, he has both completed runs on some of his own superhero favorites as well as authored extensions to his own creative universes for consumption in comic form. But unlike Whedon, Smith's primary contribution is not in creating fantastical or heroic tales; instead, what he is best known for is a different kind of fannish storytelling, focused on the considerably more ordinary lives of people who love comics as much as he does.

Kevin Smith is more fanboy than auteur, more disrupter than producer, which makes his relationship with transmedia franchises more complex. In some ways, he is the ultimate example of a curatorial fan: the owner of a comic book shop and the creator of a show dedicated to other curatorial fans and comic shop owners (mostly men), Smith's work places the fanboy on screen as well as behind the camera. His work complicates the definition of the fanboy auteur by remaining deeply embedded in fanboy culture, frequently to such an extent that he has defied the norms of a traditional directorial career trajectory and instead prioritized pseudo-independent, social media-driven avenues of production and funding that rely upon his cultivated team of fellow fanboys and his commitment to create content directly for his followers. In this chapter, we explore Smith's career through the lens of transmedia franchises, both the View Askewniverse of the most beloved of his films and his emergence as a professional fanboy who leverages his fans to tell the stories he wants to. We also consider the limitations of Smith, both as auteur and as fanboy, before concluding that Smith's presence as embodied fanboy is what grounds his success.

Smith's Transmedia Franchise: The View Askewniverse

While Kevin Smith's films are clearly referential to works in the fanboy canon—including *Star Wars*, *The Lord of the Rings*, and both DC and Marvel comics—the beating heart of his work also forms its own (roughly) internally consistent universe. Termed the "View Askewniverse" after Smith's production company, the best-known of Kevin Smith's movies (*Clerks*, *Mallrats*, *Chasing Amy*, *Dogma*, and *Jay and Silent Bob Strike Back*) include a number of recurring characters—notably, Silent Bob, played by Smith himself—as well as companies, institutions, and plot points that reach across the realistic films of the Jersey trilogy (the first three) and the more fantastical fourth and fifth movies. The later *Clerks: The Animated Series* and *Clerks II* would continue in the same vein, and several comics accompanied and filled in gaps between the main films. Over time, this set of texts grew to include cameos and self-referentiality worthy of Marvel films.

Smith's film career began when he "became something of an indie film cult hero in 1994 when his audaciously grungy, no-budget debut, 'Clerks,' was shown at Sundance and then selected for distribution by Miramax" (Townsend 2006). *Clerks* "played a big part in the independent filmmaking boom of the 1990s, and Smith's simple technique and dialogue-heavy style was a huge influence on filmmaking at the time" (Machosky 2012). The self-produced film was "a portrait of fast-mouthed misfits in dead-end jobs" (Lacey 2004), played by Smith's own friends, many of whom have been frequent on- and off-screen collaborators throughout his career.

Significantly for our purposes here, *Clerks* is, as one critic put it, "not only a movie made by a fanboy, it's one of the first movies about fanboys" (Beckerman 2006). Smith's choice to cast himself as Silent Bob, the near-silent watcher infamous for his sage one-liners, immediately made him a visible fanboy in-universe, adding to the recognizability that would become essential to his brand. This was intensified by the fact that, as Smith noted in 2006, "when Miramax sent us out on the road with *Clerks* in 1994, because the movie didn't have stars, I wound up being the face. After years of grassroots marketing every one of my movies, that personality becomes almost as important as the filmmaker" (Borrelli 2006). Several of the most quoted moments in *Clerks* emphasize Smith's—and the Askewniverse's—relationship with fanboy discourse, which is perhaps unsurprising given that Smith famously raised some of the funding by selling his comic book collection. Among others, there is a monologue on the fate of contractors blown up in the attack on the Death Star in *Star Wars: A New Hope* and a debate over the ending of *The Empire Strikes Back* versus *Return of the Jedi*. *Clerks* was so successful that it almost launched a traditional studio spin-off in the form of a TV pilot, but this project was abandoned. A similar concept became *Clerks: The Animated Series*, although only a few episodes were ever aired, with the rest released later on DVD.

However, even as early as his second film, *Mallrats*, Smith began resisting the external pressure put on him. As he described the experience in a 2006 interview, "we come out with *Clerks* where nobody is expecting anything because nobody knew who we were or what the movie was and people were pleasantly surprised. Then you make *Mallrats* and people have expectations and you don't live up to them and suddenly you're back to square one" (*Toronto Star* 2006). While *Clerks* was truly independent (although subsequently picked up for distribution by Miramax), *Mallrats* was produced on a studio budget and with expectations of greater spectacle. It was also "a critical and commercial failure" (Williams 2001). Roger Ebert offered a particularly damning criticism of Smith's move toward Hollywood:

> The year that "Clerks" played at the Cannes Film Festival, I was the chairman of a panel discussion of independent filmmakers. Most of them talked about their battles to stay free from Hollywood's playsafe strategies. But Kevin Smith cheerfully said he'd be happy to do whatever the studios wanted, if they'd pay for his films. At the time, I thought he was joking. (Ebert 1995)

Ultimately, Smith apologized for *Mallrats*, acknowledging that the type of action-oriented sequences he'd felt pressured to add as part of a larger-budget, "Hollywood" movie hadn't suited his skills. As he explained in a 2005 interview, "The studio guy was giving me notes and I didn't really agree, but he was like: 'You don't really know how to make a movie yet' so I was like yeah, I guess, and I just listened. At the end of the experience I [was] like: 'No. I did know how to make a movie and from now on it will never be like that'" (Burroughs 2005). However, despite the initial failure, *Mallrats* "has since become a 'gateway film' for many entering the View Askewniverse" (*Canberra Times* 2012). Smith noted in 2010 that "if you stick around long enough, you get respect for even the dopiest of movies, like *Mallrats*. People talk about it now as an important film, but everybody hated it when it came out" (Brownstein 2010).

This appreciation despite the critical panning is rooted in the way the film still fits easily into the Askewniverse, as Smith had already narrowed in on his audience, describing *Mallrats* in an interview as "a mainstream movie directed straight at the 15–30 year old young males" (Duritz and Smith 1996, 240). In particular, *Mallrats* continued centering and representing fanboys: two characters debate the viability of a Lois Lane/Superman pregnancy based on Kryptonian biology; Silent Bob makes use of the Jedi mind trick and wears a Batman costume as part of an elaborate plan; and, in a particularly iconic moment, Stan Lee himself offers one of the comic book-obsessed fanboys relationship advice based on an issue of *Spiderman*. Stan Lee described the role in *Mallrats* as one of his favorite on-screen moments, and years later recalled the role of relationship advisor fondly (Burlingame 2016).

Smith regained his critical acclaim with his next film, *Chasing Amy*, but it also brought a significant move away from his previous focus on fanboys. Perhaps inspired in part by his own change of circumstances and compatriots, Smith shifted his narrative to center instead on comic book creators, offering an anemic commentary on the lack of gender and racial diversity within those spaces while focusing on two white men leads. One of them,

Holden, was played by Ben Affleck in his first leading role, written specifically to give him the lead Smith felt he deserved; while Affleck's career would eventually leave Smith behind, his position in 1998 was: "I owe everything to this guy" (Schwalbach 1998).

However, though fanboys are decentered, Jay and Silent Bob—"the two Jersey stoners who have become the slacker Greek chorus to Smith's cinema of self-reference" (Strauss 2001)—still have key roles to play. Like the chorus, they provide important exposition and commentary. Silent Bob is particularly acutely Smith's stand-in here. His big moment of non-silence (Jay: "What do you look so shocked for? The fat bastard does this all the time. He thinks just 'cause he don't say anything, it'll have some huge impact when he does open his fuckin' mouth") glosses the film's title; Bob explains that, like Holden, he was intimidated when a former girlfriend, Amy, had more sexual experience than he and reacted badly, but he has since realized that was a mistake and that he can never get that good relationship back—and will be forever chasing Amy.

The film seemed to mark Smith's transition back to critical darling and independent voice. This dual move, shifting from a fannish subject position to a creator subject position (albeit perhaps a fanboy auteur subjectivity) and gesturing toward tougher issues like race and sexuality without fully engaging, marks the film as liminal. Roger Ebert's praise for the film and its handling of obsessive characters (fanboys) makes the distance between the film's subjectivity and fanboy subjectivity clear:

> He is willing to follow his characters into the subjects that obsess them, even if they seem to be straying from the plot. Here we get, for example, a hilarious speech at the Comicon about the racism and white imperialism of "The Holy Trilogy" ("Star Wars"), delivered by a wonderful character named Hooper (Dwight Ewell)—a gay black man whose militant anger is partly a put-on and partly real pain, masked in irony. (Ebert 1997)

This back-and-forth with studio production (and, indeed, the expectations of larger budget cinema) is a recurring theme in Smith's work, as both reviewers and fans expected him to continue his "independent" trajectory.

While it was lauded, *Chasing Amy* wasn't without its critics. In particular, the film caused a stir for Smith's choice to depict a self-identified lesbian entering into a romantic and sexual relationship with a man, as one reviewer noted: "It's a rude blast of gleeful provocation, a farce about emotional pain, a drama about sexual slapstick. At the Sundance Film Festival screening, those who didn't join in the standing ovation at the end bristled at Smith for pretending he knew anything about lesbians. Smith seemed to enjoy the shit storm he'd stirred up" (Travers 1997). While outsider filmmaking is certainly no guarantee of progressive attitudes about sexuality, trotting out the tired trope that lesbians are sexually available to men is part and parcel of the indeterminacy between margin and mainstream in Smith's work. Critics were varied in their judgments, with some finding the film "a surprisingly sophisticated examination of desire and sexual identity" (Strauss 2001) and others contending that "*Chasing Amy*, in which a lesbian is won over to the other side by the charms of, ahem, Ben Affleck, was borderline offensive" (*Irish Times* 2006). Smith seems to have felt the tension, describing his intentional "return to independent film and not mainstream" in an interview and noting that while he had the main character date the lesbian, "If he wound up with her I'd probably crucify myself" (Duritz and Smith 1996, 246)—presumably for triteness, though he later insisted he had always seen Alyssa as bisexual (Tucker 2010). Although Smith stepped back from making his lesbian character wholly about her relationship to a man, the shadow of fanboy misogyny would continue to lurk. As one critic noted, the film was "a window onto the way men talk about women, and men and women talk to one another, with blunt dialogue rarely heard in movies" (C. James 2006).

If *Chasing Amy*'s representations were controversial, Smith's next film, *Dogma*, "which saw Smith treat Christianity as if it were the creation of DC Comics" (*Irish Times* 2006), took it to the next level. Roger Ebert praised *Dogma* for breaking with Hollywood representational conventions in its serious yet mocking handling of Catholicism:

> There is a long tradition that commercial American movies challenge conventional piety at great risk. For a long time, any movie dealing with religion had to be run past Hollywood's resident monsignors, ministers and rabbis for approval (the habits of actual orders of nuns could not even be portrayed, which led to great ingenuity in the costume department). (Ebert 1999)

Dogma's portrayal of "a reluctant messiah who works at an abortion clinic" (Williams 2001); "a new Church program called Catholicism Wow!, symbolized by a statue of a grinning, thumbs-up Christ" (P. Howell 1999); and Alanis Morissette as God exploding the heads of angels with her voice generated intense controversy, and the film was met with protests, hate mail, and death threats.

Although this example might seem far afield from fannishness, Smith has described his own Catholicism as being a fan of God (Goddard 1997; Portman 2004) and the film as a "love letter to God" (P. Howell 1999). Simultaneously,

Smith takes a highly irreverent, if not downright trollish, approach, including joining protests of his own film, telling a reporter covering the protest: "I don't think [*Dogma*] stands for anything positive" (Blevins 2016). He described the experience on his blog, reminding readers again of his fandom—"I'm for Jesus, you're for Jesus—we just go about expressing it different ways"—and engaging the protestors respectfully:

> The head count (including us) was twenty. We held our signs and quietly prayed the Rosary with the group for about an hour (well, I prayed the rosary; Jen and Bryan are relative heathens when it comes to the Mysteries and the Memorare). I was even interviewed by a local newscrew, not as myself, during which I maintained that I was mad about the movie, and that I would not patronize it (although I couldn't help but mention that I liked the director's first film a little). A woman told me my sign wasn't appropriate (the [*Dogma* is] "Dog-Shit" one), and I apologized, offering that the movie wasn't appropriate, from what I'd been told. We agreed that it'd be better if I removed the offending word, so I did as much, rendering my sign a neutered "Dogma is Dog." (K. Smith 1999)

In this way, *Dogma* is religion fandom-adjacent in much the same way that many of Smith's works are fandom-adjacent, with one critic describing its tension as "conflict between true faith and organized religion" (Portman 2001).

Fandom also makes its way into *Dogma* though the presence of Smith's ubiquitous fanboy characters. The decision to include Jay and Silent Bob alongside not only religious figures but mainstays of Hollywood also attracted commentary:

> Jay and Silent Bob achieve nirvana, dramatically speaking, in *Dogma*. At first it's a stitch to see them in a big movie; you're enjoying the distinguished actor Alan Rickman, and watching Linda Fiorentino deliver a heartfelt performance and then—what the freak, how did Jay and Silent Bob sneak in here? The movie actually brings them along as major characters, holding screen space with as much gravity as the official coverboys Affleck and Damon. There's something a little crazy about it, and yet, especially in the final cataclysmic sequence, it works. Only a handful of people, and heavenly beings, are present for the battle for the future of the world, but Jay and Silent Bob are right on top of it. Dude! That rocks. (Horton 1999)

Ultimately, Jay and Silent Bob are present because they anchor *Dogma* to the Askewniverse. They are stand-ins not only for Smith but for his fandom, so their presence even at a near-apocalyptic scenario is only appropriate. Indeed, this suggests the value of viewing Smith's work as an ongoing dialogue with his fandom, which stands in contrast to the work of most directors: without Jay and Silent Bob, the film's overall trajectory towards the supernatural would be more fundamentally disconnected not only from fan discourse but from the arc of Smith's filmmaking.

Dogma was soon followed by *Jay and Silent Bob Strike Back*, a film that Smith called "a Valentine to his fans" (Longino 2001). The movie shifted Jay and Silent Bob from side characters to stars alongside a range of cameos, "visual motifs (a vehicle's dashboard sports the thumb-up, smiling 'Buddy Christ' figurine from Smith's religious satire 'Dogma'), inside jokes (one-liners involving monkey references to the short-lived 'Clerks' cartoon on ABC)," and potshots at Miramax, which had declined to distribute *Dogma* because of the controversy it generated (Longino 2001). *Jay and Silent Bob Strike Back* cemented the previous films as a fandom-affirming and -serving shared universe. On several levels, the film probes Smith's own position. Mark Hamill, who played villain Cock-Nocker, linked the film to Smith's fannishness, describing himself as Smith's action figure that he could now play with on a movie set instead of merely in his room (Seiler 2001). Being at once a fan and an auteur also shows in the film's representation of dissatisfaction with online critics. Jay and Silent Bob are introduced to the internet by Ben Affleck (reprising his role from *Chasing Amy* as Holden):

> Jay: All these assholes on the internet are callin' us names because of this fuckin' stupid movie.
> Holden: That's what the internet's for, slandering others anonymously! Stopping the flick isn' gonna stop that!

The trollishness displayed around protests of *Dogma* also made a return, with Smith setting up his own anti-fan site, "The Official Strike Back Against Jay and Silent Bob Strike Back" (Kornblum 2001). The film ends with a sequence of Jay and Silent Bob taking matters into their own hands by chasing down everyone who has criticized them on the internet and physically attacking them. The sequence is no less over the top than the rest of the film (which includes an animal rights-inspired rescue mission and a record use of profanity even for Smith) but positioning fan criticism as a climactic villain, opposed by fanboy leads, dramatizes Smith's split between fanboy and auteur.

While nearly all of Smith's movies are sequels to *Clerks* in a sense, relying on shared characters and a consistent universe, *Clerks II* is a direct follow-up to the fates of Dante and Randal. As one critic described it, the film is "an affectionate and funny return to the convenience store slackers of the 1994 original—but this time they're in their 30s and grappling with typical thirtysomething angst over what to do with the rest of their lives, both personally and professionally" (Goodman 2006). The film also features a new fanboy, Elias, who introduces himself as a Transformers fan and is actively involved in an online forum visually reminiscent of early iterations of Smith's own View Askew board. Moreover, "there's a hilarious extended riff on 'Star Wars' vs. 'The Lord of the Rings' that epitomizes Smith at his most comfortable and competent, both celebrating and lampooning the fan boy world of comics, movies, music and video games" (Townsend 2006). While the leads mock Elias's engagement with both the online community and the Transformers, Randal, Dante, and Elias are unabashedly presented as fanboys arguing over their preferred franchises and canons throughout the film. The fannishness was also symbolic; Smith argued that the fannish debates demonstrated that character Randal "is stuck and mired in one place in life. He is still grasping the *Star Wars* straws while most people have moved on to bigger, better things like *The Lord of the Rings*" (Cardy 2006). *Clerks II* also suggests Smith's own reflections on where he was headed, as one critic noted: "Randall's eventual epiphany about buying the ruined Quick Stop and re-opening it themselves foreshadows Smith's own development as an artist, later seguing into self-distribution and gonzo indie experiments, like Red State and Tusk" (M. Harrison 2017). Perhaps in part because of this shift in tone, *Clerks II* takes a less aggressive relationship with social media than *Jay and Silent Bob Strike Back*.

In general, Smith's portrayal of fanboys throughout the Askewniverse is loving but also mocking. As one reviewer noted of *Mallrats*, "more often than not Smith relies on dim humour and downright stupidity as the comic book-obsessed loser protagonists slide giddily about the mall from one mishap to the next" (Westbrook 2015). This is entirely common for a representation of fans in media, often "envisioned as losers with pathetic real lives sublimated into being a fan, somewhere between laughably inept and dangerously pathological" (Stanfill 2019, 52). Although engaging these negative images, Smith's portrayal is in on the joke and received accordingly. Significantly, while the View Askewniverse is only part of Smith's work, it remains its beating heart. These films' tone, subject matter, and especially the presence of Jay and Silent Bob represent what is firmly canonized as "Kevin Smith." The View Askewniverse demonstrates the ways Smith is both fanboy and auteur on multiple levels: he's the author of the text, which is steeped in geek culture, but also his body exists both behind the camera and in front of it as a fanboy character.

The Fandom of the Smith

Smith, then, both is a fan and is someone who has fans. Like any successful transmedia franchise, Smith's work has come to have its own curatorial and transformative fans, who are drawn to the world's recurring characters and to Smith himself. For example, *Clerks*, with its myriad fan references, has in turn inspired its own fan-based parodies, such as Jeff Allen's *Trooperclerks*, which Jenkins describes as an exemplar of the influence of "video store filmmakers," such as Smith and Quentin Tarantino, on "amateur digital filmmakers" (H. Jenkins 2004). These fans have also formed a community which has been praised as the site of a "fan family" by Tom Phillips (2011, 492), who notes its dependence upon participation in an "on- and offline sociality cycle" that builds close relationships situated around meet-ups and online community.

For well over a decade, the hub of Smith's fan community was the View Askewniverse Message Board. Significantly, the site grew out of fandom; it began in 1996, when "web sites had not yet become a required tool for advertising new releases, nor was there a such a thing as a dot-com economy. A U. of Michigan student, Ming Chen, decided he wanted to pay tribute to his favorite new pic, 'Clerks,' using this fresh medium, the Internet." Chen's site soon came to Smith's attention, and Smith reached out to say "that if he was ever inclined to design an official site for us, I would be more than happy to give the job to him to do" (Silberg 2000). In what would turn out to be an important choice, Smith's participation on the site and interaction with fans were integral from the beginning.

Ultimately, the board would become the hub of Smith's brand. A 2006 article noted that Smith had lately "spent much of his time, as he always does, reading and responding to internet postings on such Smith Web sites as viewaskew.com and silentbobspeaks.com. No other filmmaker has made it his business to nurture, kibitz with, heckle and engage his fans on such an intimate, day-to-day basis" (Thomson 2006). The motivation behind this uniquely high level of interaction is less clear. On the one hand, a 2000 article indicated that it was for fan benefit, saying that "Smith professes that his primary goal with the site has always been to make his audience feel like a part of the process, part of his world (Silberg 2000). By 2006, the framing was much more about how the site benefited him: "Consequently, says Smith, he's a step ahead of his distributors when it comes to understanding the tastes and attitudes of his audience" (Thomson 2006). The welcome is still up on the board's first iteration (as of September 2019), although the board itself no longer exists. The message states:

> This board has been provided for you to post questions to Writer/Director Kevin Smith. Yes, it's true, Kevin himself visits this board almost daily to answer questions. Kevin will also post updates and informaton [*sic*] on whatever he's working on at the moment, usually far before the press gets wind of it. Kevin usually answers questions based on the intelligence level and the innovativeness of the post. So let that be an early warning to you. (K. Smith 2006a)

Here, in addition to logistical details that might be found on many similar sites, there are also indications of what constitutes proper fan behavior or fan-industry relations, according to Smith: contact with the object of fandom is special and uncommon elsewhere, and fans here get insider information. Yet, he is saying, fans should also be savvy, and newbies must get up to speed. Smith shuttered the first version of the board in May 2004, migrating to a new host and leaving a message for the fans:

> I'm gonna miss this place. Waaaay back in 1996, when Ming and I were first putting together viewaskew.com, I told him I wanted to be able to do a once-a-week Q&A; with people who visit the site. He said he could do me one better, and introduced me to this board. And since then, it's been an integral part of my life; in many ways, my second home. I'm a sentimental fuck, so I'll miss this simple format. But sometimes, you've gotta grow; accept change. And all sentimentality to the side, this isn't the board. This is just the technology by which we conduct our ongoing conversations. All of you and me—everyone who posts . . . WE'RE the board. The look of the place may be changing, but the spirit? That's been the same since we started this little chat, nearly ten years ago. And that spirit will carry over to the next incarnation of this virtual clubhouse. (K. Smith 2004)

However, the second iteration of the clubhouse wasn't free: it required a $2 registration fee for all but those transferring from the original community, although that fee was donated to an anti-sexual assault group, RAINN (Lost 2018). It also wasn't long for the world, and would be plagued by trolling despite the attempt to use username registration and the small barrier of payment as a deterrent. An additional factor in the board's demise was that Smith's writing moved to a more broadcast mode as he started to confront his own fandom's scale. In one incident, he posted on his blog about hosting a signing at the comic book store he owns, expecting 200 attendees, only to encounter more than 2,000. Smith noted the change in demographics: "This was the first event at which the View Askew Message Board folks made up maybe 2% of the folks in line, with the majority of the crowd being MySpacers" (K. Smith 2006b).

As this unexpectedly voluminous attendance starts to suggest, the existence of a group of fans with strong ties to Smith was a powerful resource. Smith has even at times explicitly called on his fans to take action on his behalf. In 2006, he engaged fans as a promotional workforce, holding "a contest to see who can place the 'Clerks II' banner on the most other Web sites; the winner gets a walk-on role in a future View Askew movie" (C. James 2006). When he was removed from a Southwest Airlines flight in 2010 because they deemed him too large for a single seat, one of Smith's responses was to stir up his fans against the carrier: "With the observation 'you have a right to make noise,' Smith . . . explicitly demonstrates an indication to his supporters that protest is a viable form of action in response to feelings of persecution or having been wronged, and as such constitutes a direction for fan activism" (T. Phillips 2012, 3.8).

The most acute manifestation of Smith's sense of the power of the aggregate mass of his fans was his experiment with a version of what Suzanne Scott (2015) has called "fan-ancing" with his film *Red State*.[1] In classic trollish Smith style, he made a spectacle of his breaking of film-financing norms; "Smith outraged independent distributors when, at what had been billed as an auction, he sold the film's North American theatrical rights to himself for $20. His accompanying rant about the unworkable economic model for independent movies today offended further" (Strauss 2011). Ultimately, Smith did have a specific economic argument for why traditional distribution wasn't working for him: "At best, a distributor would pay me $4 to $5 million for the rights, then tack on another $20 million in marketing costs. . . . My regular audience only generates about $30 million, so all the people who invested in this and worked their tails off on it for peanuts would never see a profit" (Strauss 2011).

Accordingly, "Smith was determined to cut out the middle-men and take the film direct to the fans" (*Canberra Times* 2011). Key to the venture was Smith's sense that "after years of experience he knows who wants to watch his films and how to reach them" (Godfrey 2011). In the end, "on his own dime, Smith took *Red State* on a North American theatre tour where he held Q&A sessions immediately following the screenings. Smith charged a premium price for admission (upwards of $60) and was able to release his movie to the public on his terms," and moreover "on a budget of only $4 million, Smith managed to make his money back in no time at all" (Malloy 2011). On the one hand, this is a practice in which, as Luke Pebler noted of the Kickstarter campaign to "fan-ance" a *Veronica Mars* movie, "fans' devotion . . . was used as leverage to massively overpay for goods" (Chin et al. 2014, para. 2.7). On the other, as Bethan Jones contended about similar projects, these payments allow fans to "become part of the success of the project. That affords them cultural capital within fandom" (Chin et al. 2014, para. 2.8). Moreover, as Bertha Chin pointed out about the *Veronica Mars* case, fans are "funding the creative vision of the man who brought them the beloved universe" (Chin et al. 2014, para. 2.4), and they're also, as Scott (2015, 170) points out, "additionally being sold the potential to circumvent the system, if not change it entirely."

Smith has defined independence as ownership of the full process by which a creative work is received: "True independence isn't making a film and selling it to some jackass. True independence is schlepping that shit to the people yourself" (Hetherington 2017). However, critics of that self-definition point out that Smith's approach only works thanks to his earlier (and continued) affiliation with the traditional studio system and his continued fan base:

> The path that Smith took was available to him precisely because of his enormous fan-base, many of whom can be heard cheering on the footage of that fateful night at Sundance. Smith is guaranteed to pull a crowd simply by putting in an appearance; he's admired as much as a raconteur as he is a filmmaker. The irony of Smith's situation was that he had the ability to turn his back on the studios and distribution companies because he had spent fifteen years working for them. (Hetherington 2017)

Early in his career, Kevin Smith defined independent film as "a movie that's made by any means necessary" (Duritz and Smith 1996, 243). His later work demonstrates how much that definition and approach has evolved and how, in turn, he has influenced the traditional studio system through his continual experimentation with mobilizing his fandom towards more independent production. Smith's work is thus perhaps most notable for his relationship with fandom and his ability to cultivate that relationship towards continually changing economic models as his relationship with traditional Hollywood has become more and more strained. Matt Hills (2015a, 184) has argued that "affective economics does not merely allow media producers to 'exploit' fan engagement; it also calls upon producers to perform the ongoing emotional labor of a coherent 'social front' where fan-like identities and decommoditising discourses are mobilized"—and Smith was particularly well positioned to take advantage of this.

However, Smith was marketing directly to his fans long before his *Red State* project. "When his directorial cred was near its peak in 1997, Smith bought a comics and memorabilia shop in Red Bank, N.J., and rechristened it Jay and Silent Bob's Secret Stash" (Stuever 2012). In a 2001 interview, Smith characterized buying the store as giving him something to fall back on when his film career eventually ended (Moore 2001). The store and its website long featured replicas of movie-worn or inspired shirts and products, ranging from Buddy Christ dashboard figures (a la *Dogma*) to the sports-evoking jerseys that make up the majority of Smith's wardrobe.

If, on the one hand, "the fandom of Kevin Smith" refers to the body of fans who will charge into action on his behalf, the other valence is Smith's own love of fannish things. As the View Askewniverse already began to suggest, Smith is deeply fannish in his work, particularly when it comes to his most successful work. Indeed, outside the Askewniverse, Smith's career in large part is being a professional fanboy—comic book writer, comic book shop owner, pop-culture podcaster, etc. Not only does Smith own a comic book shop, but his brand as comic book shop owner enabled AMC reality show *Comic Book Men* (2012–18). One critic called the show "the anti-*Antiques Roadshow*: The guys buy, sell, talk about, and argue over the treasures of the comic-book world, and share their findings with their boss Smith through their podcast" (Strachan 2012). *Comic Book Men* is a transmedia production deeply situated in Smith's self-performance. Like his fictional fanboys, the men of *Comic Book Men* are primarily drawn from Smith's networked approach to authorship: the cast consists of the same fellow fanboys as Smith has relied upon for work on his films, shop, and podcast network. Chronic shop-loiterer Bryan Johnson and manager Walt Flanagan "appeared in several of Smith's early films, including *Mallrats*, in which they had a scene-stealing turn as Steve-Dave and Fan Boy, respectively. The characters in the movies are dismissed for their interest in comics, because that was the vibe at the time, Smith says" (Truitt 2012). Indeed, in a 2006 interview, Smith credited Flanagan with introducing him to the broader culture around comics in the first place (Kenney 2006). The show's seven-season run is exceptionally long for what is admittedly a niche reality concept, and its success is credited in part with saving the comic book shop itself from closure.

The show is particularly unusual in that it is a companion show to a podcast, part of Smith's burgeoning podcasting empire, *SModcast*. *SModcast* is a collaboration between Kevin Smith and Scott Mosier, and their initials form the first two letters of the network. *SModcast* has been ongoing since 2007 and is both the name of the network and the name of the primary podcast in the network. In 2016, Smith contended that "being able to get up and talk has kind of become my industry, as opposed to just being a filmmaker" (Law 2016). Certainly it has become a lucrative industry: "Although the weekly podcasts are free, Smith, inspired by old-school radio program formats, charges fans to come along and be part of live recordings. These were so successful he bought a 50-seat theatre in Los Angeles, Smodcastle Theatre, where his and others' podcasts are often recorded live" (Northover 2015). Indeed, by virtue of the podcasting empire, Smith started hosting weddings: "part podcast, part reality-show-style confessional, and more profanity-laden than some divorces. His weddings, at the SModcastle, his recently opened theatre, start with him interviewing the couple for 45 minutes about sex and exes, followed by a quickie ceremony. It is then all made available for free streaming on SModcast.com. The wedding package costs $5,000" (Karpel 2010). The *Comic Book Men* podcast builds on (and is recorded at times in unison with) the *SModcast* hit *Tell 'em Steve-Dave*, featuring Johnson reprising his *Mallrats* role as Steve-Dave. The most explicitly fanboy centered of Smith's podcasts is *Hollywood Babble-On*, which launched in 2010 and has included everything from comedy to a dramatic performance of Smith's own comic book series, *Batman: Cacophony*.

In addition to referencing comics in his movies and owning the store, Smith has also written comic books. "In 1998, he helped Marvel Comics relaunch *Daredevil* as a comic, and *Green Arrow* for DC Comics in 2001. In between, he had also written comic book sequels for some of his movies, including *Clerks* and *Chasing Amy*" (*Straits Times* 2003). The opportunity to write for comics is attributed to "having written a *Superman Lives* script for a Man of Steel film, starring Nicolas Cage and directed by Tim Burton. Although his *Superman* script wasn't used, it ended up on the Internet" (Schwalbach 1998), raising his profile as comic-media creator. In the subsequent two decades, Smith has written some "award-winning issues" (M. Davies 2004) while "handling legendary characters such as Batman, Daredevil and Spider-Man" (Olding 2010)—as well as "a Batman book that Comics Alliance called the worst *Dark Knight* comic ever" (Tucker 2014), which Smith blamed on writing while high. Coming as it did near the height of Smith's mainstream film visibility, Smith's run on Batman attracted commentary and comparisons with Joss Whedon:

> Now before anyone chimes in with the inevitable accusations usually aimed towards reviewers as they approach Hollywood converts, like say Joss Whedon, it should be known that I am no Kevin Smith fanboy. I've enjoyed a few of his movies (notably *Dogma* and the first *Clerks*), but I would in no way characterize myself as a die-hard Askewniverse junkie. So I'm going to put a preemptive kibosh on the argument that this book is immediately overrated due to any inherent Hollywood luster. The truth is, *Batman: Cacophony* is pretty damn good, regardless of who wrote it. (Schedeen 2008)

Smith has identified quite strongly with this comics-writing role. In a 2006 article, he said, "In an odd way, if I could pick one job, it would probably have been writing comics. However, I don't think you get to continue writing comics unless you've got the day job" (*Toronto Star* 2006).

Ultimately, much like (and depending on) the transmedia Askewniverse, Smith has parlayed his geek credibility into a transmedia career as a professional fanboy. As he noted in a 2010 interview, "I have all these outlets. When I make a movie, I get to be Richard Linklater, one of my favourite directors. When I do a podcast, I get to be Howard Stern. When I write a comic book, I'm Stan Lee. When I do a live show, I'm George Carlin" (McClatchy Newspapers 2010). Overall, Smith's brand has to some extent become that of a fanboy for all seasons—or, mostly all seasons.

Never Let a Guy Like Me Near their Franchises: Auteur Trouble

As a fanboy auteur, Smith's fannishness is unimpeachable. His auteurishness, however, is on considerably shakier ground. Despite rhetorically linking himself to a litany of auteurs as in his comment above, Smith never quite manages to be one. The film that would mark the end of Smith's traditional Hollywood studio filmmaking, *Cop Out*, demonstrates this tension with particular clarity. In some ways, it is one of the most traditional films he's ever done, but it garnered a mix of strong criticism and praise from forum fans. This prompted Smith to write a post in its defense:

> I view the flick this way: when Spielberg and Lucas made STAR WARS and RAIDERS, both were homaging the flicks of their youth—in their cases, the cliffhanger serials. Not implying COP OUT is remotely akin to the quality and ambition of SW or RAIDERS, but the ethos behind the making of this flick was borrowed from those guys: make that movie as an adult that I watched as a child. Tap into the movie buff that existed before I fell in love with *Film*. It was kinda like "Let's make a movie for the fun of it." ('cause Lord knows it wasn't for profit.) (K. Smith 2010)

Smith's framing of the issue in relation to Spielberg and Lucas is illuminating. *Cop Out* attempted to do a quite standard thing: representing an object of fandom from the perspective of a fan of that thing. However—unlike Whedon and Snyder, who are Smith's contemporaries, let alone Spielberg or Lucas—his attempt was illegible and not well-received.

Additionally, unlike these other fanboy auteurs, and despite writing the same heroes in other mediums, Smith has not been given the reins of film franchises. The way he talks about this has vacillated over the years. In 2006, Smith told the story as being pressured into franchise filmmaking: "Former Miramax boss Harvey Weinstein pleaded with Smith to do it. 'He was: "It's time for you to grow as a film-maker. Do *The Green Hornet.*" My argument was always 'Why is making *The Green Hornet* going to suddenly make me evolve or grow as a film-maker? Haven't we already seen that movie a thousand times before?'" (Cardy 2006). Smith's framing was that film franchises did not interest him. However, a year earlier, his statement about the very same franchise was that "when it started to become apparent to me that it would never be my movie, that this was a movie that the studio was going to have as much say . . . as I would, I knew I had to leave it" (Burroughs 2005), suggesting that he had been interested but found the constraints unpleasant. Prior to that, Smith said, he loved "writing comic books, but it's so much easier when your audience is about 100,000 people. Taking something that appeals to a small group and making it as mainstream as possible isn't very appetising" (Potton 2004). This suggests the very franchise-ness was in itself unappealing to Smith.

In the end, Smith's *Green Hornet* never made it to the theatres, perhaps in part because of his oft-repeated joke during Q&As that his ideal concept of a superhero film would involve the two heroes leaning against a wall chatting, occasionally going off-screen to have a battle, and then returning to dialogue. Indeed, as his 2004 preference for comics already began to suggest, the actual script (abandoned after the film deal with Miramax in 2004 fell through) became a comic book more easily than it ever was a film, as Smith described in an interview:

> They've done all these tie-ins and spin-offs, and they've been so kind in using my script as the bible to launch their whole *Green Hornet* universe. . . . At one point, I remember saying, "You don't want to do that. This is a movie, not a comic," but I think Nick [Barrucci, Dynamite Entertainment president] saw the layers in the *Green Hornet* script. He said, "You didn't intend to write a comic book series, but you accidentally did." (Phegley 2010)

The mismatch between Smith and franchise auteurism is a recurring theme. In 2014, several websites reported that Smith might be involved in some way with Snyder's *Batman vs Superman*, a rumor Smith discredited by pointing out the unlikelihood of his being involved with any major property: "C'mon, kids. . . . No major studio would let a guy like me near their franchises—even if it was for a dummy script meant solely to fool the news sites" (K. Smith 2014). This self-effacing remark is typical of Smith, and it exemplifies key features that distinguish Smith from other fanboy auteurs: humor and self-deprecation.

When Smith does get to create the object of fandom, one reason it doesn't work nearly as well as one would assume given his fanboy credibility may be due to the tone of his work, as he recounted in an interview discussing his desire to direct an episode of CW's *Arrow*:

> I was talking to Marc [Guggenheim, executive producer], and I was like, "hey man, fans keep saying they want me to direct an episode of [*Arrow*], I would love that, I wrote *Green Arrow*." He knows that. And he goes, "yeah, you know, Arrow is very dark. *Legends* [*of Tomorrow*] would be good for you." [laughs] So, I don't think they're ever gonna let me near *Arrow*, which is totally fine. (Donn 2017)

Although *Arrow* and *Legends of Tomorrow* (and *The Flash* and *Supergirl*) exist in the shared Arrowverse, and although Smith does have comic auteur bona fides, he was shunted away from the flagship show. Auteurism may not require taking the material seriously—Whedon is known for his humor—but it does require taking the auteurist self seriously, which Smith, between protesting his own films and appearing in them, does not.

That refusal to take himself seriously has surfaced even when Smith does get to direct franchise TV. Regarding 2017 *Supergirl* episode "Supergirl Lives," Smith said:

> This material is way above my pay grade: the kind of stuff I've loved watching my whole life but never tried to make myself. It's pure comic book and science fiction fantasy and it reads like it should look like a '70s album cover. In a very First World way, this is scaring the sh-t out of me. So that's gotta be the best reason to do it, right? I should challenge myself and try to do something outside of my comfort zone. Plus, it's not like I'm gonna be alone: armed with a spectacular script, I'll be surrounded by the incredible cast & crew of one of my favorite shows—and they make magic every week. So what I lack in vision and ability I'll try to make up for with boundless fan-girl enthusiasm and a willingness to learn. Thank you Andrew Kreisberg & Greg Berlanti for the misguided belief I can pull this off. I'll try to let you down gently. Up, up and away . . . (J. Johnson 2016)

Smith's current integration, even if peripheral, with the DC television universe seems particularly appropriate to his fanboy auteur positioning given the Arrowverse's deep engagement with the DC comics tradition: the shows are rife with tie-ins, crossovers, and Easter eggs that connect it to the larger DC universe. The tone is dramatically different from the Snyder-helmed DC Extended Universe (DCEU), and the diversity of characters is significantly broader. DC TV, then, is the better fit for Smith's humor and apparent desire to either have complete creative control or none at all. In 2019, Netflix announced Smith would be helming a new iteration of He-Man entitled *Masters of the Universe: Revelation*, building on the original 1980s animated franchise (Frishberg 2019), which might further this trend of franchise-leading: at the same time, his primary contribution has thus far been through his own transmedia, fan-affirming empire.

Fanboy Misogyny Strikes Back

Unlike Whedon's self-branding as a feminist, Smith's work has often been criticized for its politics. Specifically, critics have noted Smith's films' "graphic conversations about women" (Thomson 2006), and, in particular, the ways in which "Jay babbled consistently about drugs, chicks and his own sexual prowess" (Anderson 2006). *Dogma*, one critic complained, "gives way too much screen time to the recurring characters Jay and Silent Bob, played by childhood friend Jason Mewes and by Smith himself. The duo function as the movie's geek chorus, constantly framing Bethany's quest in sexual terms" (P. Howell 1999), as opposed to the religious or adventurous ones that might be seen as more fitting for the film's broader plot arc. Considering sexual orientation, when *Jay and Silent Bob Strike Back* was released, the Gay and Lesbian Alliance Against Defamation were critical of it "for glorifying anti-gay slurs and anti-gay violence," to which Smith found it appropriate to use the old saw that he has a gay brother (Longino 2001). Moreover, in the nearly one thousand news stories we canvassed for this chapter, there is not a single direct engagement with race either from Smith or about him; in fact, when he was "asked about the controversy that arose when it was revealed that Academy of Motion Picture Arts and Sciences membership is heavily skewed towards old white men, he quips, 'I'm an old white man myself—I'll be 42 in August' before adding, more seriously, that perhaps some new, younger membership might be good for the organization" (*Canberra Times* 2012). Although Smith rarely takes anything seriously, the immediate response of solidarity with old white men and then the endorsement only of the criticism of the "old" part is not exactly a ringing statement of progressivism.

At other times, Smith has specifically rejected these sorts of conservative or majoritarian politics. The final shutdown of the View Askewniverse board has been attributed by several longtime fans to fights over misogyny, particularly from Smith's friend and main forum moderator at the time, Bryan Johnson (Katy 2013). Smith has responded strongly to misogyny, as in one incident where, when he tweeted about a movie review making a dismissive remark about *Jay and Silent Bob Strike Back*, the reviewer was flooded with misogynist attacks from Smith's followers, leading to an all-caps post rejecting this type of harassment: "IF YOU LIKE ME OR ANY OF THE MOVIES/PODCASTS/CRAP I MAKE/DO . . . THEN YOU SEE WOMEN AS NOT ONLY YOUR EQUAL, BUT ALSO YOUR BETTER. SO PLEASE CONDUCT YOURSELVES IN THAT FASHION AT ALL TIMES. IN THOUGHT, WORD AND DEED" (K. Smith 2013b). Smith has been similarly critical of homophobia. In addition to being criticized as homophobic, *Jay and Silent Bob Strike Back* was also initially rated NC-17; Smith highlighted the double standard of that ruling, saying:

> Why can you be descriptive about hetero sex, like they are in all the raunchy teen movies, and then the minute you use the same terms to talk about gay sex, it's instantly offensive? That's one of the things that bothered me so much about the GLADD [sic] thing, because to me this movie is saying, "Hey, it's all sex." One gay reviewer I know, who loved the film, said I had made the first gay movie for straight teen-age boys, and I thought, "Cool, how much more subversive could a movie be?" (T. Lawson 2001)

Smith, then, is on the record on both sides of misogyny and homophobia—though, again, Bob-silent when it comes to race.

This points to a broader tension: whatever Smith's own genuine politics may be, the conservatism of mainstream fanboy identity tends to creep in every time. In January 2012, critics called attention to the lack of women in the cast of *Comic Book Men*, which was indeed an accurately gendered title. As one woman who tried out for the show explained:

> When I tried out for the project, it sounded like it could be a lot of fun. Not a lot of details were given (in fact it seemed as if they had two separate shows in mind at the time) but it was a show about comic books and they were looking for people who loved them. I know they considered at least a few women

for the show because I had several friends who auditioned as well. And guess what? One of them was chosen. My friend Zoë A. Gulliksen was filmed for the pilot but just revealed she's been cut from the show entirely. She even has audio from a podcast where Smith says she is the "perfect girl" to be on the show. (Pantozzi 2012)

Smith elaborated on the removal of the only woman in the show's cast by explaining that her inclusion didn't fit the "reality" of comic book shops:

> It's not like there aren't chicks in the show . . . there are chicks. But the reality of the comic book stores is that these are the people who work in them. There's not a woman among them. When we originally showed the idea to AMC, they said, "It's a sausage party," so we said all right, let's bring in a chick. And for the presentation we brought in and shot a chick, and it was wonderful and great, but then AMC, god bless them, said, "Well, that's not the reality of the show." (Grant 2012)

On the one hand, Smith indicated he was on board with diversifying the cast. On the other, his response to cutting the woman out was "god bless them," and he also got defensive about the critique, saying elsewhere: "I could barely do anything for myself, let alone the entire gender of women, and stuff. So my response is always, 'Go and make your show, man. I want to watch your show.' There should be a *Comic Book Women*. God willing, if this works, there will be a spinoff" (Strachan 2012). Additionally, if Johnson was a key misogynist on Smith's website, making him a central figure in this show does not seem to truly repudiate his views. Moreover, the show didn't only have a gender problem: while the interpersonal dynamics hinge on teasing between the men, many journalists noted the disproportionate targeting of Chinese American man, "Ming Chen, the store's tech expert, a Kevin Smith fan who became a Kevin Smith employee and is made to suffer verbal abuse from the other men" (Stuever 2012). Moreover, "when not picking on Ming, the men of the Secret Stash razz one another about sexuality" (Stuever 2012), indicating regressive attitudes as well. Ultimately, the case of Smith suggests that the individual fanboy, even the fanboy-auteur, can't shift the capital-F Platonic ideal Fanboy away from being a misogynist straight white dude.

Part of the disconnect may come when Smith represents and speaks for only himself as opposed to when he is subject to network pressure or other fanboys. Certainly, after the 2017 revelations about Smith mentor Harvey Weinstein's long history of abuse of women, Smith was vocal about taking responsibility:

> I'm not looking for sympathy. I know it's not my fault, but I didn't f—ing help. Because I sat out there talking about this man like he was a hero, like he was my friend, like he was my father and shit like that, and he changed my f—ing life. And I showed other people, like, "You can dream, and you can make stuff, and this man will put it out." I was singing praises of somebody that I didn't f—ing know. I didn't know the man that they keep talking about in the press. Clearly he exists, but that man never showed himself to me. It all hurts, and it didn't happen to me, but it all hurts. (Bowsher 2017)

Smith did translate his response to action: he has promised all future residuals from *Clerks* and other Miramax-distributed, Weinstein-produced films to Women in Film in addition to a $2,000 per month donation for "the rest of his life" (Bowsher 2017). Smith's public announcement of his decision to cease profiting from his previous collaboration with Weinstein inspired Ben Affleck to follow suit: "Once Kevin suggested that, I decided to do the same thing, so any further residuals that I get from a Miramax or a Weinstein movie will go either to F.I. or to RAINN. One is Film Independent, and the other is a women's organization. I just didn't want to cash any more checks from the guy, you know?" (Desta 2017)

Kevin Smith in the Flesh

The potential tension between Smith's personal politics and those of Smithland highlights the fundamental grounding of Smith as fanboy auteur: in the View Askewniverse, and in Smith as professional fanboy, it is the presence of Smith himself that serves as the guarantor of Smithian quality. It is the proof of his body—visual, audio, or physical—that makes it work. Much of Smith's brand is about being a regular guy who made it. As a self-described fanboy whose authenticity is undisputed, he occupies a position closer to his fans than even most of his fellow fanboy auteurs. This is also the case materially, as Smith's body type is larger than acceptable in Hollywood for all but the sidekick, and this mark of being a "regular person" is something to which he routinely draws attention, from his 2010 conflict with Southwest Airlines over whether he was, in his own words, "too fat to fly" to jokes about his 2018 heart attack. Further, his material body is specifically marked as fanboy, as he appears on camera consistently as a fan, whether as Kevin Smith, Professional Fan™ or as his alter ego, Silent Bob. These habits continually invite the viewer to feel close to him in a way not common among his fellow auteurs.

As part of affirming and embodying the fanboy subject-position, Smith frequently recounts his fanboy origin story, from his love of *Batman* to his outsider status as a child: "When I was a kid, sports were treated very seriously. I was into comic books, which is kind of like sports because people wear uniforms and protective headgear, and generally speaking it's good versus evil. But for some reason, my passion was always diminished, like, 'Oh, that's for kids'" (Hank 2016). This tale of comics fandom being discounted is a further point where Smith's persona converges with the generalized presumptive experience of his fans.[2] For someone so "just like you" to become a well-known auteur is itself frequently told as an unlikely success story, the truest of rags-to-riches, against-the-odds tales. Smith both resists and embraces this narrative arc in his own recounting of his journey from film school dropout to credit card-financed independent filmmaker to Hollywood director: "When I was in film school, there was this specious statistic floating around stating there were more film school students than law school students. That was one massive pool of wannabes who'd have to bottleneck into a souvenir teacup full of opportunities waiting on the other end of the rainbow" (K. Smith 2013a, 2).

Although Smith made it from the "massive pool" into the "souvenir teacup" in a way that the vast majority of his film school contemporaries did not, he identifies this as the product of hard work. This rejects the belief of Romantic authorship "that cultural production could spring, ex nihilo, from the labors of one exceptional individual" (Sinnreich 2010, 107). That is, it's not imagined to be the product of his own innate genius. In particular, in his memoir he describes his route to success using a superhero metaphor: "The only guy I ever heard of who got an amazing life literally handed to him was Hal Jordan. Don't wait for a dying alien to give you a magic ring: just do it yourself, Slappy. We can't all be Superman, but we sure as shit can train hard, and with loads of practice, we can be Batman" (K. Smith 2013a, 17). Smith's proclamation that "we can be Batman" is appropriately fanboy in style, both burnishing his credentials and serving as an in-joke about his own brief on-screen appearance in a Batman costume as part of an elaborate plot in *Mallrats*. His down-to-earth, fan-focused image has remained a constant. In 2019, writer Warren Ellis shared a story about a fan who was trying to obtain a phone call or a letter from Kevin Smith for his dying friend. Ellis reached out despite having no history with Smith, and reported the outcome on his blog: "Kevin Smith stands up, makes some calls, gets on a plane, flies all the way across America and goes to the hospital and spends an entire day with the guy's best friend. I still don't know Kevin Smith, and have never spoken to him, but here's what I know about Kevin Smith. He stands the fuck up.

And that's my Kevin Smith story" (W. Ellis 2019). In the end, Smith's message seems to be "I am Batman and so can you": he's the nerdy kid who made good and made media.

Return of Jay and Silent Bob

In 2017, Kevin Smith hosted a stunt to enter the *Guinness Book of World Records* by gathering over 250 clones of Jay and Silent Bob in screen-accurate cosplay (at 284, they succeeded) (Francisco 2017). The stunt (in the service of his *Comic Book Men* show) was a testament to ongoing fandom around him, particularly in New Jersey, but also to the particular status Jay and Silent Bob have achieved as icons unto themselves. Smith describes the 2019 iteration of the Jersey trilogy/View Askew universe as a meta-commentary on the nostalgic reboot:

> In *Jay and Silent Bob Reboot*, Jay and Silent Bob find out that Hollywood is making a reboot of that old movie that they had made about them, and they have to go cross the country to Hollywood to stop it all over again. it's literally the same f—ing movie all over again. It's a movie that makes fun of sequels and remakes and reboots while being all three at the same time. (Burlingame 2018)

Smith summarizes the impulse behind the film as revisiting his characters with stronger intentionality: "After 25 years, I know how to deploy Jay and Bob as an effective weapon, like, weaponized to make you laugh. But now I can weaponize them to give you the feels. And the older I get, that's all I care about" (A. Holmes 2019). The announcement followed closely after a more surprising announcement of Smith's intention to write and produce another Jay and Silent Bob reboot, but as a series of short films for virtual reality for STX Entertainment's Surreal division, which one reporter suggested might be successful only because of Smith's "rabid, passionate fan base eager to follow him anywhere" (Bishop 2018b). As of 2019, the VR project has not materialized. The film, however, is apparently moving ahead with a fan-friendly direct release tour. Kevin Smith and Jason Mewes announced the tour in a video while introducing themselves as "refugees from the '90s," and Smith has even accepted one fan's Twitter offer of a trade of a *Wonder Woman* book and record set from 1978 for a ticket to the tour (Jirak 2019).

Following his near-fatal heart attack, Kevin Smith has both made major health lifestyle changes and reconciled with several of his former collaborators: as of 2019, the soon-to-open *Jay and Silent Bob Reboot* looks like a testament to that community. As one reviewer enthusiastically described Smith's return to San Diego ComicCon in 2019:

> Kevin Smith is, love him or hate him, exactly like all of us. Growing up a movie fan, Smith took the extra step to actually do it and has been lucky enough to make a career in Hollywood. While critics have been less than kind to his movies in recent years, Kevin Smith continues to have fun and turn out film after film that showcase him just having fun with his friends. It is a bonus we get to laugh along with him. (Maidy 2019)

He has expressed hopes of continuing this streak, with plans to rewrite *Clerks III* with the goal of reconciling with actor Jeff Anderson, who plays Randal Graves and has refused previously to reprise the part (Burlingame 2019). One reviewer has described the progression of Smith's work to the point where he himself is both brand and content:

> Audiences have a decreasing tolerance for entertainment that feels practiced and rehearsed—they want people who shoot from the hip, say what they mean, and mean what they say. Smith delivers all of that. In an informational ecosystem where there are far too many chattering voices, people want someone who speaks loudly and directly to their interests and worldview, and Smith and the *SModcast* empire do that. We're all forced to self-promote and self-start these days, and Smith is a patron saint in that realm. Even if his time in the spotlight is in the past, few artists have more expertly navigated the present. (Riesman 2017)

Ultimately, the case of Kevin Smith shows that, while he has leveraged his fandom to build his career, his irreverence has impeded his ascension to a standard auteur position. Instead, he has a wide independent transmedia empire, whose far-flung texts and genres are held together by the presence of Smith himself.

5

Joss Whedon and the Allegedly Feminist Fanboy Auteur

> That's the genius of Joss Whedon. An unashamed feminist who freely says he always wanted his show to be a way of spreading a feminist message. (Carey 2003)

While many directors have made a fanboy identity part of their style and brand, Joss Whedon has excelled in publicly declaring his fandom and cultivating a public persona as his audience's peer. He has attracted much attention as the subject of books and studies, philosophical examination, and entire conferences dedicated to the "Whedonverse." In recent years, Whedon has become the transmedia fanboy ascendant, taking on everything from an influential run on *Astonishing X-Men* in comics to leadership of Marvel Cinematic Universe anchor film *The Avengers* and its first sequel. His involvement in tentpole media properties has generally been heralded as somewhere between great news and the arrival of a savior to provide good writing. In terms of our taxonomy, Whedon is highly affirmational, inclined to celebrate source texts and respect authorial intent more than critique or transform. On the other axis, much like Kevin Smith, he has a lot of notoriety for his own Whedonverse rather than being overwhelmingly known for his fandom of other media. This balance has shifted over the years, and currently he is known more for making media of which he himself is a fan. Whedon is both overtly fannish and enthusiastically fan friendly, verifying his credibility with fans by being an advocate for fan participation even when the industry at large is less friendly to it—as in disputes over fan creativity and *Firefly* merchandise (Hall 2013), or in his reliance on fan promotion to get his *Dr. Horrible's Singalong Blog* project off the ground (Leaver 2013; H. Jenkins 2013).

In particular, starting with *Buffy the Vampire Slayer*, Whedon gained a reputation as a feminist media-maker for his women characters who were both powerful and emotionally complex. His tendency to capitalize on familiar tropes with a twist frequently heralded as feminist continued through *Angel*, *Dollhouse*, and *Firefly/Serenity*. Indeed, Whedon's particular brand of feminism has become a benchmark for the industry, in spite of his use of racist tropes, his questionable sexual politics, and increasing awareness of his bad behavior around his actors. However, the conventional wisdom about Whedon as a feminist does not hold up well under scrutiny. His reputation for feminism is somewhere between an artifact of where gender politics were in the 1990s and entirely unearned, as his legendarily sexist *Wonder Woman* script shows. Nevertheless, we argue, his ability to perform this identity and embed it deeply into his brand has preserved his reputation against considerable scrutiny and public challenge.

Joss Whedon's direct engagement with fans and journalists through interviews, online forums, and social media is extensive: this chapter draws on highlights from both the articles and interviews in our corpus and Whedon's use of convention and forum spaces to build his reputation. We reviewed discourse centering on Whedon as fanboy over primarily the past fifteen years, with a particular focus on pieces authored by Whedon (or at least attributed to him). While this cannot possibly encompass the full discourse evoked by Whedon's engagement with fans and fannishness, it provides a representative engagement with his most (in)famous moments.

In this chapter, we begin by interrogating the role of being a feminist in Whedon's branding, arguing that, while Whedon successfully branded himself as a feminist for two decades, closer analysis and subsequent revelations demonstrate this to be more style than substance. Whedon's branding as a fanboy is more well-grounded and permeates his public persona, from his casual fashion to his works to actively participating in his own and other fandoms, though it is in tension with his auteur status. Moreover, we argue, Whedon actively leverages the illusion of intimacy enabled by Twitter and fan site Whedonesque to extract the free fan labor that has powered his career.

Whedon's Feminism between Branding and Substance

Whedon broke into the public consciousness with TV series *Buffy the Vampire Slayer*, which ran from 1996 to 2003, spawning a spin-off, *Angel*, as well as a transmedia franchise of intertied novels, video games, and comics that continued the main narrative arc even after the shows' ending. Airing first on the WB and later on UPN, the show was a big success by the standards of a small television network, and the collective "Buffyverse" would go on to draw a dedicated fandom that persists to this day. The relative novelty in 1996 of a genre show featuring a woman warrior as lead—its contemporary, *Xena: Warrior Princess*, was in first-run syndication and less widely known—immediately drew feminist readings and attention to the franchise from fans and scholars: as of September 2019, there are more than five thousand results on Google Scholar for the terms "*Buffy the Vampire Slayer*" and "feminism." The media landscape at the time particularly allowed Whedon to shine by comparison, and he credits himself with introducing feminism subversively in genre spaces: "It's like horror or, back when it was somewhat new, rap. It's a fringe art which means you will find the most egregious misogyny in there—but also the most subversive feminism" (John 2013). Moreover, Whedon worked to tightly control the transmedia elements of the franchise to preserve and encourage feminist readings of the Buffyverse. For example, the visual branding of Buffy continues in the comics, where Whedon is credited with directing artists to "draw women that look like real women," resisting the hypersexualized styles that frequently characterize comics as part of transmedia franchises (Cocca 2016, 167). This pushed back against dominant trends—and potentially marketability—while simultaneously winning fan praise (Cocca 2016).

Post-*Buffy*, being a feminist became a key part of Whedon's branding. Research has noted the attention both fans and critics pay to the "coherence" of celebrity performance on Twitter (Bulck, Claessens, and Bels 2014), and in Whedon's case, retweeting feminist criticism and news stories is an important part of this consistent self-presentation. One incident, surrounding a post by Whedon in 2007 on his own fan site, Whedonesque, is illustrative.[1] Whedon's post, "Let's watch a girl get beaten to death," was picked up and circulated across media. The thread was described in one outlet as "an interesting read, as he admits he's never had any faith in humanity, grapples with misogyny and admits to a bit of complicity himself" (Arpe 2007). The thread opens with a description of the camera phone filming of the murder of Dua Kalil, a seventeen-year-old girl who was kicked and stoned to death while a number of people watched—in some cases, as Whedon observes, "from the front row." He tries to make sense of the horrifying video in the context of media production, comparing it to the trailer for *Captivity*, a contemporaneous film firmly grounded in the torture porn genre (defined by excessive and brutal violence, like 2004 film *Saw*) and featuring the kidnapping and abuse of a woman played by Elisha Cuthbert. The genre is itself infamous for misogyny and the fetishization of violence in a twist on horror's "final girl" trope. As David Edelstein remarked in a critique of the genre: "The 'final girls' in *Wolf Creek* and *The Devil's Rejects* die ghastly deaths, and while *Hostel* ends with bloody retribution, it's set in a world in which people pay big money for the opportunity to torture and murder—a world of latent serial killers" (Edelstein 2006). *Captivity* was poorly received by reviewers and drew questions about film ethics even from reviewers not usually inclined to find movies objectionable on those grounds: as one critic wrote, "There are defenders who will argue that 'this is only a movie,' but there's something about the way the suffering is crafted that hints at darker and sicker motives" (Berardinelli 2007).

Whedon's post draws upon the parallels between the two texts, and reflects the larger concerns he sees as motivating the voyeuristic misogyny of both:

> I try to think how we got here. The theory I developed in college (shared by many I◆m sure) is one I have yet to beat: Womb Envy. Biology: women are generally smaller and weaker than men. But they're also much tougher. Put simply, men are strong enough to overpower a woman and propagate. Women are tough enough to have and nurture children, with or without the aid of a man. Oh, and they◆ve also got the equipment to do that, to be part of the life cycle, to create and bond in a way no man ever really will. Somewhere a long time ago a bunch of men got together and said, ◆If all we do is hunt and gather, let◆s make hunting and gathering the awesomest achievement, and let◆s make childbirth kinda weak and shameful.◆ It◆s a rather silly simplification, but I believe on a mass, unconscious level, it◆s entirely true. How else to explain the fact that cultures who would die to eradicate each other have always agreed on one issue? That every popular religion puts restrictions on women◆s behavior that are practically untenable? That the act of being a free, attractive, self-assertive woman is punishable by torture and death? (Whedon 2007)

The ◆ marks reproduced throughout the above quotation also appear in the original post, suggesting it was pasted directly from Microsoft Word into the (incompatible) forum box. This compositional artifact reflects the fact that the post—at 1,327 words a much longer reflection than Whedon's usual Whedonesque post—was likely composed separately as an essay. While the post begins by saying "this is not my blog," it proceeds to function as one, lacking some of the markers of rapid composition that characterize Whedon's other posts on the site, like misspellings and colloquialisms.

Despite the more deliberate composition, the post has through lines with Whedon's other commentary. As the casual racism of assuming above that rap music is uniquely misogynist already begins to suggest, Whedon's feminism was never intersectional, nor complex. Rather, it is normative and hegemonic—applauding women, like Buffy, who perform masculinely gendered activities like fighting while being unable to celebrate feminized emotion like that of the *Twilight* series, which Whedon once referred to as "Choosing Boyfriends: The Movie" (Hibberd 2013a), emphasizing a limited notion of respectability. The post above demonstrates a traditionalist feminism that foregrounds biological essentialism, reducing women to childbearing capacity (as we'll see, a common trope from Whedon) and making spurious claims about the distribution of size and strength in the human species. Women are also viewed, from this perspective, as inherently rapeable, since "men can overpower them to propagate." There are, further, echoes of Orientalist notions of brown folks in faraway lands like Iraq as uniquely savage, religious, and conservative, demonstrating the ways this particular feminism is white and Western (Mohanty 1984).

Nevertheless, the post is—albeit in a limited way—an act of feminism. Whedon not only calls attention to a horrific act of gendered violence, but calls on his "evolved" fans on Whedonesque to act:

> do something. Try something. Speaking out, showing up, writing a letter, a check, a strongly worded e-mail. Pick a cause � there are few unworthy ones. And nudge yourself past the brink of tacit support to action. Once a month, once a year, or just once. If you can�t think of what to do, there is this handy link. Even just learning enough about a subject so you can speak against an opponent eloquently makes you an unusual personage. Start with that. Any one of you would have cried out, would have intervened, had you been in that crowd in Bashiqa. Well thanks to digital technology, you�re all in it now.

In an analysis of this ending to Whedon's post, Tanya Cochran (2012, para. 2.19) describes how Whedon both pulls in his fan base and challenges them to respond using the "conflation of the fictional and nonfictional as well as his use of the second-person pronoun you. In essence, Whedon positions his readers—an audience that begins as the fan-users of WHEDONesque but quickly becomes Internet users all over the world—as voyeurs. The question is whether or not these voyeurs will stay immured in their passivity." The ability of celebrities to harness energy to a particular cause is mixed, and often more effective when it is already resonant with existing themes and ideas from the work (H. Jenkins and Shresthova 2012). The post and similar calls to action from Whedon have been linked to fan activism among Whedonverse fans, although women's empowerment is embedded in his body of work and its reception rather than something that needs to be directly attributed to the intervention of the auteur (Cochran 2012). In this way, despite the clear and troubling limitations of what counts as feminism for Whedon, he does spur awareness and urge action on gender inequality.

Whedon's fixation on childbirth cropped up again in a particularly controversial flashback sequence and follow-up conversation in his first *Avengers* film.[2] It was revealed that former assassin Natasha Romanoff, also known as Black Widow, could not bear children as a result of an operation that took place during her training. She described herself as a "monster" due to this operation, building on a pattern of representations of women as mothers or monsters in Whedon's previous work and drawing criticism for the reduction of her character. As one review noted snarkily, "That's what the Red Room did to her. It's not the loss of innocence through killing or being forced to live a life of betraying people. The greatest loss is motherhood. That's why she's a monster like the Hulk. Poor Black Widow. She leaned in, and where did it get her? She's a lonely, incomplete, monster" (Woerner and Trendacosta 2015). Whedon later explained the line as referring to Natasha's identity more broadly: "She said she was a monster because she was an assassin.... Being rendered infertile made her feel unnatural, made her feel cut off from the natural world. But it was her actions that defined her. Her murdery [sic] actions. That's what 'monster' meant" (W. Hughes 2016). However, even here infertility is foregrounded as tied to the unnatural—and, correspondingly, childbearing is presented as being natural (much like in his analysis of Dua Kalil's death years before).

As Whedon's career has developed, some of these troubling themes implicit in his earlier work have at times exited subtext for maintext. Perhaps the most infamous example of this is his 2009–2010 FOX series *Dollhouse*. Whedon points out that the show was the site of an auteur-industry conflict over its use of attractive women (and men) as reprogrammable dolls for the fantasy of the rich: as he said in an interview, "They were totally comfortable with it until [Fox owner News Corp.'s then president] Peter Chernin said, 'This sounds like prostitution.' Then Fox did an about-face that was dazzling in its speed and precision" (Hibberd 2013b). Even as Whedon acknowledges the most potentially problematic elements of the work, he holds on to the feminist interpretation in interviews: "I mean it's potentially the most offensive show in the history of television. And to me it's also the most pure feminist and empowering statement I ever made. It's somebody building themselves from nothing" (Rogers 2012). The show's questionable content (and Whedon's weak defense) would play a role in the slowly growing skepticism surrounding Whedon's feminist work.

A key incident in the trajectory of unmasking Whedon as a faux feminist came in April 2017, when his *Wonder Woman* script—written in 2006 and long mourned in fan communities for its failure to get a green light—was leaked in its entirety following the success of Patty Jenkins's film. Whedon's attempt was only one of many failures (all helmed by men) that couldn't bring the "tricky" character to screen, as Howell (2015) chronicles. The script was dissected in many circles for containing every possible cliché. Joss Whedon's description of Wonder Woman as filtered through Steve Trevor's point of view during their initial meeting refers to her simply as "THE GIRL": "To say she is beautiful is almost to miss the point. She is elemental, as natural and wild as the luminous flora surrounding. Her dark hair waterfalls to her shoulders in soft arcs and curls. Her body is curvaceous, but taut as a drawn bow" (Whedon 2006). The emphasis on a heterosexual man's perspective is so deeply embedded in the script as to be almost comical. As one writer for *The Mary Sue* commented: "The fascination with what penises look like in an all-female society when dealing with an intruder is especially 'charming.' I promise you, cis male screenwriters, left to their own devices, women are not nearly as preoccupied with what your penises look like as you are" (Jusino 2017a).

This centering of heterosexual masculinity also comes into play elsewhere with Whedon. In a 2012 interview, he went on at length about the uselessness of feminist criticism to understanding film while suggesting he had a more authentic entrypoint into gender in film because of his male gaze:

> The reason I felt like I had an in that most of my classmates didn't in my feminism classes was, I was a fucking guy, first and last. Male gaze? I was wearing those goggles every day. I was the enemy. I absolutely knew what the enemy was. I had sympathy for the devil. Not in a horrific way, but in a normal way. Sometimes you need to celebrate the darkness. (Rogers 2012)

The disturbing choice of phrase, "I was the enemy," is perhaps prescient given how thoroughly Whedon was eventually shown to fail at feminism. However, his brand as the feminist fanboy auteur horror, science fiction, and comics desperately need to save themselves from predictable and tedious misogyny was always marked by incidents of this sort. It extends even to the strange man-obsession of his first bio section in his profile on Twitter: "Ladies man, man's man, man about town . . . Java man, Isle of Man, Mandroid, Man Who Would Be King Ralph, girly man."

When his failures of feminism have been critiqued, Whedon has responded not with soul-searching to try to be a better feminist but with defensiveness. When an episode of the show GeekU on the question of "Joss Whedon—Feminist" that contained criticisms of *Dollhouse* was posted to Whedonesque (DeathIsYourGift 2009), Whedon replied the next day, and instead of addressing the central thesis, he initially commented on the potential sexism represented by his characters' footwear. He noted, "Eliza: Yeah, she's wearing some pretty intense boots, particularly as Taffy. That's Eliza. She absolutely likes to turn up the heat wherever she thinks it's appropriate—or close enough—and it's part of her persona. My girl flaunts. I got no problem with it." This is fascinating not only for its deflection of the subject at hand but for locating the choice of costuming with the actor, who he describes with the possessive "my girl." Perhaps pressed by the continued conversation, Whedon added another post twenty-four minutes later that expounded on his position:

> I wasn't going to touch the whole feminism debate, but I'm wacky sometimes. All I'll say is this: what I say about myself and my intentions should have nothing to do with your experience of my work. As Hitchcock said, "Trust the tale, not the teller." Some "feminist" works reinforce stereotypes, some "exploitive" works provide textured kick-ass female roles. Mostly everyone does both. If you view a piece solely from the perspective of the writer's INTENTION—or one specific part of that intention—it's harder to have a true response to how the work makes you feel.

Whedon makes a double move here, ostensibly killing himself as an author and emphasizing the agency of the reader to reinterpret and contextualize a work at the same time as he reinforces that he had feminist "INTENTION." His reference to "exploitive" works that can include "kick-ass female roles" is particularly telling as it almost directly reproduces criticism of both *Buffy* and *Dollhouse*, which rely upon tropes of "strong women" while demonstrating an obsession with femininized vulnerability and victimhood. The irony that he had just insisted on the primacy of intent in his earlier post seems to have escaped him.

Similarly, in response to the backlash over *Wonder Woman*, Whedon doubled down on the value of his original script: "I don't know which parts people didn't like, but . . . I think it's great. . . . People say that it's not woke enough. I think they're not looking at the big picture" (Desta 2018); in an even more impressive understatement, he referred to himself as not "the most woke individual who ever lived at that time." The interview followed the announcement that Whedon would no longer be directing the Batgirl movie, in a surprising move for DC. Given DC's own infamous weakness on inclusivity—indeed, so lacking in acumen that an entire countdown clock online counts the "days since DC has done something stupid"[3]—their move to distance themselves from Whedon suggests that his heralded days as feminist fanboy might be drawing to an end.

Whedon's defensiveness goes hand in hand with shifting any and all blame for his texts. In particular, he has historically benefited from the separation that Derek Johnson (2013) terms the "auteur-producer divide": he escapes blame even when his texts are deemed flawed by fandom, profiting from a model that creates a divide between artistic vision and industrial production. One reviewer noted that his success in utilizing this separation has allowed Whedon to disclaim the *Buffy* film entirely, and the fandom has in many cases followed suit: "Perhaps part of the reason the *Buffy movie* is so disliked among fans of the TV show is because Whedon has been so open about his problems with it—it's easy to feel angry on his behalf, or to wish the movie had come out the way he wanted it" (Dobbs 2012).

Whedon excels at simultaneously blaming the influence of studios and networks as well as the desires of the audience members themselves for limiting the activism of his works. He has frequently relied upon a veneer of accessibility to reinforce the perception of his work as activism: in one interview, he observed: "If I made 'Buffy the Lesbian Separatist,' a series of lectures on PBS on why there should be feminism, no one would be coming to the party, and it would be boring. The idea of changing culture is important to me, and it can only be done in a popular medium" (Nussbaum 2002). The very framing of the joke is confrontational: feminists cannot be trusted to "sell" feminism, his words imply—only men offering a gentle, less "separatist," consumable feminism can reach the masses. The comment also invokes the lavender menace often used to divide and conquer feminism—the specter of the lesbian as the most extreme feminist (A. Rich 1980).

Similar to his dismissal of feminist film theory above, at times Whedon even lambasts feminism itself. In an interview on his 2015 decision to leave Twitter, Whedon claimed that harassment wasn't his major reason for leaving the platform:

> I saw a lot of people say, "Well, the social justice warriors destroyed one of their own!" It's like, Nope. That didn't happen. I have been attacked by mili-

tant feminists since I got on Twitter. That's something I'm used to. Every breed of feminism is attacking every other breed, and every subsection of liberalism is always busy attacking another subsection of liberalism, because god forbid they should all band together and actually fight for the cause. (Vary 2015b)

The reference to "social justice warriors," a term typically used as derogatory in conservative internet discourse (though sometimes adopted as a positive self-identification by activists), suggests at least some engagement with such discourse. The characterization of gender-based critiques as "attacks by militant feminists" is also part and parcel of this brand of conservatism. Indeed, in this interview he spoke with some regret about his self-branding as feminist: "I've said before, when you declare yourself politically, you destroy yourself artistically.... Because suddenly that's the litmus test for everything you do—for example, in my case, feminism. If you don't live up to the litmus test of feminism in this one instance, then you're a misogynist. It circles directly back upon you" (Vary 2015b). Whedon's words suggest he is haunted by his own self-branding. The implication is that he believes he might have been held to a lower standard, and appreciated for the efforts he made, if he hadn't embraced feminism as a brand so strongly from the outset. While his conclusions are debatable, there is certainly a change of tone here from Whedon's early, enthusiastic declarations of feminist identity.

The strength of Whedon's feminist fanboy brand enabled him to get away with minor creepiness, androcentrism, and even more overt forms of misogyny for a surprisingly long time. However, there were signs as early as *Buffy* that his feminism was not actually substantive. Notably, Whedon's use of the women in his shows as placeholders for his own experience is rarely veiled: in the director's commentary to the first season, it is revealed that "Cordelia's rejection of Jesse in the Bronze in 'Welcome to the Hellmouth' is word for word from Joss's own life" (Lavery 2002). The uncomfortable use of characters such as Cordelia for Whedon's projection and fantasy is a theme across his work. This projection extended from characters to actors, leading to an uncomfortable interview exchange in 2012 around Whedon as an outsider who has never been to a Hollywood party:

> Wired: You mean gawking at preternaturally attractive people is not a reason [to go]?
> Whedon: Have you seen the women on my shows?
> Wired: Good point. (Rogers 2012)

Whedon has no need to go where the attractive people are, he claims, because he has proprietary access to women on his shows. Such incidents are part of a recurring uncomfortableness in how Whedon engages with the women in his media projects. That this access to his actors was quite literal burst into the public consciousness with the publication of an open letter from Joss Whedon's ex-wife, Kai Cole, that included an indictment of his feminist persona:

> I believed, everyone believed, that he was one of the good guys, committed to fighting for women's rights, committed to our marriage, and to the women he worked with. But I now see how he used his relationship with me as a shield, both during and after our marriage, so no one would question his relationships with other women or scrutinize his writing as anything other than feminist. (Cole 2017)

The piece goes on at length about Whedon's affairs and is strongly linked with the #MeToo movement, calling out Whedon as among those using the veneer of feminism to abuse women, including his wife. Overall, while Whedon successfully branded himself as feminist for two decades, closer analysis and subsequent revelations demonstrate this to be more style than substance.

Scruffy Jeans and Internet Squee: Performing the Fanboy

If feminism has been one key aspect of Whedon's brand, fannishness is the other. He often positions himself as an everyfan, and is also positioned as such by others. This persona has endured through what are now more than two decades of interviews and internet postings, as Whedon has struck a consistent self-presentation anchored in his continually reaffirmed status as fanboy. The opening to a fan biography paints an accessible portrait: "In his scruffy jeans and baggy button-down camp shirt, Whedon doesn't look much like a Hollywood mogul . . . his lopsided grin makes you think more of the video-store clerk he once was than the man who created one of the most beloved television shows of all time (Havens 2003, 1). This type of description fits the tropes of the fanboy auteur: like Kevin Smith and his *Clerks* origins, Whedon maintains the trappings of his former life.

Additionally, fannishness is baked into many or even most of Whedon's projects, even unexpected ones. Following his shift away from television and in the midst of the changing economics of studios and digital distribution in the late 2000s, Whedon directed three projects notable for their fannishness.

These projects, ranging from the superhero parody web serial *Dr. Horrible* (discussed at more length later) to the horror comedy and cliché collection *Cabin in the Woods* to the fan remake of Shakespeare's *Much Ado About Nothing*, could be seen as in line with the "transformative" fandom more frequently associated with the fangirl author (S. Scott 2019). However, these works are still strongly curatorial, reflecting both Whedon's fanboy brand and a savvy understanding of how to harness existing fandom to circulate and build new properties. Perhaps Whedon's most recognizably fannish production and an outlier among his work, *Cabin in the Woods* is frequently read as a sardonic fan letter to the horror genre. The movie was already in theatres when Whedon's big-budget *Avengers* film was released, and was described by one reviewer as "a brilliant genre-bending dark comedy made by horror fans for horror fans" (Wilson 2012). Whedon also established his fannishness farther afield with *Much Ado About Nothing*, which was heralded as a "surprise" from the "overachieving" Whedon (Itzkoff 2011). The film is highly rooted in an unexpected fandom, drawing on Whedon's self-proclaimed status as Shakespeare fanboy (Holl 2017).

However, perhaps the ultimate realization of Whedon's status as fanboy auteur is *The Avengers*. He identifies this success as rooted in fandom; he told one reporter that "I kept telling my mom that reading comic books would pay off" (John 2013). When asked about taking on the blockbuster, he described it as a realization of a long-held dream, referencing classic markers of authentic comics fandom:

> The icy cold part is, I've wanted to make a comic book movie all my life, I've wanted to make a summer tent-pole movie all my life. I loved the book as a kid. I feel empathy for the characters. I have a take on the material. And this feels right. Now, that's not so cold that artistic integrity isn't involved, because I can't live without it. I had the luxury of never doing a job I didn't at least initially love. And I even include working in a video store. (Rogers 2012)

The rhetoric of the everyfan is strongly present in Whedon's wording—and holds echoes of Kevin Smith and other fanboy auteurs who hold closely to a discursive position as a "lucky geek." Indeed, Henry Barnes (2012) referred to *The Avengers* as carrying "the mark of a piece of expensively assembled fan fiction," although given that comics themselves are already deeply mutli-authored and reboot-ridden, such a descriptor is if anything a reminder of how little mainstream film critics tend to understand transformative fan fiction practices. The film also included Joss Whedon's signature brand of feminism, opening on Black Widow and offering a version of the character that actress Scarlett Johansson still credits as a major influence: "He just is such a huge believer of strong female characters and storylines, and he really celebrated the character's flaws and wanted to bring them to light.... Just having his support and him wanting to shine the light on that character really made a huge difference" (Bleznak 2019).[4] However, much like the above reviewer's reflexive denigration of fan fiction, Whedon is careful to indicate his auteur-ness, assuring his listeners that his fannishness does not get in the way of "artistic integrity." This insistence that fannishness not overwhelm auteur status reflects an ongoing tension in Whedon's position.

While Whedon is frequently attributed fanboy status by others in many venues, his self-establishment as a fanboy can perhaps best be seen through his engagement on his own fan site, Whedonesque. Although its "About" page emphasizes the platform's independence as a "non-profit platform for fans" (Vermeulen n.d.), the site has often been mischaracterized by the wider media, linking Whedonesque to Whedon himself and suggesting it serves as an official website akin to Smith's viewaskew.com. This slippage between fan and auteur with Whedonesque's ownership is quite apt for its content as well. Whedon first joined his own fansite in 2004. One of his earliest posts, from August 11, 2005, is centered on fannishness, establishing his credibility as fanboy:

Joss Luvs Veronica.

This is my attempt at posting my own thread. My peeps and I just finished a crazed Veronica Marsathon, and I can no longer restrain myself. Best. Show. Ever. Seriously, I've never gotten more wrapped up in a show I wasn't making, and maybe even more than those. Crazy crisp dialogue. Incredibly tight plotting. Big emotion, I mean BIG, and charsimatic actors and I was just DYING from the mystery and the relationships and PAIN, this show knows from pain and no, I don't care, laugh all you want, I had to share this. These guys know what they're doing on a level that intimidates me. It's the Harry Potter of shows. There. I said it. People should do whatever they can to check out this first season so the second won't be a spoiler fest. I'm nutty.

I'm a little calmer now. Oh God, no I'm not! Wait. Wait. Okay. Some of you may already be all up on this, and some may disagree, but I'm urging peeps to check it out, 'cause there is great TV afoot, and who doesn't want that? Thank you for your time.

Still not calm! Wait . . . wait . . . (Whedon 2005a)

The combination of misspellings and colloquialisms (from the use of "peeps" and dramatic periods to the all caps used for the word "DYING") is not unlike the typical fan post on the site, taken perhaps to farcical extremes. In particular, the deployment of both a Harry Potter comparison and the "Best. X. Ever" formulation—which entered geek culture from fictional superfan Comic Book Guy of *The Simpsons*—locates Whedon in fandom. Several of the replies to this post reinforced the "one of us" interpretation, with commenter orphea noting "YAY! Joss goes all fangeeky like the rest of us mere mortals!" This expression of fandom escalated into a cameo for Whedon on the show, in a savvy cross-fan base marketing move that drew attention to Whedon as the show's "No. 1 fan," as he was proclaimed in the title of an *Entertainment Weekly* piece he himself wrote (Whedon 2005b). The article is unusual both as a news piece written by Whedon himself and as directly addressing fellow auteur Rob Thomas as an outlet for his own questioning fandom around the show's DVD release: "So where's a commentary, Rob? The extras are frustratingly thin" (Whedon 2005b). The combined impact of these texts serves to affirm Whedon's sincerity in his fandom.

Whedon also positions himself as fannish through in-person interaction in fan spaces. As he describes, ComicCon became a hub of his social interaction due to *Buffy* and its reception:

> It's an ego boost—not gonna lie. It's also where all of my friends gather. I was always about interacting with people partially because I was so gratified that people would care. Partially there's a business aspect to it—be decent [to people]; that will help. And there's a real connection. Someone will say, "You helped me through a hard time in my life with this show." For a long time I thought, "That's so sweet and lovely they're responding to the work." And then I realized, "Oh, I was helping me through a hard time with that show, too." I was a different version of them. We're almost like a support group. (Rogers 2012)

Here, Whedon explicitly identifies himself as "a different version" of his fans and creates slippage between fans and (industry) friends, but he also maintains himself as media-maker and as separate from them. Ultimately, Whedon's fan identity permeates his public persona, from his casual fashion to his works to actively participating in his own and other fandoms.

Leveraging Fandom: From Internet Intimacy to Labor

Whedon's engagement on Whedonesque did more than burnish his fan credentials. It also helped cultivate his general relationship to his fans. During his membership on Whedonesque, Whedon posted thirty-four threads and

159 comments, with the most recent coming in 2016. While these are small absolute numbers, particularly compared to the average fan who might post daily or weekly, they are impressive given the apparent low return of participation on a fan site compared to other venues available to him such as the entertainment press. His continual presence on Whedonesque (albeit relatively limited when placed in the context of approximately thirteen years of use) allowed him to build an accessible online persona as he added comments further cementing his fandom of everything from *How I Met Your Mother* (CBS, 2005–2014) to the paperboy musical *Newsies* (1992). His participation, unsurprisingly, drew fan attention; the "joss" account's presence as a commenter had the potential to disrupt and redirect any thread. While the interface distinguishes his presence from other contributors only minimally—his username changed from the default yellow to a bold purple, and, in a nod to his everyfan status. his name displays simply as "joss" and his bio makes no direct reference to his work—Whedon is nevertheless distinguished both by design and by practice. Indeed, his very presence on his own fan site elevated it as a subcultural hub, allowing Whedonesque to boast additional "insider" information drawn from this "fan-producer proximity" (Chin and Hills 2008).

This practice of internet intimacy continued into Whedon's later use of Twitter. At the same time as he has gained broad fame and auteurist power, he has used Twitter to maintain his branding as an outsider. The association of Twitter and "authentic" celebrity disclosure has been attributed by Nick Muntean and Anne Helen Petersen (2009) to the "ostensible spontaneity" of the tweets, a descriptor of the apparent "extemporary intimacy" that fits well with Whedon's style. Whedon joined Twitter in May 2013, well after early adopters: his initial account was called @JossActual, gaining 20,000 followers in two weeks. This wasn't actually his first account (he claimed responsibility, at least, for the *Much Ado About Nothing* marketing account established a few months earlier in March), but it was the first marked with promises of political authenticity, as his first two tweets established. The first read: "It's me! Joss! My own account! No more hiding under studio skirts! I'm FREE! @MuchAdoFilm @AgentsofSHIELD @Marvel @roadsidetweets #free." The second read: "MY account! I got strong opinions! I'm gettin' POLITICAL! (Heads up, LEMURS.) And making wry observations about mundane stuff!"[5] Whedon's rhetoric implied that the promotional emphasis he'd previously placed on Twitter (with the *Much Ado About Nothing* account) and his silence on recent political issues was a result of studio concerns, positioning himself as the "rebel" and the studios—whom he nevertheless tags in the tweet—as his silencers.

This performative rebellion has continued to be a staple of Whedon's Twitter use. After a departure, he rejoined Twitter on September 14, 2016, using the handle @joss—the same handle he used on Whedonesque. His bio on Twitter has continued to be extravagantly casual: as of May 12, 2018, it read: "writer, actor, rapper, dreamer, quarterback, astronaut, floozy." The sense of authenticity is reinforced by bringing a more intense political performance to this space. Whedon posted a tweet on April 4, 2018, reacting to the Trump presidency: "Donald trump is killing this country. Some of it quickly, some slowly, but he spoils and destroys everything he touches. He emboldens monsters, wielding guns, governmental power, or just smug doublespeak. Or Russia. My hate and sadness are exhausting. Die, Don. Just quietly die" (Zanottie 2018). As a result of terms of service violation reports filed on the tweet, his account was briefly suspended, but he returned on April 6, tweeting a reference to *The Breakfast Club* (1985) along with a reaffirmation of the political stance: "Well I was put in twitter suspension but luckily there was also a jock, a weird girl, a socialite and a rebel and it turns out we're all the same or something (?) anyway they all hooked up and I had to write this tweet so I'm not sure, trump still killing the country tho lol"—notably, here again he's positioned as the geek through taking the place of the Anthony Michael Hall character (Whedon 2018). He continues to provoke on Twitter: as of August 2019, his bio read "for starters, abolish ICE," and his Fourth of July tweet that year bemoaned the state of the country (Whedon 2019).

Alice Marwick and danah boyd (2011) remind us that the illusion of intimacy enabled by Twitter (and, indeed, Whedonesque before it) must not be confused with an "equalizer" of discourse, as fans continue to occupy an observer position and can mostly respond or amplify without expectation of being "seen" in return. Whedon has proven particularly talented at maintaining this sense of intimacy: his earlier habits on Whedonesque of occasionally joining in replies built the sense that any participant on the forum might have the opportunity for this type of direct connection, allowing even those who hadn't been the object of engagement to bask in a sense of shared attention. The "context collapse" of multiple audiences (Marwick and boyd 2011) is amplified when we consider Whedon's Twitter engagement with people ranging from fellow film celebrities to media critics, authors, and even the Whedonesque account.

That the flattening of fan-auteur hierarchy is ultimately illusory is key. Whedon has acted, explicitly and implicitly, as a leader of his fans even from his initial postings on Whedonesque. In particular, he has led his fans toward actively supporting his work. Much of the discourse around Whedon's work is fan-centered: his "cult" following ensures a regular dissection of his words, intentions, and next moves that began at the time of his earliest work and continues through to his current status as multi-franchise titan, and this has been both actively cultivated and strategically deployed. Any of his posts to the Whedonesque community (particularly his comments on other people's threads) appear in the context of ongoing fan discussion and are therefore discussed at length. He first used his account on the site for promotional purposes with an April 27, 2005, post, using a combination of humor and self-deprecation to connect with his fan base: "Screenings announced / by me! 10 screenings next week. It's all on the offical board, eh? I'd link ya but i'm me! I still can't work the mmmihmmenineograph machine." The post received 199 comments, including some from Whedon himself (with one further building the persona through a pretend-fake fan post gushing over his own work). Here, Whedon performs a lack of authority in the very same post as his undiminished authority drives attention to his work. Whedon frequently turned to the site to make direct announcements, including a post on February 2, 2007, regarding his departure from the *Wonder Woman* film. This adds to the sense of exclusivity and suggests Whedon's prioritization of his invested fan base as the first audience for his big announcements.

Whedonesque is often perceived as an official site—the top search results for the term "Whedon" as of February 2019 were fan-run sites Whedonesque and Whedonverse Network—which calls attention to the fact that Whedon *has* no official site. While other auteurs are known for hosting their own sites and branding (e.g., Kevin Smith, J. K. Rowling), Whedon's decision to capitalize on a fan-run effort placed his brand partly in the hands of the fandom. This might seem like an odd oversight for a director who understands fandom, yet this seemingly uncontrolled choice is key to Whedon's leverage of the internet to manage his brand, reliant upon this frequent conflation of his most prominent fan sites with his own image. It also shifts the responsibility for maintenance to the loyal Whedonites. This tension between being an auteur and maintaining plausible fan credibility is most visible in these uses of the site to promote his work, emphasizing that Whedon's career has relied extensively on fan labor.

This question of whose labor powers Joss Whedon's success arises again and again. During the 2007–2008 Writers Guild of America strike, Whedon took advantage of his online visibility to self-fund and circulate *Dr. Horrible's Singalong Blog*, a superhero musical parody; its unprecedented success built on what Tama Leaver (2013) calls Whedon's "paratextual aura," harnessing the audience from fan conventions, Whedonesque.com, and other fan goodwill to promote the series. The character of Dr. Horrible himself became a symbol of the online threat of new media, appearing at the 2009 Emmy

Awards—hosted by actor Neil Patrick Harris—in what Hudson (2015) calls "a hilarious salute to an auditorium full of old-media dinosaurs, allowing them a collective codgers' 'harumph' at the technical limitations of internet video streaming even as Neil Patrick Harris's online alter ego accurately predicted the demise of their critical mass-dependent, schedule-oriented business model." The move seemed to be a testament to Whedon's range and vision, coming as it did in the very early days of digital distribution.

However, an overemphasis on Whedon as the fanboy auteur ignores the powerful role played by fangirls in the work's success. *Dr. Horrible* capitalized upon the visibility of leading lady Felicia Day, whose YouTube work and cameo appearances across transmedia franchises have helped cement her status as professional fangirl. Day has longstanding links to Whedon, as she had previously appeared on Season 8 of *Buffy*. Day's web series *The Guild* was actually an inspiration for Whedon's approach to releasing *Dr. Horrible*, and Whedon credits Day with explaining Twitter and social media marketing concepts (Littleton 2015). The first episode of *The Guild* had been released a year earlier and represented an early success in web content, as she describes:

> In 2006 I wrote a script called "The Guild." It was a comedy about online gamers that I initially wrote as a 1/2 hour TV series, but turned into a web series after everyone rejected it, and my co-producer Kim Evey said, "Hey, you should do this for the web, because that's where gamers are." This was right after YouTube STARTED, so I was like, "Okay?" After our first upload though, the summer of 2007, I knew I wanted to do this show for the web as long as I could. (Day n.d.)

The Guild continued through 2013, running for six seasons and seventy episodes, representing a more large-scale and long term production than Whedon's use of web distribution for auteur side projects.

However, Day wasn't the only fangirl on whom *Dr. Horrible* piggybacked. In the "Frequently (soon to be) Asked Questions" section of the *Dr. Horrible* website, Whedon calls on fans to labor in support of the project in answering the question, "What can WE do to help this musical extravaganza?"

> What you always do, peeps! What you're already doing. Spread the word. Rock some banners, widgets, diggs . . . let people know who wouldn't ordinarily know. It wouldn't hurt if this really was an event. Good for the business, good for the community—communitIES: Hollywood, internet, artists around the world, comic-book fans, musical fans (and even the rather vocal community of people who hate both but will still dig on this). Proving we can turn

Dr Horrible into a viable economic proposition as well as an awesome goof will only inspire more people to lay themselves out in the same way. It's time for the dissemination of the artistic process. Create more for less. You are the ones that can make that happen. Wow. I had no idea how important you guys were. I'm a little afraid of you. (Whedon n.d.)

Here Whedon is relying explicitly on fans to do promotional labor for him in a way that is usually disguised (Stanfill 2019). In particular, he explains all the things that are needed in enough depth to be actionable, and he's transparent about the economic benefit of doing so. Like leveraging Day, Twitter, and Whedonesque, this shifts the work of supporting Whedon's brand elsewhere than the man himself. In the end, as much as Whedon's brand relies on framing himself as a fan, he also leverages the actions of his actual fans, turning largely illusory internet intimacy into a willingness to do free labor.

Conclusion: Joss Jossing Joss

As *TV Tropes* notes, being "Jossed"—named for Whedon—is when a fan creation "built upon canonical elements is abruptly disproved by further canon" (n.d.). In important ways, this is exactly what has happened to Whedon himself in recent years, as the feminist brand built on canonical elements of his texts and persona was disproved by subsequent revelations about him. Accordingly, his brand has fallen on hard times of late. On August 21, 2017, the Whedonesque weblog (active since 2002) announced its closure. This announcement came the day after Kai Cole's (2017) post, discussed above, that asserted Whedon's feminist persona to be a sham. The final post to Whedonesque does not directly cite the controversy, and in a statement the founder made no direct connection, but many of the comments noted the timing and questioned the connection and appropriateness of the response (Plaugic 2017). The post also directly references donations to support treatment of Complex PTSD, and most media outlets immediately connected the events (Jusino 2017b). Joss himself remained silent. The fandom response continues to be divided. Whedonesque still exists as of September 2019, but it is no longer a home for new content. While, of course, Whedonesque is not the sum total of Whedon fandom, given how heavily he has relied on having an army of fans, the end of a website sometimes seen as official does not bode well for his continued ability to leverage those fans.

However, those hoping that a white man with both credible accusations of abuse and a visible history of being inappropriate with women might actually experience consequences seem likely to be disappointed. Even following the closure of the site, Whedon engages with Whedonesque on Twitter, and the account continues to post Whedon and other fandom-related content and commentary. The Whedonesque Twitter bio still reads: "Twitter account for the now legendary http://Whedonesque.com. Elder statesfan" as of September 2019. The feminist fanboy's legacy in work and fandom lives on in spite of the controversy. Although his involvement with Marvel ended in 2015 with *Avengers: Age of Ultron*, and his last DC project was *Justice League* (2017), Whedon is apparently still seen as bankable. In July 2018, it was announced that Whedon's new show was "ordered straight to series at HBO" after "a competitive situation with multiple bidders, including streaming giant Netflix" (Goldberg 2018). At the same time, the show's premise seems likely to invite Whedon's usual weaknesses. As Suzanne Scott (2018a; 2018b) noted on Twitter, "this is a VICTORIAN PERIOD PIECE which feels by design to be a get out of jail free card for bad representational decisions," adding that "the Victorian context will structurally heighten the trademark feminist ethos, but also conveniently give him an out on his longstanding issues around race. Joss may be many things, but he's not dumb." Early critiques of the casting announcements for the show, entitled *The Nevers*, note that his feminist brand seems to be wearing thin: "These days, Whedon's passion for traumatized, ass-kicking waifs feels more like a fetish than feminism, with fans cracking jokes about how long it will take before one of his Victorian heroines goes barefoot onscreen. If you were hoping that Whedon had listened to the feminist criticism of his work, these character descriptions strongly suggest he did not" (Baker-Whitelaw 2019).

6

Zack Snyder and the Professional Toxic Fanboy

> You could call it "high-brow" comics, but to me, that comic book was just pretty sexy! I had a buddy who tried getting me into "normal" comic books, but I was all like, "No one is having sex or killing each other. This isn't really doing it for me." I was a little broken, that way. So when *Watchmen* came along, I was, "This is more my scene."
> —Zack Snyder (Jeff Jensen 2008)

Unlike many of the fan auteurs profiled here, Zack Snyder has followed a trajectory of near-continuous production hyperfocused on the cinema. He has also been heralded as the purest of fanboys. In 2011, a writer for the *New York Times* dubbed him "Hollywood's Leading Geek," observing the essential appeal of his fanboy credibility:

> Snyder is a native son of the geekverse . . . his clout really stems from his ability to speak geek culture's language, both aesthetically and promotionally, and his fearlessness about working on that culture's holiest ground, whether he's remaking a zombie movie that geeks believe to be George Romero's finest hour . . . or adapting graphic novels by comicdom's most esteemed creators. (Pappademas 2011)

In particular, Snyder's work demonstrates both an essential fidelity to the source material he loves and a desire for more: as suggested in the quotation from him above, more sex, more violence, more hypermasculine affirmation. In this way, he is at the extreme end of both the axes of our taxonomy. He is known only for making media out of his own fandom; even his original projects function to a large extent as homages. He's also so affirmational that he distills these media into ever more concentrated form. Moreover, he is fannish in another sense; upon closer examination, it begins to seem as if Snyder is not only the purest fanboy auteur, but a startlingly comprehensive embodiment of the very worst stereotypes of fandom. His work has been noted as childish, violence-obsessed, and misogynist, which has earned him criticism from the public and commentators alike. He also hasn't tended to triumph at the box office, particularly relative to his massive budgets. (Who watches the Watchmen? Nobody, apparently.)

At the same time, however, Snyder has a powerfully invested fan following, which he engages and cultivates through social media. Snyder has built his brand on this direct appeal and acclaim from fans rather than critics, as can be seen from his online reviews. Metacritic offers an impressive insight into Snyder's career, with twelve movies rated as of September 5, 2019: one positive (*Wonder Woman*, over which he had minimal control), one negative (*Sucker Punch*, 33/100), and ten falling into the "mixed" category. However, the user scores tell a different story—namely, that of his passionate fan base: 6.5/10 for *Justice League* (45/100 from critics); 6.1 for *Suicide Squad* (40 from critics); 7.0 for *Batman v Superman* (44 from critics); 7.5 for *Man of Steel* (55 from critics); and even a 6.3 for the much-maligned *Sucker Punch* ("Zack Snyder Movies Profile" n.d.). At every turn, fan ratings are at least 20 percent higher than those of critics. This combination of fannishness and contested auteur status has made Snyder's canon one of the most argued-over, and highly defended, in the current popular culture ecosystem.

In this chapter, we draw on both news stories about Snyder and a collection of more than nine hundred tweets posted in May 2018 following the announcement that the filmmaker was pursuing an adaptation of Ayn Rand's *The Fountainhead*. We begin by interrogating Snyder's aspirations to auteur status, arguing that they are in tension with his one-note style that always gets darker, grittier, and more violent, no matter what. Next, we contend that Snyder's tendency toward a high opinion of himself and unwillingness to expand beyond a circumscribed approach join his strong cinematic aesthetic trend towards a masculinity rooted in extreme violence and routine misogyny to make him the archetypical toxic fanboy. We then explore his intense fan following, as well as how he engages and cultivates fans through social media.

Slow-Mo and the Art of Self-Aggrandizement

Despite widespread disdain for Snyder's work from film critics, he stands out among the figures surveyed in this book for his clear aspirations to be counted among film auteurs, and to have his style and approach elevated in popular film discourse. This interest in his own canonization comes through in how he discusses the filmmakers he sees as his aspirational peers, as he noted in one interview: "When you go see any Martin Scorsese movie or Quentin Tarantino movie, you don't know what the f— is going to happen.... You just don't know, because that individual is capable of anything. There's a madman driving the boat. And I mean that in the best possible way" (Leonard 2016). These choices (hypermasculine auteurs, icons of "serious" film) suggest Snyder has a goal of elevated status even as he is associated with franchise material and popcorn action flicks. This auteurist self-image lends itself to self-aggrandizing rhetoric. His 2004–2019 production company with his wife, Deborah Snyder, Cruel & Unusual Films, described itself as "a destination for fresh and unique material, Cruel and Unusual Films maintains a mandate of taking on projects that are unique and sometimes outside the box, basing its approach to filmmaking on not being derivative, but rather innovative in every way" ("Cruel & Unusual Motion Picture Company" 2018). This framing emphasizing innovation is particularly ironic against reports that "when Zack Snyder and Henry Cavill disagreed about Superman's psychology, they would both do push-ups until someone gave in" (Begley 2016)—not exactly an auteurist creative method. Snyder's sense of his own artistic superiority even comes at the expense of more recognized auteurs, as when he adapted comics legend Frank Miller's 300 and Miller noted that he wasn't allowed much input: "I realized that with this film there was only room for one director and that is Zack. I visited the set just to check it out and I got to see a combat scene and got to know some of the crew and cast, but this is Zack's movie from start to finish" (Staff 2006).

Snyder's high opinion of himself is definitely ideologically consistent with some of his other choices. As one tweet in response to the announcement that Snyder planned to make *The Fountainhead* said: "Nothing has ever made more sense than this. You know he reads *The Fountainhead* at night and tells himself that critics trying to keep the masses malleable is the reason his films keep doing poorly."[1] It is believable to this commenter that Snyder is himself like the protagonist of *The Fountainhead*: sure of his own genius and blaming others who fail to recognize it. A journalist noted that this may explain why Snyder's superhero films were so unusual: "In a deeply ironic twist, Snyder said recently that he is interested in turning Ayn Rand's 'The Fountainhead' into a movie. It's a novel whose author believed that self-interest was the highest moral calling, a philosophy literally the opposite of that of both Batman and Superman. Warners, did you even talk to this guy before hiring him?" (Gross 2016).

Snyder has built his persona in part upon a rejection of criticism. At best, he seems surprised when he finds his work less than adored, as when, before *Justice League*, Snyder called many of his harshest critics together to address the response to *Batman v Superman*: "It did catch me off guard . . . I have had to, in my mind, make an adjustment. I do think that the tone of Justice League has changed because of what the fans have said" (Buchanan 2016). Alternately, Snyder sometimes attempts to evade grappling with criticism altogether. One particularly sarcastic reviewer noted of Snyder's response to the terrible reviews on *BvS*:

> So how does *BvS* director Zack Snyder feel about all of this? "I'm a comic book guy and I made the movie based as much as I could on that aesthetic," Snyder told Yahoo. "And so I don't know how else to do it 100 percent, so it is what it is." Basically a non-answer, but it's up to you to decide how many tears would have to start slowly streaming down Snyder's face for you to start actually feeling kind of bad for him. (N. Jones 2016)

Snyder's firmest rejections of criticism led another critic to comment that "examining the manner in which Snyder sells his own films is a business for which face-palming was invented. In reaction to the accusations that *300* operated as neo-fascistic propaganda, Snyder simply shrugged off all who deigned to extract subtext from this worryingly ornate war opus" (D. Jenkins 2016)—this about a film described by another journalist as "probably the Nazi-est movie Hollywood has ever made." The same critic added: "*300* is what Leni Riefenstahl might have come up with, given the CGI budget" (Romney 2007). Snyder also falls back on his proclaimed status as visionary particularly heavily when his work is questioned. "I understand the canon. I'm not crazy. I know what these characters need from a mythological standpoint" (Child 2014). One important aspect here is that, while often these kinds of proclamations about auteurs' uniqueness and vision are the stuff of studio PR, this is how Snyder talks about his own work—and it's also a departure from the more humble "I can't believe I got so lucky" trope we see from people like Whedon.

Snyder's distinctive style is inescapable, and has been critiqued as overtly reliant upon repetition. One critic points out that his first film was a strong warning of the qualities that would overtake Snyder's cinema-to-come: "And, yeah, of course, there's a lot wrong with the movie—listless performances, bizarre plot contrivances, pointless slow motion—but that's sort of the point. It's as Zack Snyder as a movie gets, for better and for worse" (Purdom 2017). He does it well, but he does exactly one thing: dark, gritty, and violent. One critic observes that Snyder is now trapped in a repetitive style that he cannot help but defend: "The problem with keeping the same filming style is that it needs to evolve with the artist or else they will be stuck in a permanent state of uninspired arrested development. This is where Snyder currently finds himself, a slave to conventions and predictability" (Espino 2016). In relation to *Justice League*, a critic directly called on Snyder to "change up the playbook (and stop brooding)" (Guerrasio 2017). Significantly, while auteurs almost definitionally have a distinctive and identifiable style, the complaints about Snyder seem to be because the style isn't always appropriate to the material; in other words, his selection of projects is often at odds with the way he makes films. Overall, then, Snyder seemingly has a self-concept as an auteur—Tarantinoesque, too much of a genius to be recognized, and with a distinctive style.

It's important to acknowledge that Snyder has been well loved by many, and his work has been heralded by other creators (including those on which he formed his fandom). He has been praised by *Watchmen* illustrator Dave Gibbons, who "loved" his adaptation (even if writer Alan Moore wanted nothing to do with any adaptations) (*Alpha Magazine* 2009). *Dark Knight* trilogy director Christopher Nolan also "heaped lavish praise . . . calling the filmmaker's Superman blockbuster far more challenging than his own *Batman* franchise" (*The Advertiser* 2012). Critics, too, appreciate him: one called *Watchmen* "a stunning achievement" (*Gold Coast Sun* 2009). Another characterized Snyder as righting the ship on Superman, whose previous "ventures on to the big screen however, have somehow failed to capture just what a man with god-like powers is capable of. Until now" (*South Burnett Times and Rural Weekly* 2013). When it became known that *Justice League* "(reportedly) marks the end of Zack Snyder's efforts with the DC Extended Universe," one headline proclaimed the "End Of An Era"; indeed, the title went on, "Zack Snyder's vision for superhero movies is over, and you should be sorry to see it go" (Bunch 2018b).

However, just as many commentators, if not more, decline to view Snyder nearly so positively. He has been criticized by Kevin Smith, who contended that "there seems to be a fundamental lack of understanding of what those characters are about" in *Batman v Superman* (Child 2016b). Comics luminary Grant Morrison similarly criticized how Snyder's approach to Wonder Woman in the same film "failed to honour the vision of her creator" (Child 2015b). Outside the world of other auteurs, *BvS* was nominated for eight

Razzies—the awards given annually for the worst in film—and won four (Seth Kelley 2017). If the headline above said Snyder's era would be missed, another asked "why are DC's films so bad? ... The answer is Zack Snyder" (Rose 2016). Another headline was, improbably, blunter about Snyder's auteurial stylings: "*Sucker Punch* Sucks" (*Sunday Tribune* 2011). Thus, Snyder's auteur status is both self-proclaimed and a site of external contestation.

The Most Stereotypical Fanboy of Them All

Snyder's habits of thinking highly of himself and sticking to a narrow media comfort zone are also part of what makes him the archetypical toxic fanboy, a term Anastasia Salter and Bridget Blodgett (2017, 11) have noted has shifted with the mainstreaming of geek culture:

> The consumers of the mass culture of geekdom ... have often done so despite criticism of these works as trivial or juvenile. Protectiveness of these mediums thus comes with the territory of geekdom ... [yet] the outsider status of these mediums has diminished significantly. ... Geeks used to the marginalization of their chosen media and fandoms have been given a choice: embrace the new popularity and surge of interest and production of these works, or defend the terrain from those less dedicated, who have never suffered from their geekdom. Many geeks have visibly chosen the latter, playing out a culture war over the turf of geek identity.

Such toxic fanboys—a term that here refers to an emphasis on their own subject position and on exclusivity that can destroy affinity communities—are thus characterized by their self-perception as victims, defending their marginalized culture against infiltration.

It is thus unsurprising that another key characteristic of this stereotype is childishness. This is certainly a feature of the content of Snyder's films: after all, *Batman v Superman* seemed to exist mostly as an answer to the playground-level fanboy question, "Who would win in a fight?" But Snyder also willingly describes himself as needing adult supervision. He established a production company with his wife, whose influence on the work is not well documented and mostly ignored, and he has pushed off accusations of inequality in the partnership.[2] However, the way he described their relationship in an interview is notable:

> The old Hollywood version was incredibly [*sic*] sexist, a romanticized Vincent van Gogh version of the muse. And then the grown-up version has come all

the way around to Debbie going, "Listen, these are the things you need to get done to make our machine work." The muse becomes the chairman of the board in a weird way. Debbie keeps me sane. If I was single, I would just live at the stage and then go to the gym and sleep. (Siegel 2016)

To be a grown-up, according to Snyder, is to have his wife be his mother—in charge of everything and making sure he does more than indulge the parts of his job he likes, which doesn't sound very adult at all. The trope of a self-centered man and a hypercompetent wife is familiar from media, but considerably more disturbing outside of fiction.

Snyder also typifies the toxic fanboy stereotype in that he has a strong attachment to a toxic masculinity rooted in extreme violence, evident throughout his filmography. His first film, *Dawn of the Dead*, marked his feature debut following a successful career making music videos and commercials.[3] As a remake of the original George Romero film (1978), it was a fitting beginning for an auteur who would go on to almost never use original material, instead becoming known for taking familiar geek cultural enterprises and making them what would eventually be known as "Snyderesque"—that is, darker, grittier, and more violent. It also began his trajectory of making things he was a fan of. When Romero died, Snyder would make one of his rare tweets in appreciation: "The world has lost a master. Thank you for the inspiration. You changed my life with your art. You will be missed. #georgeromero #dotd" (Snyder 2017). Unfortunately for Snyder, Romero had at best faint praise: "It was better than I expected. I thought it was a good action film. The first 15, 20 minutes were terrific, but it sort of lost its reason for being. It was more of a video game. I'm not terrified of things running at me; it's like *Space Invaders*. There was nothing going on underneath" (Walters 2005).

Despite Romero's lukewarm reaction to *Dawn of the Dead*, the film's commercial success was enough to open up a world of possibilities to Snyder—an interesting counterpoint to the lack of opportunities extended to others like Patty Jenkins after an initial success. Snyder immediately tasked himself with bringing some of the most iconically violent comic books to the screen, despite prevailing opinions that those same works might in fact be unfilmable. The first of these, *300* (2006), took as its source material a 1990s-era comic series by Frank Miller and Lynn Varley. Miller is his own institution, known for comics that are not only violent to the point of fetishism but also for conservative politics and at times demonstrable, on-the-page racism. His most infamous work, *Holy Terror*, is a post-9/11 version of Batman that proved too horrifying even for DC Comics to publish. *300* is similarly a "(decadent) East-meets-(noble)West [*sic*] showdown" (Craft 2007). It's also, particularly in Snyder's rendition, hyperviolent. "Violence has rarely been so deliriously aestheticised. Snyder goes full-out with CGI's capacity to turn actors' bodies into manipulable objects: soldiers have their heads sliced off in mid-dash. One Spartan youth, thus decapitated, keels over like a felled statue; it's a horrifying image, yet hypnotically graceful" (Romney 2007). Fascinatingly, Snyder identified this aestheticization of violence as particularly appealing to women: "It's still a battle, and it's still brutal, but it's done in such a beautiful way that I don't think it affects me in the same way. So, I'm really happy and I keep saying, 'Women will really like this film; there's a lot here for women to see'" (Daswani 2007).

Snyder's follow-up project, *Watchmen*, was much the same. One journalist noted that, post-*300*, "Snyder still exults in gratuitous splatter (sawed-off limbs, dangling human entrails, a very random display of adolescent vampirism)" (Chang 2009). Another commented that "when a movie character says that the alleys run with blood, it's usually hyperbole. In 'Watchmen,' the alleys really do run with blood" (Kloer 2009). However, those familiar with the graphic novel found that the violence diminished rather than enhanced the film:

> The film, on the other hand, obfuscates this nuance by virtue of its unending chain of blood and gore, both more graphic than that presented in the graphic novel and perceived more quickly, as a series of moving images progressing at a continuous pace rather than of static ones, the pace of which may be determined by the reader. In the context of the film, this incident in the early life of Rorschach is just another example of Snyder's blood-soaked aesthetic. (Henry 2017)

The critic's preference for the comic experience of *Watchmen* recalls Scott McCloud's description of closure, or the work the reader does of navigating the meaning between panels: this expressive space and work is collapsed by Snyder's straightforward focus on violence, which McCloud might term "over-powering" (McCloud 1994, 64). This sort of flattening out of meaning in favor of gore is consistent with Snyder shrugging off analysis of *300*'s fascism, but is at odds with his auteurist self-image.

Next up for Snyder was a strange cartoon—yet the signature hyperviolence remained. As one critic noted:

> Snyder loves nothing more than to slow the computer-animated action down to a crawl, the better to show raindrops splattering on feathers, or razor-carrying owls in mortal combat. (This from the producers of *Happy Feet*?) If he does it six or seven times more than is strictly necessary, he's also careful with the details. Feathers fly but little blood is spilled, and the film clings precariously to its PG rating (Knight 2010)

This, despite the film being dubbed "owl-tra-violent." This would be just a side note not worth dwelling on, except that it shows how very dedicated Snyder is to his violence that it would be such a key feature of a children's cartoon that walks right up to the edge of being too violent for its rating.

While some of Snyder's source material was already extremely violent, this was not the case with *Superman*. Accordingly, news of his association with *Man of Steel* as his first DC project drew immediate speculation: it was one thing to imagine the gritty director taking on *Batman*, but a hyperviolent *Superman* was a marked departure from previous cinematic versions of the hero. Responses to the film reflected that divide, as one reviewer compellingly writes:

> Director Zack Snyder (*Watchmen*) and screenwriters Christopher Nolan and David Goyer (the *Dark Knight* film trilogy) can't seem to wrap their brains around the idea of Man of Steel containing tension without violence, or a meaningful victory based on anything but martial strength. This is surprising from Nolan, but it's a problem endemic to Snyder's work, and part of what makes him such a baffling choice to helm this movie: He's all flash and no substance. This is the guy who felt the need to add rape to a Frank Miller story, and played Rorschach in *Watchmen* as an unambiguous antihero. (I'm not even going to touch *Sucker Punch*.) And somebody decided it was a good idea to give him *Superman*. (Edidin 2013)

In this way, Snyder's narrow artistic range is identified as particularly ill-suited here. As one critic noted, "it's a mystery why Snyder believes that prison rape, sex, and death are what people want to see in superhero films—that comic book fans who love Superman really wanted to see him start killing people" (Abad-Santos 2016).

Batman v Superman continued the trend. As one reviewer commented, "Gone is the Batman who refuses to kill, let alone hold a gun. This Batman flattens cars (along with their baddie passengers) and shoots assault rifles like it's nobody's business" (*Bangkok Post* 2016). Another commentator mirrored Snyder's aestheticization of violence in their summary: "Gun barrels unleash spinning cylinders of hot metal in lustrous slow motion, a female victim tumbles to the floor amidst a cascade of milky white pearls from her broken necklace, exploding vehicles pirouette through the night-time air during a high-velocity chase" (*Hull Daily Mail* 2016). It is, in a word, Snyderesque. Interestingly, this kind of discussion of violence—extreme, aestheticized, or otherwise—is absent from coverage of *Justice League*. Perhaps there was just enough involvement from Joss Whedon, who finished the film after Snyder's daughter died in 2017, to mitigate its Snyderness—which would also explain why Snyder fans are so insistent on seeing the so-called "Snyder cut," as we will discuss below.

Ultimately, Snyder's style relies on provocation and builds on the Alan Moore school of superheroes: the darker, the grittier, and the more violent, the better. This is perhaps unsurprising given that a profile of Snyder's professed favorite films included conflicted, hypermasculine antihero Western *The Searchers* starring John Wayne; Stanley Kubrick's violent *A Clockwork Orange* (whose tagline is "being the adventures of a young man whose principal interests are rape, ultra-violence, and Beethoven"); *Star Wars*; and the Mad Max sequel *The Road Warrior*, which Snyder describes as "violent and sophisticated. It feels uncompromising" (Earl 2017). Snyder's conflation of violence and sophistication is telling, and borne out by his work.

Third, Snyder instantiates the fan stereotype of toxic masculinity with substantial misogyny. This is on clearest display with *Sucker Punch*, which would take the hypermasculine to new extremes using, fittingly, the context and aesthetics of video games by way of an insane asylum dedicated to the mental destruction of women. One reviewer defends the movie, suggesting that it was an ultimately unsuccessful attempt at allegory for the abuse of women:

> Snyder's grim vision fell short because he didn't employ the tools he had well enough. The dark journey in *Sucker Punch* is a wildly over-the-top reflection of a world that many people were unwilling or unable to see at that point. He undermined his own work by not giving us enough story, ending up with a movie that feels more exploitative than reflective. *Sucker Punch* is meant to be an examination of sexism and the multiple planes on which it exists. This was 2011, remember. Harvey Weinstein was still a movie mogul. Bill Cosby was still a beloved comic and former TV star. The world was waking up more and more, but we were a long way off from Time's Up. The clock was still ticking back then, even if no one could quite hear it. (Rosenberg 2018)

Even this most generous reading of the film doesn't have a particularly positive take on it, and the majority are far harsher. One reviewer of Snyder's later works noted that *Sucker Punch* should have served as the greatest bulletin of the director's intentions, particularly with regard to the screen fantasy depiction of women: "Another warning sign should have been 2011's *Sucker Punch*, Snyder's first original screenplay: a tale of female empowerment that felt closer to a glossy rape fantasy. Think nubile women in schoolgirl-stripper outfits with samurai swords leaping out of CGI fireballs in super-slow-mo. THIS! IS! SNYDER!" (Rose 2016). For this reviewer, these troubling aspects are entirely in line with Snyder's overall style. However, Snyder contends to this day (as of a 2019 interview) that the film's message has been misinterpreted, in part due to changes to the voiceover (which he called a "contrived post-production mechanism") by the studio: "I'm always shocked that it was so badly misunderstood. I always said that it was a commentary on sexism and geek culture. Someone would ask me, 'Why did you film the girls this way?' And I'd say, 'Well you did!' *Sucker Punch* is a fuck you to a lot of people who will watch it" (D. Harrington 2019). His characterization of his work passes the blame for objectification of the women onto the audience, suggesting that it is their gaze that is misogynist, not the film. This self-characterization of the film still acknowledges the fundamental appeal of the chosen directorial gaze to the presumed misogynist audience while simultaneously disclaiming that audience as the film's target. It also speaks to Snyder's reputation that it was assumed that he must be playing the violence against women straight given how frequent it has been in his work; there was not a widespread interpretation that the film was a critique.

Indeed, this misogyny and eroticization of rape was present even in his earlier films. In a departure from Snyder's usual fanboy fidelity, the Jupiter character in *Watchmen* was changed. Yet, in keeping with his fanboy toxicity, the changes are rooted in misogyny:

> Jupiter is a nothing character. She's relegated to a prop. She appears to exist only to wear said sexy costume (that the character in the book dislikes), and Akerman plays her in such a way that she just appears to seek male approval and nothing else. In fact, the hard edges that make her annoying in the book are smoothed over in the film, into a version of syrupy femininity that's totally digestible for the male gaze. (Lim 2010)

While the original *Watchmen* comic had its share of problematic elements, Snyder particularly leans in on the characterizations in a way that forefronts the men and even turns an erotic lens on a rape sequence.

These characteristics also cropped up with subsequent films. One critic commented that "Snyder only executive produced *Suicide Squad* but it retains his trademarks of casual sexism, operatic violence, music-video montages and general teenage-boy fantasy" (Rose 2016). Further, there was a great deal of controversy over the way that, after the more practical and less objectifying costumes of *Wonder Woman*, *Justice League*'s Amazons were in "'tiny leather bikinis'" (Rigler 2017). Snyder's future projects seem to promise more of the same. One user tweeted that "'The Fountainhead' is a logical next step for Zack Snyder after the misogynistic rape fantasy that was 'Sucker Punch.'" Another described it as "returning to his comfort zone of films starring heroes who commit sex crimes." In all of these ways, then, Snyder's filmography constructs him as the epitome of a toxic fanboy.

One Fanboy to Lead Them All

Despite epitomizing toxic masculinity—or perhaps because of it—Snyder has a following that puts the "fan" in fanatic. One journalist proclaimed that "Snyder has become something of a nerd king, an auteur for comic-book fans who consider him one of three directors (along with Sam Raimi and Christopher Nolan) who can be trusted with their beloved material" (Bowles 2009). Snyder's fan following is, of course, deeply intertwined with his own fan identity. He has a reputation for his adaptations sticking closely to the source: there are sixty-six mentions of "faithful" in the 307 pages of press data. He also personally proclaims his fannishness as part of establishing his creative authority: "I'm a fan of the character and fan of the canon and I understand what Superman is about when it comes to his personal mythology as it exists in comic books" (*Daily News of Los Angeles* 2011). At times, this is even a more affective attachment: "I wanted to get a chance to see the *Superman* movie I'd always wanted to see. That really drove me to the attention to detail, and trying to get every little aspect correct" (Daswani 2013).

Snyder's following makes some of these same arguments. A *Fountainhead* tweeter contended that "snyder made the best superman movie to date and the most cómic accurate versión of superman." One reviewer similarly argued that, just as 1980s comics "deconstructed our impression of superheroes and of comic book storytelling, taking apart the past and reassembling it," Snyder was doing the same, "and he envisioned something ambitious and bold—an entire superhero cinematic approach that starts off by positing a new type of world in which superhero [sic] exist, deconstructing the genre itself right in front of our eyes and building something unlike any we'd seen before in superhero cinema" (M. Hughes 2018). This sort of exaltation is incredibly common. One of the Urban Dictionary definitions of "Zack Snyder" proclaims: "His realistic, religious, and philosophical movies are too much for the average person to decipher" ("Zack Snyder" n.d.). While one wonders what's realistic about super-slow motion, the post is indicative of the types of responses from Snyder's fans. Another *Fountainhead* tweeter similarly insisted that "the passion he puts into his craft, as well as his obvious interest in an array of complex philosophys prove that he has the intellect to critically adapt the Fountainhead." Another fan asserted that Snyder had pursued *The Fountainhead* because "he doesn't like the easy path to glory." In this way, we can see how the fanaticism that surrounds Snyder is that of a pure fanboy anointed, and his version of hypermasculine fidelity to his vision is passionately defended by his fan base.

This devotion leads fans to refuse any criticism of Snyder just as much as he himself refuses criticism. One reporter opens his piece on local reactions to *BvS* with the summary line: "Don't always believe what the critics say" (Mihm 2016), which is a fairly accurate summary of the most common defense of Snyder from his fans, who argue that critics cannot appreciate what Snyder brings to his work. As another journalist comments, "The more scorn reviewers pour on Zack Snyder's box-office triumph, the more audiences are determined to see it" (Child 2016a)—though rather than "audiences," this might be more accurately rendered if it said "fans." The Urban Dictionary definition for "Zack Snyder" also points to another important part of the fan response to him, his central role in the perceived MCU / DC Extended Universe (DCEU) rivalry. The idea that Marvel's success is because of undiscerning audiences is quite common: "Most people have been accustomed to the bland, unimaginative, basic, and low risk MCU. . . . Most people are either too ignorant or too afraid to admit Zack and the DCEU's superiority to the MCU" ("Zack Snyder" n.d.). Similarly, one of the *Fountainhead* tweeters contended that it was a logical project because "dude was taking aim at Whedon-esque faux feminism, the nihilism of the MCU, and the hollow ethics of American culture and politics from the start." The fundamental defense of Snyder as a fanboy-turned-auteur is that anyone who doesn't appreciate Snyder is ignorant, caught up in the inferior work of Marvel's less fan-anointed leadership, or both. This emphasis on purity recalls what Salter and Blodgett describe as geek masculinity's self-defensive reaction to being "under siege": "to preserve geek cultural spaces for participants who share this same set of values without ever having these values tested or challenged" (2017, 193). The *Fountainhead* tweets have several mentions that critics are "biased" against Snyder. They also speak pejoratively of "liberty foes," "wokes," and the ever-maligned "SJWs," pointing to the perhaps-unsurprising overlap of an auteur who exudes toxic masculinity with a reactionary fan base.

Given that, the fact that his fans have also engaged in systematic harassment of those perceived not to support Snyder is perhaps also to be expected. Former DC Entertainment president Diane Nelson was attacked for posting a tweet saying she was looking forward to the upcoming Joker movie, thanks to a line perceived as an attack on Snyder: "What DC should have been doing since Nolan. Even if die hard fans struggle with his vision. #goodmoviesaregoodmovies." Eventually, she deleted her Twitter account after attacks from Snyder fanboys:

> the backlash was reportedly strong, with one fan accusing her for being a "snake in the grass," and not supporting Snyder's vision while at DC (which is funny considering Warner Bros. and DC entrusted him to direct three movies). The response was apparently enough for Nelson to delete her Twitter

account, though not before denying she was deliberately snubbing Snyder: "I happen to count Zack Snyder among those things, if you are insinuating otherwise. No snake here." (Hibberd 2018)

This sort of pile-on is a familiar tactic from reactionary fan bases, seen in cases like the 2014 #Gamergate backlash against women in video games, the 2016 mass-downvoting of the trailer for the all-woman *Ghostbusters* reboot, and the successful 2018 campaign to get *Star Wars* comic book writer Chuck Wendig fired, which may or may not have substantial overlap with those who worship Snyder.

Snyder's departure as the leading voice in the DCEU was contentious and, to many fanboys, a sign of DC's betrayal of an auteur's clearly essential vision. Years after Snyder's *Justice League* was taken over by Whedon in post-production, some fans are still petitioning for the release of the "true" Snyder cut of the film so that they can enjoy its obvious superiority. Following the critical failure of two Snyder DCEU films, a petition to remove Snyder from *Justice League* gained 18,000+ signatures (Change.org n.d.)—but the petition for a Snyder director's cut of *Justice League* received ten times more, over 179,000 by the time it closed (Change.org n.d.). The desire for this version is so great that it has given rise to borderline conspiracy theories:

> The ongoing saga of the Snyder Cut of *Justice League*, a rare version of the film which preserves the pristine vision of director Zack Snyder, continues. Last week, we learned the shocking news that there is not just one Snyder Cut of *Justice League*, but two, as Cyborg actor Ray Fisher confirmed that Snyder shot at least two movies worth of footage before being replaced by alleged fake feminist Joss Whedon, who replaced all of Snyder's badass Superman scenes with scenes where Cyborg says "booyah." (Terror 2018)

A layperson might be forgiven for misunderstanding film production practices to think that "two movies worth of footage" means "two full films exist," but the idea that Whedon removed all of Snyder's Superman scenes wholesale is quite farfetched, and it speaks again to the perceived opposition between supporting Whedon and Snyder. The intensity of the fan desire for the Snyder cut has also led them to leverage Snyder's physical location to advocate for it—they had a banner flown near his office in Burbank and, upon finding out Snyder was located near the ComicCon venue, pressed to find out if he would be in attendance and confirm a *Justice League* cut—he wasn't, and he didn't (Begley 2018).

Eventually, Snyder acknowledged the fans pushing for his cut to be released. As one journalist described:

Zack Snyder has officially recognized the release the Snyder Cut movement after a charity campaign to raise money for the American Foundation for Suicide Prevention reached its goal, resulting in a plane flying a "Release the Snyder Cut" banner over Warner Bros. Burbank offices. The original *Justice League* director still has an office on the Burbank lot, so he was also able to include a video of the plane and banner in his post on the social network, Vero. (Colbert 2018a)

Although *Justice League* has been a larger and more fever-pitch campaign, it wasn't the first such attempt from his fans: "When word leaked online that Warner Brothers were pressuring Snyder to stick with a two-hour running time, a fan petition called Campaign for a three-hour *Watchmen* movie was launched online" (E. Butler 2009). Overall, the Snyder fanboys believe so strongly in their ability to influence discourse that an article on Screen Rant suggests that Warner Brothers "will eventually have to find a way to appease them," calling on the studio to release the original screenplay, create a graphic novel of Snyder's version, or find some other way to meet their demand (Colbert 2018c).

Snyder, of course, doesn't control what his fans do, whether harassment or incessant petitioning—but he does, as with the example of the Snyder cut, engage them in ways that help to maintain their attention to him. He has long released sneak peeks and teases this way: "Director Zack Snyder has ramped up the hype again for the upcoming *Batman v Superman: Dawn of Justice*. On Thursday, the director uploaded new picture of the famous Batmobile, as it will appear in the movie, to his Twitter account" (Sobolewski 2014). More recently on niche social platform Vero, Snyder answers questions regarding details from the production and exults in the references and visual choices of the work. For example, Snyder explained the choice of phallic symbols for the alien pods in *Superman* as part of a post on the symbolism, concluding: "the amount of reasons why dildos is too many to count" (*Outlaw* 2018b)—which is itself almost unbearably Snyderesque in its celebration of hegemonic masculinity and unwillingness to engage critically. Even news coverage has noted the extent to which he has fueled interest in the Snyder cut by dropping continual hints of deleted cameos and scenes in his Vero posts:

> There's been no shortage of coverage on the "Snyder Cut" of *Justice League* in the last year since the theatrical version of the movie hit theaters. Somewhat surprisingly, it's been Snyder who has been the source of most of the discussion too. Even though he's left most of social media and has largely remained out of the public eye following the death of his daughter, he's very interactive

on Vero, and routinely drops new hints about his various plans with DC. It's given him an outlet to connect to his supporters, and has even set up reference challenges in the past. (Hood 2018)

In this way, Snyder's social media use, much like Rowling's, acts to continually re-center him as the font of all information and meaning.

The choice of platform is also interesting. Vero, an app reportedly created by a friend of Snyder's, doesn't allow sharing outside of the site and thus is mostly recirculated through screenshots (J. Alexander 2017a). By contrast, Snyder rarely uses Twitter (there are 124 tweets live as of September 2019). For a long time, his pinned tweet invited users of Twitter to join him on Vero, where his short film *Snow Steam Iron* was released. By using Vero, Snyder avoids some of the controversy surrounding his work just by being both away from the main discussions that his film inspired and surrounded as much as possible by his own fans. One critic notes that Snyder fans originally dominated Vero until changes in Instagram brought a flood of new users looking for an alternative: "prior to the influx of users, Vero was primarily home to Snyder and his most devoted fans, who waited for Snyder to post stills from upcoming movies (J. Alexander 2018a). This platform dominance may have given him an even larger audience. One of the key aspects of Vero is that "there are granular controls for both sharing and following. On the sharing side, you can control the audience of your post on a sliding scale from 'close friend' to followers. You can also choose which categories of your friends' posts you want to see; it's possible to follow someone only for their music recommendations, for example" (Newton 2018). While it's impossible to know exactly how Snyder uses the platform—since nonpublic posts wouldn't be visible to us, by definition—the ability to strictly control both what others see from him and what he sees from others is consistent with his unwillingness to listen to critics and interest in presenting himself as superior. It's also very unlike Whedon or Smith's approach to using fan-designated spaces that they own (Smith) or that are specifically dedicated to them (Whedon).

Notably, one of Snyder's most substantial 2019 interviews was granted as an exclusive to a fan who solicited the piece through Vero. In that discussion, Snyder noted that the current political landscape was putting his plan for a *Fountainhead* TV series (apparently no longer a film) on hold: "*The Fountainhead*.... It's still important to me, but it's a really touchy subject right now. People will think it's hardcore right-wing propaganda, but I don't view it like that. I just think the story is super fun and crazy and melodramatic about architecture and sex." He added, "It's about time we get a different president so we don't take shit so seriously!" (D. Harrington 2019). Snyder also discussed his other ongoing projects: a Netflix film entitled *Army of the Dead* and a film centered on a war correspondent in Afghanistan entitled *The Last Photograph*. Snyder did not attend the 2019 San Diego ComicCon due to filming on his latest zombie film—despite efforts of his fans, who raised $20,000 for billboards asking for the release of the Snyder cut (Gardner 2019).

Snyder After DC?

As of this writing, Snyder has apparently left the building at DC. The most recent film in the franchise, *Aquaman* (2018), was described by one reviewer as a "course correction" from Snyder, noting that "Snyder's movies, like *Man of Steel*, *Batman vs. Superman: Dawn of Justice* [sic] and even parts of *Justice League*, lacked the inspirational superhero feel that Marvel Studios perfected. It's mostly been dark, bleak stories, although Gal Gadot as Wonder Woman rectified that somewhat" (Matadeen 2018). The break also seems apparent from his behavior, as one fan commented:

> Zack Snyder seems to be free of whatever shackles [of] confidentiality that Warner Bros. had him under. The DC Extended Universe architect has recently been very candid and vocal with fans who are still inquiring about what could've been with Justice League, based on everything from speculation to examination of concept art and unused footage from Snyder's early version of the film. (*Outlaw* 2018a)

Overall, the Snyder era of DC seems to be over. Snyder's influence is instead felt elsewhere; the dystopian superhero satire *The Boys* (Amazon, 2019-present) has in-world films featuring corrupt heroes that draw on Snyder's version of the DC Universe (N. Romano 2019). As showrunner Eric Kripke sums up: "Every time they make a superhero thing, they're making a Zack Snyder movie . . . we wanted the Vought superhero movies to be a little full of themselves" (N. Romano 2019).

However, Snyder's shadow is long at DC, too. He was only a producer on *Aquaman* (2018), but Jason Momoa, in the words of one headline, "Won't Let Warner Bros. Distance Aquaman From Zack Snyder":

> It doesn't simply stop at reminding people Snyder was the one to cast him, either. He even went as far to link *Aquaman* to Arthur Curry's final scene in Zack Snyder's cut of *Justice League*. This understandably caused a bit of a stir, considering the studio has been quiet on the much-discussed alternate cut of

the movie, with sources reportedly only saying they have no intent to release it. But that didn't stop Momoa. When asked about the cut directly in another interview, he threw his support behind it completely, saying "F*** yeah, I want to see it!" (Colbert 2018b)

While fandom of Snyder may be expected from an actor who infamously once bragged that on *Game of Thrones* he got to "rape beautiful women" (*Guardian* staff 2017), Momoa isn't the only one to hold on to Snyder's involvement in the franchise. Director James Wan got feedback from Snyder on an early cut:

> Yeah, I showed Zack [Snyder] my Directors Cut pretty much right after I finished it and he gave me his thumbs up. He was really complementary about it. He basically gave his blessing to me to go finish the movie, because he knew how huge of an undertaking I had with the visual effects. What he saw was a lot of blue screen, a lot of pre-viz and a lot of storyboards. You photograph your storyboard's [*sic*] and you cut it into the film and so it was very very rough and crude. But, I think the human element is there that played and I think he and Debbie [Snyder] were very complementary about it. They gave us their blessing. (Dumarog 2018)

Snyder, that is, may generate the same loyalty among his collaborators as he has from his fans.

Snyder himself does seem to be moving on. He announced his new brand on Vero on January 7, 2019. Given his tendency to ultraviolence, the words carried an extra twist: "Although Cruel & Unusual Films will always be a proud part of our legacy, our new and exciting future creative endeavors will be mined, chiseled and honed in THE STONE QUARRY" (*Outlaw* 2019). It's unclear what the change in metaphor will bring to Snyder's brand, but the intentional reimagining comes at a time when Snyder's departure from the cinematic universe he built seems clearly cemented. Setting aside continual teasers and *Justice League* "truth" reveals on Vero, Snyder's departure from DC is complete, his status as the anointed fanboy is, at least in that universe, apparently at an end. However, his work on action horror film *Army of the Dead* for Netflix suggests a willingness to consider further reinvention: he's even returned to Twitter to promote his work on the movie (Trumbore 2019).

7

Patty Jenkins, Ryan Coogler, Taika Waititi, and the Fan Auteur as L'autre

> I met with Warner Bros. right after I made *Monster* [an indie hit, her only previous feature] more than 10 years ago, and I said, "I want to make *Wonder Woman*." I've always been moved by the idea of movies that are personal but still have a huge reach. *Superman* had that effect on me when I was a kid—it rocked my world. That kind of movie was always the brass ring of what I wanted to do with my career
> —Patty Jenkins, as told to Rebecca Ford. (2016)

The fanboys ascendant described in this volume have taken different trajectories to developing their personas while occupying similar narratives in popular media. Many of those fanboys have been defined both in their early life and in their career by a relationship to comics and superheroes, a popular culture space where fandom is prominent. The gatekeeping of comics fandom is legendary, and recent escalations in Comicsgate, an alt-right movement directed at resisting the so-called threats of inclusivity and diversity in comics, have only intensified it. Indeed, Comicsgate points to some of the men profiled in this book as heroes from among their own ranks: those who occupied the fanboy origin story, admired their heroes, aspired to direct their tales, and succeeded in living the dream.¹ Such a fanboy-turned-leader is expected to provide characters faithful to his youth, and to place value on the white men assumed to be the core of comics. Then again, the industry itself doesn't take a very different approach. Patty Jenkins describes this as the self-fulfilling prophecy of fanboys-turned-auteurs:

> As long as your main interest is teenage boys, then the No 1 obvious person to write that story is a grown teenage boy and the No 1 person to direct it is a grown teenage boy. Ultimately so many things come down to money, but particularly when it comes to superheroes—people really thought that only men loved action movies and only men would go see a superhero movie. And then the few movies they tried to do with women superheroes didn't quite work out. (Hoby 2017a)

Ultimately, most fanboy auteurs conform to the Comicsgate narrative. Nearly every superhero film ever made has been directed by a white man (Riesman 2018).

Yet the comic book shops that harbor toxic hypermasculinity have also held more diverse heroes for decades. Media has been slower to catch up, even though those characters have in turn inspired fans-turned-directors. 2017–18 was a key period for expanding fan auteurs beyond white men in major media franchises, as a series of films garnered intense attention for the change in who was behind the camera: Patty Jenkins's *Wonder Woman*, Ryan Coogler's *Black Panther*, and Taika Waititi's *Thor: Ragnarok* are all inseparable from their directors in popular reception and the speculations (and criticisms) that accompanied their respective releases. These three directors are all fans who've taken the helm of major franchises, drawing characters from the fanboy space in a way almost guaranteed to draw resentment for their outsider status. Two of these films that broke this mold of superhero stories through important choices in directing, casting, and storytelling are often put into conversation: Jenkins's *Wonder Woman* and Coogler's *Black Panther*. Less talked-about alongside them, but perhaps equally important in the history of superhero cinema, Taika Waititi's *Thor: Ragnarok* turned Thor's colonial empire on its head, bringing its hero to face his violent origins and ultimately burning the Viking-esque nation down.

Jenkins, Coogler, Waititi, and several others are at the forefront of a change in the fan auteur pattern that has been quite slow to develop, but has been heralded, falsely, as abrupt and revolutionary. These directors have found a shakier path to helming franchises than Whedon and Snyder and, once there, face far greater scrutiny for their actions. In a sea of white men as leads and directors, these films attracted attention and speculation. Their directors were frequently assumed to be (or actually) disempowered in major decisions—certainly, none of them got to cast their lead. The unexpected, disproportionate success of their films (particularly *Wonder Woman*, which stands as the critical flagship of an otherwise troubled DC Extended Universe) has been similarly hyped, used to suggest that barriers are breaking down and inclusivity in superhero films has already been achieved. With the success of *Captain Marvel* in theatres (helmed by a directing team that included one woman), the narrative of the successful outsider fan has become even more prominent. By examining how these outsiders have occupied and challenged the fanboy auteur trajectory, we can see some of the most problematic elements of this narrative on display, and how even outsiders can end up primarily serving as defenders of the status quo.

This chapter focuses primarily on Jenkins and Coogler, drawing on more than 950 news stories about each of them; Waititi is less often framed as a fan auteur and so was not the subject of a full investigation but rather addressed in a more limited way as a comparison case. First, we consider how these auteurs are similar to others, deploying the origin story of being fans since their youth. Next, we interrogate how Jenkins and Coogler in particular are the subject of a mountain of superlatives, nearly always framed as being the "most," the "best," or the "first" at something. Third, we argue that the auteur as Other tends to be held responsible for the continued success of their entire category. Fourth, we parse out the uneven availability of opportunity for such figures, their successes notwithstanding. Finally, we investigate how representation in these films is presented as tightly interwoven with the identities of the auteurs.

Wonder Woman in the Schoolyard: Fan Credentials and Origin Stories

Like more traditional fanboy auteurs, Jenkins, Coogler, and Waititi deploy the origin story of being fans since their youth. Jenkins narrates her trajectory to *Wonder Woman* as starting from childhood affection for the character: "I was that kid on the schoolyard who saw Lynda Carter and went racing out to where all the other kids were playing in the playground and said, 'I want to be Wonder Woman!'" (Kegu 2017). In terms of our taxonomy, Jenkins is highly known for making media of her own fandom, on par with E L James, Steven Moffat, or Zack Snyder. However, on the other axis she's more moderately transformative than James (or, as we will see, Waititi or the Wachowskis), with one foot planted firmly in fidelity. In a similar origin story, Ryan Coogler described in an interview being introduced to *Black Panther* after asking an employee of a comic shop to suggest a book about a Black hero: "I wanted to find a comic book character that looked like me and not just one that was on the sidelines . . . and I walk in and ask the guy at the desk that day, and say, 'Hey man, you got any comic books here about black people, you know, like with a black superhero?' And he was like, 'Oh, yeah, as a matter of fact, we got this one'" (Greene 2018). Coogler is also, as was frequently noted in the press coverage for *Creed*, a fan of the *Rocky* series. In addition to two of his three feature films to date being derived from his own fandoms, Coogler is more transformative than any other man in our sample except Waititi. Waititi, though described as "an outspoken fan of the original Akira manga" (Lau 2017), isn't known for making media he's a fan of—and in fact "hadn't read many *Thor* comics before being tasked with Ragnarok" (Admiraal 2018). Waititi is nevertheless quite transformative; as one commentator notes, by contrast to "previous Marvel films which feature Robert Downey Jr as a billionaire smart-ass dropping glib one-liners," in *Ragnarok* "the lead character—the superhero, the guy the film is named after—is generally the butt of the joke," which the journalist describes as "distinctly Māori in tone, in rhythm and as a kind of philosophical outlook" (Taipua 2017).

Moreover, all three directors also speak openly of the emotional attachment they have to the material. Not only did Jenkins love Wonder Woman as a girl, but she felt empowered by her, too. "When you were her in your head, you were like, 'that bully over there, I'm gonna go stop them'—and I look like Lynda Carter while I'm doing it. . . . It was this wish fulfillment of being like the greatest version of yourself—of the woman you could fantasize" (Kegu 2017). Waititi directly frames his directorial approach as paying forward his childhood experience: "I wanted to make the audience feel how I did as a kid reading comics" (Admiraal 2018). Coogler even brings the attachment forward to the present: "I grew up reading these comic books and watching all these movies. If I really thought about the fact that I'm making one of these things right now, with people I know and love, I would break down emotionally. I wouldn't be no good to anybody" (Ugwu 2018). In this way, the fan auteur maintains some of its key contours even in its otherwise most divergent cases.

The Most-Best-First* (*For an Other): Superlatives True, False, and Weird

In other ways, however, the differences between these directors is clearly marked. Jenkins and Coogler in particular (as well as DuVernay, as we will discuss in the conclusion) are nearly always discussed in the context of being the most, the best, or the first at something. There is, in particular, a lot of emphasis on the matching of lead and director for both of them. One journalist points out that *Wonder Woman* is "the first mainstream solo superhero film that has a woman at the center (Gal Gadot) of it and a woman (Patty Jenkins, director) at the helm" (*News International* 2017). Correspondingly, *Black Panther* "is the first major superhero movie with an African protagonist; the first to star a majority black cast; and in Ryan Coogler ('Creed', 'Fruitvale Station'), the first to employ a black writer and director" (Ugwu 2018).

At other times, the superlative status of the content and the director are treated separately. The wait for *Black Panther* was a long one, and some reviewers attribute the film's success, in part, to being the first of its kind: "Audiences wanting superheroes who looked like T'Challa had to watch and wait as Iron Man, Batman, Captain America, Thor, Spider-Man, Ghost Rider, the Punisher and Daredevil got one or more shots at cinematic glory. Meanwhile, black audiences had to settle for supporting roles in *Iron Man* and one-offs like Will Smith's (underrated and $624 million-grossing) *Hancock* and Halle Berry's *Catwoman*" (Mendelson 2018b). There is much more emphasis on T'Challa as the first African protagonist than on Coogler's status, with the only mention of the latter being variations on "the first of the Marvel movies to be directed by an African American" (Romei 2018). Waititi, of course, was the first man of color to direct a film in the MCU. Jenkins has a wider variety of firsts attributed to her: *Wonder Woman* is the first "major superhero film" (Strauss 2017), "summer superhero movie" (Davis 2017), and "big-budget superhero movie" (Sakoui 2017) directed by a woman; Jenkins is the first woman to direct a "film that grossed over $100 million in its opening weekend" (Sblendorio, Bitette, and Honan 2017) and/or "movie with a $100 million budget" (*USA Today* 2017). Another writer notes that Jenkins is "not only the first female director of a superhero movie period, but now also holds the record for the best domestic box office debut for a female director" (Swenson 2017).

However, many of these statements of first-ness are not, in fact, accurate. To begin with claims about Jenkins, comic adaptations more broadly have had women directors, with notable films including Rachel Talalay's *Tank Girl* (1995), Deborah Kaplan's *Josie and the Pussycats* (2001), Shari Springer Berman's *American Splendor* (2003), and Marielle Heller's *The Diary of a Teenage Girl* (2015). Previous women directors may be overlooked because women have primarily engaged the superhero genre through animation. In fact, one of them even directed her own *Wonder Woman*: Lauren Montgomery, who has directed a number of direct-to-DVD DC superhero films, including a

2009 *Wonder Woman* movie, without generating too much commentary.[2] Moreover, Jenkins is not even the first woman to direct *this particular* movie version of *Wonder Woman*: she replaced Michelle MacLaren. Jenkins is also actually "the second female director to command a budget of more than $100 million" (Hoby 2017b), after Kathryn Bigelow.

Similarly, others pointed out that labeling *Black Panther* the first Black movie superhero was incorrect: 1998's *Blade* not only predated the film but, according to one journalist "served as a proof of concept for Marvel's jump into the world of big budget licensed filmmaking" (Bunch 2018a). There was also "NBA superstar, Shaquille O'Neal's, superhero turn as 'Steel' in 1997" (China Daily 2018). Moreover, it wasn't even "the first megabudget superhero film to star a black man" (Bunch 2018a)—that honor goes to Will Smith's *Hancock* (2008). Others point out that even if not the first, it's been a while since there was a Black superhero film: *Blade* was released "way back in 1998" (Ahsan 2016). Beyond the lead not being new, Bunch added: "Fine, but 'Black Panther' has to be the first superhero film directed by a black person, right? That would be news to Robert Townsend, who directed 'The Meteor Man' in 1993, a full quarter century ago" (Bunch 2018a). However, other writers insisted that, while "black superheroes are not groundbreaking in 2018, of course," nevertheless "Netflix's 'Luke Cage,' Wesley Snipes's 'Blade' and other on screen examples hardly compare to this gorgeous, effortlessly assured, big budget version" (Wenzel 2018)—and it is also "the one with the most 'African' storyline" (de Souza 2018).

Despite these exaggerated or even false claims, there is also a great deal of praise for these two films based on their actual characteristics, both their quality and their success. One journalist called *Black Panther* "the best Marvel movie so far, *by* far" (Ehrlich 2018). Another predicted that it "may end up being . . . the film for which the whole MCU project is best remembered" (Murray 2018). However, the praise also takes on some interesting contours. When one writer declared that *Black Panther* is "flashier, sassier and cooler than most of what has gone before" and "way more exciting than most of the company's offerings of late" (McLean 2018), he walked right up to the edge of the stereotypes that Black men are inherently cool and Black women inherently sassy. As for *Wonder Woman*, multiple journalists described it as the best DC or superhero movie since *The Dark Knight* (Child 2017; D. Ellis 2017; *South China Morning Post* 2017). One writer noted as well that, among the films in the DCEU, "so far, Patty Jenkins' standalone 'Wonder Woman' film is the only one well received by critics" (*Philippines Daily Inquirer* 2017). In these ways, then, alongside being attributed groundbreaking status for the race or gender of their casts and directors, these movies are also judged qualitatively as good.

The films also, of course, had huge quantitative success. First, *Black Panther* had "best first-day presales of any Marvel movie on the ticket site Fandango.com" (Truitt 2018a). Then, it had "one of the top five opening weekends of all time" (Sonaiya Kelley 2018). In the end, it reached, by one measure, "the third highest-grossing film domestically in history ($699.6 million) and the ninth highest-grossing film worldwide ($1.3 billion)" (Katz 2018).[3] The quantification of *Wonder Woman*'s success ranged from the relatively narrow statement that it was "the highest grossing superhero origin film of all time and was the biggest money earner this summer" (Daniell 2017b) to more broadly being "the most successful DC Comics movie ever" (B. Alexander and Mandell 2017) or, even, most dramatically, the "top live action superhero" at Warner Bros. (Betancourt 2017b). In terms of raw sales, one source identified *Wonder Woman* as "the second-highest grossing film of the year in Canada and the US" (Hoyle 2017). Another, including international sales, said that it was "the eighth highest-grossing film of 2017" (Nair 2017).

However, in keeping with being the first for their categories, the films are often walled off with a proverbial asterisk indicating otherness as the movies are classified as "the best x" for a white woman or Black man. One journalist notes that *Black Panther* is "already considered a brilliant milestone in African-American big-budget moviemaking" (Coyle 2018a)—but apparently it's not a milestone in terms of general big-budget moviemaking. Another journalist, while helpfully situating *Black Panther* and Coogler in relation to other Black films and directors, downplays that the grosses are huge for *anybody*: "It nearly doubles 'Furious 7' as the best opening for a black-directed film. It is triple the best previous record (held by 'Straight Outta Compton') for initial weekend of a film with a primarily black cast" (*Daily Times* 2018). When a writer points out that *Black Panther* is "the most expensive movie with a largely Black ensemble" (Coyle 2018c), it elides how that budget figure is less than those for films with predominantly white casts (*Black Panther*: $200 million; *Solo: A Star Wars Story*: $275 million; *Avengers: Infinity War*: $316 million). *Wonder Woman* is discussed in similar terms: "the most expensive film ever shot by a person with two XX [*sic*] chromosomes (its $150 million budget surpasses Kathryn Bigelow's $100 million K-19: The Widowmaker)" (Siegel 2017). It makes one begin to wonder if these are the All-Stars of the Farm League. Jenkins is given similar superlatives as Coogler, with "the biggest opening weekend for a female-directed film, a record previously held by 50 Shades of Grey" (*The Satellite* 2017b), but she also gets called "the most important female film director in the business today" (Siegel 2017). She's certainly the most highly paid, as the *Wonder Woman 1984* "deal, reported to be in the range of $7 million to $9 million, makes Jenkins the highest-paid female filmmaker in history" (London Free Press 2017). Yet for all that, the old saw invalidating the relevance or even existence of structural inequality still shows up: we are still told that *Wonder Woman* is "a rare big-budget blockbuster from a director who happens to be a woman" (Bahr 2017).

Indeed, at times journalists seem so eager to identify *Wonder Woman* and *Black Panther* in terms of milestones that they select some rather weird ones. *Black Panther* is "the biggest non-'Star Wars' opener since 'Jurassic World' (with a prime June release date) nearly three years ago" (*Daily Times* 2018); say that three times fast. Its superlatives are often this specific. Did you know that it's the "biggest non-sequel opening weekend, biggest solo superhero launch, biggest long holiday opening weekend and biggest Monday grosser"? (*Express Web Desk* 2018). For its part, *Wonder Woman* is sliced and diced as "the highest-grossing live-action film directed by a woman" (Yamato 2017), "the highest-grossing film ever by a solo woman director" (*Washington Post* 2018) and "the most profitable live-action film ever directed by a woman" (Robey 2017)—all of which are because a woman, Jennifer Lee, was one of the directors of animated film *Frozen*, which had a Disney-sized financial footprint. But Jenkins gets the list treatment as well, with *Wonder Woman* described as "the top-grossing movie in North America, having already broken records as the biggest opening for a female director, largest opening of a female-led comic book adaptation and sixth largest June opening of all time" (Rubinoff 2017).

All Hail the Franchise Savior* (*Conditions May Apply)

Beyond being described as the "best" and the "most," an important strand of the narrative is that these auteurs will save their respective franchises. One headline proclaims that, post-*Black Panther*, "Ryan Coogler suddenly finds himself at the center of Marvel cinematic universe" (*Philippines Daily Inquirer* 2018)—despite the fact that the MCU would common-sensically seem to be centered on the *Avengers* films that all the others are structured to feed into. However, there's a clear sense of improvement over the MCU baseline: "It's gripping, funny, and full of spectacle, but it also feels like a turning point, one where the studio has finally recognized that its movies can be about more than just selling the next installment. In the process, the studio has ended up with one of the most enthralling entries in its entire universe" (Bishop 2018a). The idea of saving franchises is explicitly invoked with Jenkins, who is hailed as saving at least "DC Comics' Films. From themselves" (Braun 2017), the box office (*Times & Transcript* 2017), and even pop culture itself (Hadsall

2017). Moreover, *Wonder Woman* is termed "the first masterpiece in Warner Bros. and DC Entertainments [*sic*] *Justice League* era" (Betancourt 2017a). Prior to its release, one journalist hoped the film "could be the type of epic, not-directed-by-Zack Snyder masterpiece of a cinematic journey many fans felt DC Comics characters were always capable of producing" (*The Star* 2017). This distinction from Snyder apparently shares the belief that his works are not masterpieces. In fact, Jenkins is routinely described as superior to Snyder, as in "at least this standalone film is in the hands of Patty Jenkins (director of *Monster*) and not Zack Snyder (cinema's greatest monster)" (Hertz 2017).

To be the savior of a franchise is a burden, but to be the Other while you're at it increases the weight. While Snyder in particular held on to the reins of the DCEU through failure after critical failure, Comicsgate and other critics are waiting to declare the woman superhero "over," or the *Black Panther* director a one-trick flash in the pan, such that the auteur as Other is held responsible for their entire category. Jenkins describes her thought process in choosing to pass on a project in precisely these terms: "And I thought, 'If I take this, it'll be a big disservice to women. If I take this knowing it's going to be trouble and then it looks like it was me, that's going to be a problem. If they do it with a man, it will just be yet another mistake that the studio made. But with me, it's going to look like I dropped the ball, and it's going to send a very bad message" (Siegel 2017). In Hollywood, as in so much of life, marginalized people are always perceived to represent their entire group in a way that majoritarian populations are never called to do. Thus, *Wonder Woman* is described as "carrying the weight of whether female-led superhero movies will continue to be greenlit and funded by Hollywood studios" (*The Satellite* 2017a).

The situation is similar with *Black Panther*, whose grosses "could help make the film a game-changer for black cinema and diversity behind the camera for years to come" (Levin 2018): do well, and more people get chances. One journalist discussed at length the "Coogler Effect" and the impact on other Black directors:

> So, can *Black Panther* open doors that should've been kicked down long ago? Is the Coogler Effect real? In small measure, it already looks to be producing dividends with superhero films from [Ava] DuVernay and, potentially, [Spike] Lee. It should be noted that *New Gods* marks DuVernay as the second woman to oversee a DC tentpole (following Patty Jenkins' *Wonder Woman*), no small feat given the scarcity with which black women filmmakers are granted the opportunity to shepherd franchise films. There's also the stellar Gina Prince-Bythewood (*Love & Basketball*, *Beyond the Lights*), who is set to direct *Silver*

& Black, a Spider-Man spinoff for Sony that follows the twined adventures of *Silver Sable* and *Black Cat*. She and DuVernay are now among the first black women entrusted with studio-backed superhero epics. (Parham 2018)

The ability of these fan auteurs to open doors for others is certainly helpful, but it's also unfortunate that they apparently have to do so for such opportunities to be extended.

In fact, the success of *Wonder Woman* and *Black Panther* is called "the diversity market trend" and credited with an increase in other studios "slotting ethnic superhero movies into their own pipelines" (*China Daily* 2018). All three of the films explored in this chapter and their directors are often directly compared to each other. Articles particularly placed *Wonder Woman* and *Black Panther* in an implicit battle for most successful marginalized superhero film, with significant coverage following the news that *Black Panther* had out-earned *Wonder Woman* at the box office (McNary 2018). Both films were cited alongside other marginalized cinema hits (such as Jordan Peele's *Get Out*) as a sign of a turn in the tides: "inclusion is paying—and often, it's paying off big time" (Coyle 2018b). *Wonder Woman* came first and therefore tends to anchor comparisons: *Black Panther* was described on its premiere date as "perhaps even approaching the blockbuster status attained last summer by another Hollywood myth-buster, 'Wonder Woman'" (B. Barnes 2018). However, there is a disturbing amount of "All the Women Are White, All the Blacks Are Men" (Hull, Scott, and Smith 1993), where "women" and "Black people" are treated as entirely separate categories: "Much like 'Wonder Woman' did last summer when it crystallized the sentiment expressed in the 2017 Women's March, and gave women and girls a superhero role model who was much more than a pretty face and a skimpy costume, 'Black Panther' gives black Americans an opportunity to see themselves in the role of hero" (Lamberson 2018). Some journalists did remember that Black women are women as they made these comparisons: "Like the Amazons before them, Okoye, Nakia and Black Panther's female fighting force Dora Milaje continue to do wonders for women on the big screen" (Truitt 2018b). The linkage between the two was also emphasized when Jenkins was directly asked to weigh in on *Black Panther* and "called the film's success 'incredibly meaningful'" (*News International* 2018).

With the final film chronologically, Coogler also "follows New Zealander Taika Waititi, who directed the terrific *Thor: Ragnarok* (2017), in being a nonwhite director of a Marvel movie" (Romei 2018)—which is true, yet awkwardly Othering. Both are particularly described as putting their own "stamp" on the films (Augustine 2018; Maddox 2018). This is a good thing, as another comparison makes clear: *Black Panther* "also injects a fresh dose of adrenaline into the superhero genre, just like *Thor: Ragnarok*" (Mukherjee 2018). In this way, while the Other as auteur improves their franchise, they do so in the shadow of Otherness.

Auteur-ish: Uneven Opportunity and Creative Control

These auteurs are not only socially marginalized but also industrially. All of the Othered directors profiled in this chapter took a longer, or more successful, route to their big-budget films than similar figures among white men directors. At the end of an interview in 2004, Patty Jenkins said she was writing the next project and suggested that it would be easier to get financed due to *Monster*'s success: "I think making a film that you think is good and you believe in is going to be difficult forever. It will be easier to cast and easier to get financed [due to *Monster*], and then it will be harder to stay as focused" (Patrizio 2004). That proved to be painfully untrue: Jenkins would not make another feature film until *Wonder Woman*, instead working in the world of television. Interpretations of this trajectory have varied. Several articles contended that "Jenkins has struggled to find movie work since *Monster*" (Child 2015a), but others disagreed: "Even though *Wonder Woman* is only her second feature, Jenkins's work has always been steady. Hollywood has never stopped trying to get her to make films" (Bahr 2017). Jenkins's own words may provide the best insight: "I'm not offered things that are authentic to me very often" (Hoby 2017b). That is, she may have struggled with regard to work she was willing to take. This was particularly related to a belief that she was hired because she was a woman. In the more dismissive reddit formulation, "She really only got the part cause WB was actively looking for a female director" ("R/Movies—Why Hasn't Patty Jenkins Directed a Feature Film in 14 Years until Wonder Woman?" 2017). Even professionals insisted that Jenkins's gender was integral to securing the job: "Warner also needed to find a female creative vision for the project and would have faced outrage from fans and bloggers if it had gone for the 'safer' option of an established male film-maker" (Child 2015a). The contention that there would have been backlash for hiring a man may be true, but it's not a vote of confidence in Jenkins. Of course, Greg Silverman, Warner Bros' head of development, insisted "it was never about the best female director" (McClintock 2015)—which PR would dictate he had to say whether it was true or not.

Interestingly, this was not a claim made about Coogler—even though so few white people know how to light for Black actors that insisting on a Black director would probably have been for the best. Coogler does share the slow road to franchise auteurship with Jenkins, however. An article on Coogler's "ascent" parallels his rise with several white directors (Colin Trevorrow and Jon Watts) but notes that Coogler's path took "slightly longer":

> The success of *Fruitvale Station*, which won the Grand Jury and Audience Awards at Sundance, led both Coogler and [actor Michael B.] Jordan to collaborate for the second of three times as director and star of the remarkably entertaining *Creed* in 2015. The film, a new entry in the long-running *Rocky* franchise, tells the story of Apollo Creed's son Adonis (Jordan), who ends up being trained by the Italian Stallion (Sylvester Stallone) himself before a heavyweight fight in the United Kingdom. That well-received film earned $173.5 million on a $35 [million] budget—and then led Coogler to the much bigger world of Marvel. (Spiegel 2018)

Coogler, that is, had to be both critically acclaimed and a box-office heavyweight to get into Marvel—not something required of white men in the franchise.

As this question about whether and how they get jobs indicates, the level of opportunity for the Othered auteur is lesser. Jenkins's pay increased between seven and nine times after *Wonder Woman*'s success (the exact figure wasn't released), and she also got "a 'significant' percentage of the back end. Jenkins was paid $1 million for the first *Wonder Woman*; she was not credited with the screenplay or the story" (Sliver, 2017)—though the fact that she wasn't signed for her sequel, when locking personnel in to multi-film contracts is usually standard, both showed her lack of status and gave her negotiation leverage. Jenkins is also not invited to have the same aspirations as other directors, who regularly lay claim to heroes and franchises. Even at the height of *Wonder Woman*'s success, when asked what she would like to direct next Jenkins deferred on a direct answer: "It's no secret that I love *Superman* but right now I'm just happy doing *Wonder Woman*" (Outlaw 2017).

The lack of opportunities may have much to do with the fact that these auteurs are perceived as particularly risky. The coverage accompanying the announcement framed Jenkins as a risky choice, as critics noted:

> On Wednesday, an article in *The Hollywood Reporter* blatantly asked, "Can Patty Jenkins make the superhero world safe for female directors? Warner Bros. gambles $150 million on its first woman-centered comic book movie with a filmmaker whose only prior big-screen credit was an $8 million indie." As many people on Twitter were quick to point out, the use of the word "gamble" is indicative of how women directors are treated in Hollywood. Yes,

it's true that the budget for Jenkins's first film, *Monster*, the 2003 drama about serial killer Aileen Wuornos, was small potatoes compared to the budget for *Wonder Woman*. (It still managed to win Charlize Theron the Academy Award for Best Actress.) But directors of smaller films (and even TV shows) getting hired to head dramatically bigger productions isn't unusual—it's just normally something that happens to white men. (Beck 2017)

Similarly, one article on his negotiations referred to Waititi as an "interesting" choice (Admin. 2015). "Interesting" is less inherently loaded than "risky," but still emphasizes that this is not who normally gets these opportunities. By contrast, what's deemed risky is not Coogler but the Blackness of his film:

> *Black Panther* isn't the first comic book movie to feature a black hero, as the *Blade* trilogy did that years ago, but it is the first ever to feature a predominantly black cast. There were plenty who felt this was a risky bet in some ways, even for Marvel Studios, who have earned a ton of good faith with audiences over the years. Risky or not, it's a bet that paid off handsomely and one that provided Hollywood with an important lesson. (R. Scott 2018)

This focus on the person of Jenkins but the contents of *Black Panther* was a recurring theme across the data.

The perceived risk or slower professional trajectory for the Othered auteur then affects whether they are trusted and how much creative control they have. Jenkins noted that "so as long as Zack and I both understood the trajectory of where *Wonder Woman* goes and it makes sense in her future in his films, then I was free to tell whatever story I wanted" (Daniell 2017a). While the intent was to insist that she *did* have freedom, it ends up showing that Snyder's thumb was on the scale. Trust was definitely not extended to Jenkins; speculation on her departing started right from the announcement that she had been hired, with a narrative of Jenkins as potentially "difficult" taking hold thanks to her departure from *Thor: The Dark World*. One article asked:

> Will Jenkins be able to hold onto the role? Since her feature film *Monster* (2003) she has had great difficulty with a second film project. Despite several episodes of TV under her belt (*Entourage*, *The Killing*) she has yet to have a second feature film. Her work on both Thor: *The Dark World* and *Jane Got A Gun* fell victim to "creative differences" and disagreements. Given the reasons cited for MacLaren's departure just a few days ago [creative differences], can Jenkins hold onto the DC gig? (Seabrook 2015)

"Creative differences" might be a face-saving code word for when things aren't working out, but at face value it implies conflict between directorial vision and control higher up the chain. Before *Wonder Woman*'s release, an internal memo claimed the film was a "mess," causing Jenkins to take to Twitter to refute the claims: "Real lasso of truth, time, will reveal that letter to be false soon enough. But lame something so transparent in its agenda gets traction" (P. Jenkins 2016). For his part, one article mentioned that "Coogler persuaded executives to let him bring some familiar faces, including *Fruitvale Station* director of photography Rachel Morrison, *Creed* production designer Hannah Beachler and his long-time editor Michael Shawver" (*Sunday Tribune* 2018). While this was intended to be proof that Coogler had escaped Marvel's "uniformly cookie-cutter vibe," the fact that he needed permission to choose his own support staff shows the same franchise overlord problem.

It's also notable that none of the three got to cast their lead. Waititi was the farthest from the point of casting, inheriting Chris Hemsworth after four previous films. The other two, however, were just shy of having creative input. Coogler spoke of the challenge: "When I first started talking with Marvel, you guys were in post[-production on *Civil War*]. Making a film where your lead actor has been cast by somebody is scary. It terrified me. And I knew Chadwick was crazy talented and I didn't know him at the time yet" (Anderton 2018). Jenkins's account is similar: "I had never met Gal and when I heard that Zack Snyder had cast her as Wonder Woman in *Batman v Superman*, my heart skipped a beat.... That doesnt [sic] always work out" (*The Nation* 2017). Although in both cases the directors went on to express happiness with who they ended up with, it does reemphasize the lack of control.

However, at other times they do seem to have control. One article about Marvel parent Disney said that "rather than assign the cinematic equivalent of widget-makers to write and direct their flagship projects, they've hired filmmakers culled from the world of indies and film festivals: Ava DuVernay for 'A Wrinkle in Time,' Ryan Coogler for 'Black Panther,' Alex Ross Perry for 'Winnie-the-Pooh' and David Lowery for 'Pete's Dragon'" (Hornaday 2016). Similarly, it was treated as laudable that "from the time talks with Warner Bros. began, back in 2005, Jenkins held fast to her original narrative for the heroine" (Woerner 2017)—even though it meant that they wouldn't hire her for ten more years. Sometimes these directors are even directly attributed the term "auteur": MCU hired "an auteur African-American director (Ryan Coogler of 'Fruit-vale Station' [sic] and 'Creed')" (Tillet 2018); "it should not be overlooked that Jenkins has made something very close to a personal auteurist vision here" (Daniell 2017b).

Representation between Politics and Universality

The most talked-about characteristic of both *Wonder Woman* and *Black Panther* is their representation, which gets tightly interwoven with the identities of the auteurs in a way that it does not for white men or even for Waititi. There is so much discussion of representation that it's impossible to fully engage here; we will instead focus primarily on the auteurs' own words about representation and inclusion. Indeed, representation is the place where the subjects of this chapter most diverge from each other, with Jenkins largely retreating into white feminism, by contrast to Coogler and Waititi being more overtly political.

To begin with Jenkins, she was to some extent between a rock and a hard place with *Wonder Woman*. Some, like director James Cameron, complained that the character wasn't tough enough, while others argued she was tilted too far toward eye candy. In effect, some thought she should be more of what men approve of and some thought she was too much of that already. Jenkins has defended many of her choices directly, including following Cameron's suggestion that *Wonder Woman* is a step backward from Sarah Connor's "grit." Jenkins replied on Twitter with an image of text that read in part:

> James Cameron's inability to understand what *Wonder Woman* is, or stands for, to women all over the world is unsurprising as, though he is a great filmmaker, he is not a woman. Strong women are great. . . . But if women have to always be hard, tough and troubled to be strong, and we aren't free to be multidimensional . . . then we haven't come very far, have we. I believe women can and should be EVERYTHING, just like male lead characters should be. There is no right and wrong kind of powerful woman. And the massive female audience who made the film [the] hit it is, can surely choose and judge their own icons of progress. (P. Jenkins 2017)

There's certainly a compelling case that "troubled and hard" is a narrow and limited model of strength, which calls for variety and multidimensionality. However, Jenkins seems less to want more options than being "hard and tough" than simply to refuse them altogether. In her choices for Wonder Woman's fighting style, she said, "if you watch closely she never stabs anybody—she's knocking guns out of hands," adding a physical demonstration in which "she mimes precise and focused self-defence"; this would be just a characterization decision like any other, except that she describes this as being "very cautious with her attitude" (Hoby 2017b). The link between being less physically violent and having the right kind of "attitude" is telling.

As this begins to suggest, there's concern that Jenkins may have swung *Wonder Woman* too far toward very conventional femininity. In the same Twitter post discussed above, she advocated that we "celebrate an icon of women everywhere because she is attractive and loving" (P. Jenkins 2017), and doing so *because* she's attractive might give us pause. Certainly, Wonder Woman's revealing outfit attracted criticism. Jenkins's response was to say:

> When people get super critical about her outfit, who's the one getting crazy about what a woman wears? That's who she is; that's Wonder Woman. I want her to look like my childhood fantasy. It's not the male gaze that's made little girls buy princess dolls for all these years. They're into it. And so we're into it. Who's been the fan base that's kept Wonder Woman alive all these years? Women. So let her be every glorious thing that she is. Including hot and beautiful and sexy and loving and great and kind. (Woerner 2017)

This comment has a number of issues. One appreciates Jenkins's honesty about matching up to her childhood fandom and commitment to rounded characters, but the idea that the male gaze is irrelevant is laughable. Wonder Woman was something of a fetish object for William Moulton Marston, who "insisted that Wonder Woman be chained or otherwise bound in every issue, telling his DC editor that 'women enjoy submission'" (Cavna 2017). Men have decided her look more or less ever since, and little girls, like the rest of us, "have no means of registering their demand for products that are not offered to them" (Herman and Chomsky 1988, 339). The fetishistic and perhaps even hypersexual appearance was certainly mitigated in Jenkins's rendition; feminist writer Jessica Valenti (2017), among others, waxed poetic about "watching the Amazon women of Themyscira practice fighting, their strength and athleticism on full display; the battle scene where their bodies flew through the air, beautiful but not sexualized." However, the association of Wonder Woman with sexualization remains.

Concern over sexual objectification was particularly acute given that Brett Ratner's involvement with the first *Wonder Woman* film collided a feminist hero with a set that harbored a man accused by multiple women of sexual assault and harassment. The rumor that Gal Gadot had used her success to have him removed launched many speculative articles. Gadot's comment on Ratner not being involved with the second *Wonder Woman* following accusations of assault and harassment was as follows: "The truth is, there's so many people involved in making this movie, it's not just me, and they all echoed the same sentiments. . . . Everyone knew what was the right thing to do" (Rosa 2017). Jenkins herself rarely spoke out directly regarding the contemporaneous #MeToo and #TimesUp movements around sexual assault and harassment, only addressing some of her own experience: "The second I wanted to be a director there were constant flirtations and inappropriate overtures and requests to have meetings in weird places." While this is consistent with the ways Jenkins overall shies away from controversy, her positioning on Time's "Person of the Year" runner-up list was particularly ironic: in the year of #MeToo, she was the only woman on the runner-up list (alongside Donald Trump and Kim Jong Un). However, one important, tangible change with Jenkins in the directorial seat for the *Wonder Woman* sequel is the production's status as the first film using the new Producers Guild of America policies to "combat sexual harassment and misconduct on film and TV sets" (Rosa, 2018).

Ultimately, Jenkins's relationship to gender politics is best understood as somewhere between postfeminist and white feminist. At some moments, she rejects structural inequalities to emphasize individual advancement, making comments in interviews like, "I have always wanted to be last-wave feminism, where you're so feminist, you're not thinking about it at all. Where you're like, 'Of course this superhero is the greatest superhero of all time. Oh, she's a woman? I wasn't even thinking about that!'" (Setoodeh 2017). At other times, she rejects "feminism" as something for the character to embrace: "[Wonder Woman] doesn't have a chip on her shoulder. That was something I felt . . . that I really brought in. We had a lot of conversations about feminism and her point of view. She's not a feminist. It never occurred to her that she would treat somebody differently to somebody else, which is the stronger statement" (Harold 2017). This is a kind of universalism that structurally relies on having whiteness and heterosexuality and wealth—on gender being one's only source of marginalization. Indeed, Jenkins even invokes universality explicitly:

> I think that there was an idea that only a very small, certain kind of people liked action movies or superhero movies, whatever, and that's where the money was. I think what things like *The Hunger Games* and *Divergent* are starting to change is, everybody sees there's a universal story to be told with other people and there's also universal money to be made with all kinds of people who want to see it. (C. M. Smith 2017)

Jenkins also invokes a sort of gender essentialism more often found in previous waves of feminism with comments such as "I'm sure there's a long history of belief that certain jobs are masculine. . . . But why a director would fall into that [category] makes me very confused. Because it feels like a very natural job for a woman. It's incredibly maternal in a way.

You're caretaking all of these sorts of things" (Siegel 2017). The idea that women are inherently any kind of way similarly takes the white woman's experience as universal. Jenkins is, at times, even hostile to the mention of structural concerns: "'I can't take on the history of 50 percent of the population just because I'm a woman,' says Jenkins, bristling when asked about the heavy responsibility of directing *Wonder Woman*" (Siegel 2017). While resistance to the burden is fair, alongside the other aspects of her gender politics, it becomes further evidence of her drive to be as apolitical as possible.

Coogler, by contrast, recognizes representation as less of a burden than a responsibility. He notes that "as more content gets made, more opportunities like ours can come about for folks. But you've got to put your foot on the gas when it comes to that or things can go back to where they were" (*Sunday Tribune* 2018). This sense that change must actively be pursued is different than many others, and important. In speaking about Disney as a studio, he praised them for a meaningful commitment to representation:

> When you look at Disney with [Tendo Nagenda, executive vice president for production at Walt Disney Studios, and Nate Moore, a producer at Marvel Studios and an executive producer of "Black Panther"], it's a place that's interested in representation, not just for the sake of representation, but representation because that's what works, that's what's going to make quality stuff that the world is going to embrace, that's what leads to success. (Ugwu 2018)

In this way, doing representation well matters, as in his own statement that "I'm not qualified just because I look like this" (*Sunday Tribune* 2018). That is, being part of the African diaspora didn't make him an expert in Africa, even if typical Hollywood interchangeability might have treated him as one. He explicitly visited the continent to do research, which he discusses in deeply personal terms: "This movie brought me closer to my roots. This movie took me to the continent of Africa, which is somewhere I wanted to go since my mom and dad sat me down and told me I was black, you know what I mean?" (J. Weiss 2017). Coogler also uses "us" liberally to link himself to African Americans and Black people more broadly; the other auteurs don't overtly connect themselves to specific groups.

Beyond general commitment to representation, Coogler explicitly talks about power and inequality. Speaking about gender in his film, he said:

> What we wanted to do was build a society that's both based on the source material and also pulled from historical content, looking at the history and

role of women in African society, specifically precolonial African society. We saw tons of examples of women who had high-ranking political positions and were respected as warriors. We wanted to push that idea forward in this film.... It's about a king, but he's able to be king because of these incredible women around him. These women who were empowered to be great at the things they chose to be great at. (*Philippines Daily Inquirer* 2018)

This is similar to women's position in his film's production: "They're incredible artists and having them on this film meant everything.... Women had their hands all over the film" (Bell 2018). This way of overtly addressing systems also came through in Coogler's response to Donald Trump's comments calling African nations, among others, "shithole countries," which happened directly before *Black Panther* was released. Asked to respond to those stereotypes, Coogler made a point of historicizing: "The narrative about the continent that we know is actually a fairly recent narrative, if you think about human history. It's a narrative that was born out of what happened when the countries of Africa were conquered" (Ugwu 2018).

This willingness to directly address inequality is where Coogler and Waititi meet. Waititi, for example, was willing to call out his home country of New Zealand in an interview, describing it as "racist as f***" (Ramos 2018). He also directly addressed the issue of cultural appropriation, a concern which raised some hackles around *Black Panther* creating a mash-up culture for Wakanda out of aspects from many African nations (de Souza 2018). By contrast, Waititi said that

> while some of the design and look of *Thor: Ragnarok* is inspired by Australia and New Zealand, he says, "I was very careful in these design meetings.... You need to follow-up by saying 'don't copy that, but use it as inspiration,' because the next thing you know you have 50 people who have appropriated all these like beautiful ancient designs without asking what they mean, or who owns them, or for any permission." (Bizzaca 2017)

Indigeneity surfaced repeatedly in the film, even in a simple example that Valkyrie "shows up in a spaceship in the colours of the Aboriginal flag, amid massive fireworks show, because why be subtle when you can be awesome instead" (Taipua 2017). At a deeper level, while filming in Australia, Waititi "lobbied Marvel Studios to include support for a group of Aboriginal filmmakers to follow the production on set, making sure that that his work gave back to the people of the land in which he was a guest. Furthermore, he made sure the production acknowledged the Yugambeh people" (Taipua 2017). This direct engagement with systemic issues is particular to these directors, and it is an important part of putting them into conversation.

Coogler and Waititi also both work through issues of colonialism. Coogler's Wakanda is utopian on many levels, of course, but "part of the movie's emotional and visual appeal lies in the fact that Wakanda has never been colonized" (Tillet 2018). Moreover, beyond the absence of colonialism, there's the expressive possibility this enables: "Free of imperialist violence, the country developed the most technologically advanced society on the planet" (Ingram 2018). In this way, it's clear why many view *Black Panther* as "more than just a movie. It's an unapologetic celebration of cultures seldom seen in a blockbuster movie, that many say couldn't have come at a better time" (Streeter 2018). Waititi's engagement with colonialism is far less utopian; rather than colonialism never happening, it's revealed to be the crime underpinning Asgard's wealth when it comes home to roost in the form of Thor's destructive sister, Hela. While the first *Thor* film noted some of the dangers of colonization in the form of Loki, the stolen child of an enemy people raised with no knowledge of his identity or origin, *Thor: Ragnarok* took the narrative full circle. Thor grappling with Asgard's history and ultimately destroying it rather than letting Hela continue her colonization spree is a potent political framing for contemporary beneficiaries of colonial pasts. This was particularly so given Asgard's vaguely Viking aesthetic, as currently "medieval Vikings . . . function as a signal to white supremacists" (Kim 2019). This makes *Ragnarok* particularly powerful as "a multiracial and postcolonial counternarrative to the white Viking narrative circulating through the alt-right digital ecosystem" (Kim 2019).

However, for all their representational successes in some respects, all three of these films fail to include LGBTQ+ people in any meaningful way. The relative lack of attention to this compared to dissecting other aspects of representation demonstrates that the presence of Othered directors in the chair tends to divert criticism from the representation that goes unfulfilled, particularly in cases where the comics are ultimately more progressive than what makes the cut on-screen. However, GLAAD critiqued all three of the directors analyzed here for the lack of queer representation in their films:

> Despite the fact that *Wonder Woman*, *Black Panther*, and *Thor: Ragnarok* all featured characters that are canonically queer in the comic books, none of the films made mention of the fact. In the latter two films' case, scenes that explicitly acknowledged that Okoye and Valkyrie are both queer women were considered before ultimately being left on the cutting room floor. (Pulliam-Moore 2018)

Indeed, while *Wonder Woman* had a throwaway line that "when it comes to procreation, men are essential, but for pleasure, not necessary," it was both plausibly deniable and the result of improvisation between the actors rather than scripted (J. Alexander 2017b). A *Saturday Night Live* skit parodied the apparent lack of queer characters on *Wonder Woman*'s Amazon island and in doing so skewered the implied romance between two characters on the battlefield with a reminder that "the whole thing seems so super gay" (Kristian 2017). Moreover, much like Rowling's extratextual pronouncements, the confirmation that Valkyrie is indeed bisexual came first from interviews with actor Tessa Thompson instead of the text itself (Nicholson 2017). However, director Waititi's influence on turning that subtext into text in the upcoming *Thor: Love and Thunder*—which promises both the inclusion of Natalie Portman as Thor and Tessa Thompson as an openly queer warrior king—is promising. The statement that Thompson's Valkyrie will be "searching for a queen" made waves on the internet, with Captain Marvel as a fan favorite choice (Sherlock 2019). It's important, then, to parse out what does and doesn't come to fruition from Othered directors. Although there is some ability to expand beyond their own group in representation, there are still absences.

Conclusion: Sky High Expectations?

Given the combination of progress on inclusion with massive success represented by these three auteurs, there is now a sense of far greater possibility. Jenkins, in particular, has acquired something of a fandom of her own, inspiring fan cosplay of herself (T. Heyman 2018) as well as, like Ava DuVernay, a Barbie doll, about which she tweeted: "Can't express how totally mind blowing and delightful it is to have your childhood favorite resemble you!! Thank you @Barbie, for this incredible honor, and for celebrating all kinds of women, everywhere. What a great way to inspire the girls of tomorrow!" (P. Jenkins 2018). As exciting as the recognition may be, this kind of singling out underscores that change is still in its early days. As Marvel president Kevin Feige noted, "With ['Ant-Man and the Wasp'] and now with 'Captain Marvel' and many movies to be announced in the near future, I'm anxious for the time where it's not a novelty that there is a female-led superhero movie but it is a norm" (Russo 2018).

In fact, the ways these few films have been so spectacularly lucrative has produced some unfortunate side effects:

> *Captain Marvel*, directed by Anna Boden and Ryan Fleck, is probably going to be a huge hit next March. But it need not match *Wonder Woman* and it has

no business being saddled with the expectations of being a $1 billion+ global grosser. Nobody expected *Black Panther* to do *Black Panther* business back in February just as few of us expected *Wonder Woman* to do *Wonder Woman* business in the summer of 2017. *Captain Marvel*, like *Wonder Woman 1984*, *Birds of Prey* and *Black Widow*, can be a winner without breaking records. When you have enough of these, they stop having to prove a damn thing. (Mendelson 2018c)

As it happens, *Captain Marvel* lived up to some of these high expectations, passing $1 billion in the box office to land respectably at seventh in Marvel's slate of hits (Abad-Santos 2019). A sequel to the film was confirmed at ComicCon in 2019. Yet this exception doesn't mean that the problem of inflated expectations is solved, and as *Birds of Prey* screenwriter Christina Hodson notes, this challenge is still awaiting the next generation of Othered directors in the superhero space: "Just because we're talking about it now and just because [*Wonder Woman* director] Patty Jenkins kicked a—, it doesn't mean everything's fixed. And I think we just gotta be mindful. But one or two big movies, like out there front and center, don't change the fact that the numbers are really, really bad" (Gonzalez 2018).

The low overall numbers are part of what make Jenkins's white feminism so disappointing: as one of the only visible women in this type of directorial space, she has an opportunity to amplify the larger need for change, but she doesn't always use it. The more directly political stances taken by Coogler and Waititi show that being more intentional is certainly possible. At the same time, it's important to recognize that tokenized figures are continually called upon to be representative in ways they didn't volunteer for. The directors examined here share an unexpected level of attention on their politics and a disproportionate ability to be heard, which can make their position untenable unless and until they're not a novelty speaking for all directors like them. Thus, whether their success produces a broader shift still remains to be seen.

Conclusion: Fanboy Backlash and the Futures of Fan Auteurs

> There is an element of wish fulfillment to the film that many female critics latched onto—a hero's story, but with specific touches that make it clear who the target audience is meant to be. Jupiter lives a life that seems inconsequential to her, then has a universe of possibilities open up in front of her. Her journey requires an acceptance of nobility, changing in and out of incredible outfits, proposals of marriage, harrowing chase sequences, and a hunky guy who attaches himself to her side from the moment they lock eyes. It's better than a princess narrative because it's not about being whisked away to a castle, never to toil or worry again–in fact, the narrative is basically the opposite of that in every way—and hits beats for its female audience that are often looked down upon by action films. (Asher-Perrin 2016)

In January 2019, *Black Panther* received an Academy Award nomination for Best Picture. The nomination has been interpreted as pandering to the fan base, but it was also predicted to increase viewership for the telecast, looking to *Black Panther* and the fanboy auteur as potential salvation. As one critic observes:

> But T'Challa may need to slide on his sleek suit for one more important rescue: *Black Panther* may have to save the Oscars. In an era when the awards show has lost audience, relevance, and its place as a communal cultural moment, Coogler's comic-book movie delivered on all three, and did so with

a level of style and craft that rose above its peers in the genre. *Black Panther* doesn't need the Oscars to have its place in history cemented, but the Oscars may need *Black Panther*. (Keegan 2018)

This move was not without resistance. Briefly, the Academy of Motion Picture Arts and Sciences committee floated a "Best Popular Film" award as a potential way to navigate between the concerns of prestige film and more popular audiences. The immediate social media reaction to the phrasing and implied distinction from the "actual" Best Picture caused the Academy to reverse course, at least for now. However, the incident highlighted the fundamental tension between the box-office-dominating world of fanboy auteurs and the prestige engines of Hollywood. As of September 2019, the top-grossing films worldwide are littered with fanboy franchises: *Avengers: Endgame* (1), *Star Wars: The Force Awakens* (4), *Avengers: Infinity War* (5), *Marvel's The Avengers* (8), *Avengers: Age of Ultron* (10), *Black Panther* (11), and *Harry Potter and the Deathly Hallows Part 2* (12) (Box Office Mojo n.d.). Yet despite (or maybe because of) this box-office clout, respect from the prestige side of the industry is in short supply—and, indeed *Green Book*, a feel-good film about racism being solved through interracial friendship, took the top honor at the 2019 Oscars. The gap between prestige and box-office success is one place where the fan auteur intervenes in the contemporary moment—to attempt to bridge the two. On the one hand, fan franchises are becoming increasingly authored. On the other, auteurs are increasingly asked to adapt to the fanboy world, but are not always successful in that adaptation.

With the rise of the fan franchise as box-office staple, the gaze of the fan seems inescapable; the gaze of the fan auteur may be even more so. The establishment of the fan auteur becomes increasingly necessary as the franchises that shape the current conversations in popular culture (and, in turn, form the "canon" for the sometimes subversive and transformative gaze of fandom) are frequently sustained beyond the involvement of the original auteur. The drive to continuation often leads to a desire for continuity or at least fidelity. This leads almost inexorably to the fanboy solution—the far corner of our taxonomy where the auteur is both thoroughly a fan of the material and thoroughly affirmational. Unlike the fan authors and canon-revisionists who occupy the non-affiliated and unendowed spaces of online communities and fan fiction, these fan auteurs are anointed for their appreciation of the original, and thus most frequently engage, at least to some extent, in cycles of reverence, replication, and referentiality that offer fan service to their kindred spirits. Those same fanboy-kin are viewed as the keepers of the franchise's longevity: without fidelity to the nostalgic gaze, the franchise might drop out of sight. By contrast, the more transformational fangirl auteur gaze seems to offer (and author) a disruption; perhaps unsurprisingly, that disruption is viewed with suspicion, rejected, and contained as much as possible by the forces of normative regulation. Such normativity is wielded nearly as much by the fanboys who still occupy a primary position relative to the media franchises that dominate the landscape as it is by the formal keepers of franchises.

It is against this background that the fan auteurs we've examined thus far have different relationships with their franchises and their own fan identities. Steven Moffat and E L James are the purest examples of fans-turned-auteur in the sense that they're both strongly known for their fandom, but the results of that position have been very different for each. While Moffat's fanboy ascendant attitude has mostly won him acclaim (with some grumbling, particularly from fans subject to his trolling and dismissal), E L James is a continual subject of mockery for her fannishness. Coverage of her most recent book, *The Mister*, has been especially derisive, particularly questioning the marketing of it as her first "original" novel considering how closely it hews to the tropes of its genre. One critic covering the announcement referred to the book as "probably exactly what you'd expect" (*Vogue* 2019). Meanwhile, J. K. Rowling suffers continual problems navigating her auteur status while modeling an extremely affirmational type of fandom under the scrutiny of fans ready for her to step aside as keeper of the canon.

Some fanboys have set the bar for keeping both their fanboy status and a positive support community within fandom, emphasizing a personal connection with their audiences through online interaction that, while reimagined with each iteration and platform, endures. Kevin Smith has used his fanboy status and audience to propel himself outside of traditional Hollywood productions and enable continual creative opportunities for not only himself but also his community. Joss Whedon, by contrast, has moved from outsider fanboy to ultimate insider, shifting from making works viewed as feminist critique of tropes to being the definer (and defender) of regressive stereotypes. For his part, Zack Snyder has moved from insider to the apparent outskirts, but recent news suggests he is on his way back to the center, with his dedicated fan base following every step of the way.

Those who occupy a more uneasy relationship with their fan identity are marked as outsiders from the start. Patty Jenkins and Ryan Coogler have ascended within the DC and Marvel universes, respectively, and the success of their work is unassailable, yet both are cautious in their social media usage and, along with Taika Waititi, they continue to be marked as Othered in news coverage and fan reception. The need to navigate this position then impacts their ability to act as franchise heads. Overall, what we have seen so far is that the story of the fan auteur is one of tensions between the fan pole and the auteur one, and this is particularly the case at the point where the two make contact: social media. In this final chapter, we explore this tension and its implications for the future of fan-centric franchising.

Here, we contrast two cases of fangirl auteurs—the Wachowski sisters and Ava DuVernay—with the rise of fan backlash. On the one hand, we argue, media-makers can no longer opt out of the spaces and patterns of fan engagement. This brings a great deal of risk as campaigns for hiring and firing—sincere or otherwise—are an increasingly widely used tactic in fandoms and the culture wars alike. On the other hand, DuVernay and the Wachowski sisters are interesting cases whose established auteur status enabled them to move into fan franchises. The Wachowskis have historically avoided the spotlight and have embraced outsiderhood only recently. DuVernay, by contrast, takes an overtly political approach to being a public figure, directly naming systems of inequality and the media industry's issues as well as making a strong use of Twitter as a platform. We end with a consideration of some other possible futures; proliferating fannish media can allow a wider variety of auteurs, but tentpole properties continue to be haunted by the specter of mainstream fan rage.

Fanboys Strike Back: Social Media Scandals and other Risky Encounters

The fan auteur is the product of a moment with increasingly blurry boundaries between fan and creator. One part of this, as we've discussed in this book, is fans becoming official creators. However, the other part is the extent to which fans have contact with creators. From one direction, this is an opportunity for industry to recruit and exploit the most docile, useful fans (Stanfill 2019). At the same time, however, there is always an excess of fannishness that industry's best-laid plans can never contain. Coordinated campaigns of fan harassment against media creators, such as the one known as #Gamergate, are now infamous, but even more quotidian examples show increased contact across the fan/media-maker boundary. The writers' rooms of television shows increasingly have Twitter accounts, and routinely find themselves subject to the scrutiny and angry tweets of fans (Navar-Gill 2018; Navar-Gill and Stanfill 2018). Hotly disputed moments, like the unnecessary death of lesbian character Lexa in *The 100* (CW, 2014–20), become battlegrounds, with show creators many times coming to issue apologies. The option to disengage is no longer available to those who create geek culture; much like George RR Martin, subject to questioning regarding his elusive next book in any public setting, auteurs will be asked to answer to their fans. Auteurs and franchises find themselves under the potentially hostile gaze of fans, creating a cycle that demands their performance for an audience that can be quick to pass judgement.

Media-makers can't opt out of the spaces and patterns of fan engagement: the expectations of accessibility and visibility are now built into the profession. Yet social media is uneven terrain. Traits that are well-received in fanboy auteurs (such as Snyder's excessive posting regarding the details of his true auteurial intentions on *Justice League*) are ill-received from their counterparts (as in the reaction to Rowling's continued additions to the Harry Potter canon). The fangirl auteur is expected to make similar use of social media and be available for continual critique and harassment, but her defenders are unlikely to campaign in the manner of Snyder's horde demanding to see his cut of *Justice League*, and the consequences of missteps, for her, are greater. Even the most successful women, such as E L James and J. K. Rowling, fall into contentious patterns in their use of social media and visibility. Again and again, women, particularly women of color, have abandoned their social media presence following campaigns of harassment, only to return because to not be present is as (or more) dangerous to their continued careers and relevance.

However, the fanboy auteur's ability to control reception and discourse is also diminishing. While many auteurs got their start in social media on platforms they controlled or influenced heavily, such as Joss Whedon at Whedonesque and Kevin Smith's viewaskew.com message boards, most auteurs now have to rely upon visibility in platforms with more diverse audiences. Zack Snyder's attempt to work outside of conventional social media spaces by using niche platform Vero has been somewhat effective, but is unlikely to be a successful strategy for mainstream promotion of his forthcoming films and new franchise. Others adopting the fanboy auteur approach or trying to fit the mold set by those who started their careers at a time dominated by more enthusiast-focused and thus fan-friendly social media platforms (as opposed to porous spaces such as Twitter) are likely to find the stakes and consequences have risen significantly.

Even outside of geek cultural spaces, auteurs such as Shonda Rhimes and Gina Rodriguez are building their media empires while keeping a similar veneer of accessibility to their fans. In an interview, Rhimes discusses this practice as essential, saying of her Shondaland.com website that "what I love about it is that it is a place not just for fans of the shows, but for any of the people who live in the universe of thinking about things in a much more inclusive way to enjoy themselves, to read, to have a conversation." She adds,

"I think I'm fortunate in that I have an audience of followers that is 12 to 75," noting that the website "really is about talking to all of them" (Recode Staff 2017). However, Rhimes also noted that—on this platform she controls, an outlier in the contemporary moment—"We have yet to open it up to the comments. We've had a lot of talks about this.... We've yet to open up all of our comments on our discussion parts, because we've really been talking about how to do that, and how to do it well and responsibly because it is getting worse out there, I think" (Recode Staff 2017). Rhimes has similarly created distance from fans on Twitter, explaining, "I used to use it more as a way of talking to the people who watch the shows," and her retreat is because it's "awesome when you're sending people off to medical school and they're telling you they became doctors because of you. But it's not awesome when they're saying they're gonna kill themselves if Callie and Arizona break up, because you made them know that they were gay and it was okay" (Recode Staff 2017). Such uncertain engagements are now par for the course, both within and outside geek media.

This same expectation of accessibility extends to many of the visible contributors to creative projects, as James Gunn's now-notorious firing from Disney's *Guardians of the Galaxy* sequel reminded many in Hollywood. Gunn was targeted by an alt-right campaign for his criticism of Donald Trump; the campaign dredged up old tweets "joking" about pedophilia and rape, bringing negative attention that Disney ultimately decided they could not afford (Fleming Jr. 2018). One critic noted the risky precedent this firing sets:

> The capitalist machine tried to respond in such a way that looks morally responsible and so fired him. But in reality, James Gunn's specific case was not black and white and needed careful, deliberate consideration.... Subsequently, the film's stars have all come out against the decision, an army of other celebrities have all called out Disney, a petition to reinstate Gunn has gained over 400,000 signatures, and Hollywood has actually empowered internet trolls and created a dangerous precedent. By trying to behave morally responsible, [sic] this decision caused chaos, not positive change. (Karim 2018)

The petition begins with a statement from its initiator, Chandler Edwards, noting, "The other thing is if you do this to Gunn you have to do it for all the other directors who have said some crappy joke sometime in their life, which is all of them, cause I doubt there's one human on this planet who hasn't made a shitty joke once or twice in there [sic] life" (Edwards 2018). It must be said that the point that vast swaths of media workers would face consequences if held to the same standard is less a defense of Gunn than an indictment of

Hollywood and/or American culture. Nevertheless, Gunn offered a similar defense in his tweets following the resurfacing of the jokes: "I used to make a lot of offensive jokes. I don't anymore. I don't blame my past self for this, but I like myself more and feel like a more full human being and creator today. Love you to you all" (Gunn 2018). Gunn left Twitter for eight months after this tweet, dated July 19, 2018. However, Gunn's story, unusually, has a happy ending: a corporate reversal of the decision was announced in March 2019, resolving the demands of the cast but placing the film in a new scheduling limbo caused by Gunn's overcommitted film slate (Fleming Jr. 2019).

The combination of disingenuous targeting and overzealous corporate risk management that precipitated Gunn's firing is an emergent trend that is an entire book in itself. Significantly, such tactics are on the rise. Writer Chuck Wendig's firing from a Marvel comic series over tweets criticizing Republicans in the wake of the contentious September 2018 confirmation of Brett Kavanaugh to the US Supreme Court, coming as it did quickly on the heels of James Gunn's, offers a similar warning. As Wendig noted in a tweet following the event: "To conclude: this is really quite chilling. And it breaks my heart. I am very sad, and worried for the country I live in, and the world, and for creative people all around. Courage to you all. I have a dire fear this is going to get a whole lot worse before it gets better" (Wendig 2018).

However, the long-term consequences for white men anointed in the auteur role seem often to be minimal. Well before he was reinstated to *Guardians of the Galaxy Vol. 3*, it was announced that James Gunn's *The Suicide Squad* would be produced by none other than Zack Snyder (Bezanidis 2019). By contrast, Wendig, who was championing the marginalized rather than mocking them in his social media "faux pas," has not returned to high-profile franchise work as of this writing. Social media is risky, but, as is true in as so many cases, the risk is uneven.

Fangirls Ascending: Wachowski Sisters Reloaded

In this context of ascendant fan(boy) auteurs and social media peril, a pair of examples become especially interesting. The Wachowski sisters first came to prominence with their successful and acclaimed transmedia *Matrix* franchise. In this work, they were marked as auteurs, but not as fans. In fact, Lana Wachowski has been vocal in rejecting the entire franchise concept, for example describing Superman as a "product" too predictable to be compellingly transformed in mainstream narrative: "I don't like Superman. . . . Superman is very simple, and he's a product, like Coca-Cola. You know, the Coca-Cola

Bottling Company is never going to kill Coca-Cola. And that's the same thing with Superman. Our relationship to him as a culture is unchanging" (McWeeny 2015). In the same interview, she credits 9/11 for a cultural shift towards safety, noting that the last original property to succeed was James Cameron's *Avatar* (2009). She further suggests that we have lost our interest in originality: "Nowadays, people who write about movies are obsessed with derivative material in a way they never were before ... they hunger for familiarity, and they actually have a suspicion of originality" (Vary 2015a). Much as with the Coca-Cola example, repetition and financial success go hand in hand in media to a large extent. The fan franchise auteurs we discuss here are well represented across the top 100 films: *Marvel's The Avengers* and *Avengers: Age of Ultron* (Whedon); and *Black Panther* (Coogler), but also all eight of Rowling's Harry Potter films (12, 44, 50, 54, 55, 59, 64, 85), plus *Fantastic Beasts and Where To Find Them* (82). Snyder's maligned *Batman v Superman* lands at 67, while *Thor: Ragnarok* is at 74. And *Wonder Woman* sits at 79 (Author 2019).

While *The Matrix Reloaded* has been edged out of the top 100 recently (it now comes in at 107), it still stands as enough of a success to allow the Wachowksi sisters room for their more experimental work, which hasn't yet reached the same levels of financial success as their *Matrix* films. In 2015, they released a movie that in some ways is the perfect embodiment of fangirl desires: *Jupiter Ascending*. Being auteurs, that is, is what enabled them to dabble in fandom, and from that position they have been rather transformative. The film was critically panned, a failure at the box office, and would likely not exist if not for the pedigree of its *Matrix*-proven directors. One critic describes the plot as the ultimate example of wish fulfillment for a certain type of fan:

> The plot is this: the Wachowskis were given an extraordinary amount of money to make whatever the hell they wanted, and what they wanted to make is exactly what we all, secretly, deep down, want to make: the big-screen adaptation of that *Stargate* fanfic you wrote when you were fourteen that really went off the rails and began to inhabit its own universe, complete with original characters, wolf-men, and bees. (Maggs 2015)

The film, that is, has a fannish positionality even if it is not strictly rooted in a particular fandom, and it remains a critical touchstone for understanding fangirl desires writ large. As one reviewer summarized: "for some, it was the Holy Grail of everything they ever wanted in a movie and hadn't known to ask for" (Asher-Perrin 2016).

Another critic observed that the film offers almost the perfect parallel to fanboy narratives such as *Aquaman*:

> If *Jupiter Ascending* is the self-indulgent fanfiction fantasies of [a] nerdy 13-year-old girl brought to starting life, *Aquaman* is the same but for a jock-y 13-year-old boy. Cultural critics can argue over what it means that the latter is destined to make a gagillion more dollars than the former, but let it be said that the appeal of both films is closer than some fans might admit. (Baron 2018)

As the closest thing to a post-Snyder DC Universe film, *Aquaman* is notably less toxic in its depiction of masculinity. However, as a fanboy fairy tale, it certainly succeeds: its hero finds himself heir to a throne and sought after by a fierce underwater redhead who, like *The Matrix*'s Trinity and other seekers of "The One" before her, needs him to come to the rescue of her fantastical world. It is also, despite these familiar and potentially trite narrative aspects, a resounding success, and has been heralded as a turning point for DC.

The Wachowskis have an unusual trajectory to fangirl auteurship for another reason: they are trans women who transitioned mid-career. Although it has become a tired trope that people who formerly moved through the world as men suddenly experience the marginalization women knew all along and "get it," it's nevertheless the case that the Wachowskis previously occupied a different relationship with their industry and audience and were given a flexibility with blockbuster production post-*Matrix* more consistent with their previously publicly presented gender identity. As fangirl auteurs, they have had less power; they have also faced more outright critique for their work's "fangirl" associations—as if *The Matrix*'s Neo was not wish fulfillment, too.

One of the forms of power the Wachowski sisters formerly had was the capacity to resist being public figures. Post-*Matrix*, their contract "included a no-press clause. Avoiding the scrutinizing glare of the industry press, they gave no interviews and did no publicity" (Hemon 2012). As Lilly noted in an interview, "My desire for anonymity is rooted in two things.... An aversion to celebrity (I like walking into a comics shop and nobody knowing who I am) and the fact that there's something nicely egalitarian about anonymity. You know, equality and shit" (Hemon 2012). This anonymity did not endure, however. Lana describes the press as a tool that the release of *Jupiter Ascending* demanded: "Yeah, press is kind of like a tool. You have to pay for the privilege of what we get to do for our work" (Weintraub 2015). The Wachowskis themselves have suffered from media attention, particularly in threats of outing prior to Lilly Wachowski's public coming out in 2016.

She wrote in her announcement about living in fear of a tabloid-style "Sex Change Shocker" headline, describing how a reporter's threat of a reveal forced her announcement:

> My sister Lana and I have largely avoided the press. I find talking about my art frustratingly tedious and talking about myself a wholly mortifying experience. I knew at some point I would have to come out publicly. You know, when you're living as an out transgender person it's . . . kind of difficult to hide. I just wanted—needed some time to get my head right, to feel comfortable. But apparently I don't get to decide this. (Baim 2016)

Reticent directors like the Wachowski sisters can no longer escape the need to publicly perform in the fan auteur era. They have accepted increased interaction and visibility to the press as an inevitable part of continuing to produce films, taking on an uneasy relationship with the fangirl auteur identity while rejecting the franchise loyalty and pre-branded content that characterizes the output of many of their peers.

However, despite increasingly playing by the rules of fan auteurship, the Wachowskis have maintained some of their resistance. In particular, Lana discussed working on *Jupiter Ascending* from an outsider status:

> There are ideas that have resonated through our work since the beginning – the nature of identity, and the struggle against institutional oppression. Those things will always be a part of us. We're natural outsiders. I'm an out trans person with pink hair! But we're more courageous as storytellers now. We're better and braver and we take bigger chances. We don't want to tell simple stories about good guys and bad guys. We try to make movies that are unique and complex. (Huddleston 2015)

In the end, though moving into the position of the fangirl auteur brought a distinct loss of their former leverage, it also opened up more of a capacity to embrace outsiderhood. That status will be complicated and challenged by Lana Wachowski's announced role directing a fourth Matrix film (Kroll 2019).

Ava DuVernay and the Future of the Fangirl Auteur

Ava DuVernay took a similar path as the Wachowski sisters: from auteur to fan. She built a reputation on so-called serious films, including the narrative of grief *I Will Follow* (2010), incarceration critique and love story *Middle of Nowhere* (2014), and her powerful career-building hip-hop documentary

This Is the Life (2006). Her early work was decidedly not situated in geek or franchise culture, and instead challenged American racism head-on, particularly her film *Selma* (2014), which chronicled the voting rights work of Martin Luther King Jr. Her work in this vein attracted critical praise but no awards, and she played a visible role in the 2015 #OscarsSoWhite discourse. Yet DuVernay's career took a turn to the geek side with the announcement that she would direct Disney's *A Wrinkle in Time*. Madeline L'Engle's *A Wrinkle in Time* is a fangirl staple: a science fiction-fantasy quest centering on a girl's journey across the universe to rescue her father, with the guidance of three women (at least, broadly understood) as mentors. After *A Wrinkle in Time*, DuVernay is moving into more fanboy-centric terrain: the DC Extended Universe (DCEU). As a self-identified comics fan, she is now the director of a film based on a surprisingly obscure property from within that universe, New Gods. Asked about her reaction when asked to direct *New Gods* during a Twitter chat with fans, DuVernay clarified that she had initiated the conversation: "I actually said: 'Hey Guys, I wanna make a New Gods movie.' Then someone said ok. #AskAva" (DuVernay 2018b). This speaks to her auteur position within the industry. Indeed, J. J. Abrams, when asked which women he would like to see direct a *Star Wars* movie, said, "To me, the knee-jerk reaction if I had to [name someone] is Ava DuVernay.... She is as much a fan of genre movies ... and hearing her talk about not just *Star Wars* but hearing her talk about those kinds of films is evidence that she would just kill it" (Child 2015c). DuVernay, that is, is proclaimed both fan and auteur by one of the most fannish auteurs of them all.

Much like Jenkins and Coogler, DuVernay is the subject of frequent superlatives. Coverage of her directorial role on *Wrinkle* often centered on her position as the first black woman to direct a film with a budget over $100 million. As one article emphasized:

> DuVernay ... joins a tiny group of women live-action directors who have worked at such budget levels—Kathryn Bigelow for the 2002 movie "K-19: The Widowmaker," and Patty Jenkins, who is directing next year's "Wonder Woman" movie. Among live-action directors of color, she is also in elite company, a group which includes "Star Trek Beyond" director Justin Lin, "Fantastic Four: Rise of the Silver Surfer" director Tim Story and "Fast 8" director F. Gary Gray. As a woman of color helming a live-action studio tentpole movie, she will be in a category of one. (Keegan 2016)

However, DuVernay departs from her superlative compatriots by addressing her position head on. In her own statement on Twitter about the milestone of being the first black woman to direct a film grossing $100 million, DuVernay pointed to the larger structural problems: "Lovely room to be in. But can't wait for more sisters to be here too. #Onward" (DuVernay 2018c).

This is consistent with DuVernay's overtly political approach to being a public figure. Unlike many of the auteurs we consider in this book, she is not only deeply aware of systems of inequality, but willing to speak forthrightly about them. In interviews, DuVernay directly addressed comparisons of her work to the few other women to ascend these ranks, including Patty Jenkins, while noting that her view of science fiction and fantasy would bring something entirely different:

> You're seeing worlds being built from the point of view of a black woman from Compton.... So, when I'm told, 'Create a planet.' My planet is going to look different from my white male counterparts' planet, which we've seen 97 percent of the time, so you're used to seeing this that [sic]. So, is this going to be as fallible, as interesting, as intriguing? These are all questions that we've only barely been able to ask with Patty Jenkins's great work in *Wonder Woman*. What do worlds through a woman visionary's lens even look like? (Stefansky 2017)

This kind of engagement with her different position and questions of diversity is routine for DuVernay.

In interviews, she often describes her commitment to broadening and diversifying representation. Speaking of *Wrinkle*'s guides Mrs. Who, Mrs. Whatsit, and Mrs. Which, she said, "My whole process with this film was, what if? . . . With these women, I wondered, could we make them women of different ages, body types, races? Could we bring in culture, bring in history in their costumes? And in the women themselves, could we just reflect a fuller breadth of femininity?" (S. R. Weiss 2017). Yet, despite this framing of open-endedness, her casting choices were very deliberate, including the choice to make Meg's friend and companion on her journey a white boy:

> because that was so powerful, to show a white boy following a black girl through the movie. I've never seen that.... I mean, I have a crew of thousands of people, and it's not lost on me that I have white men coming up to me all day long like, 'What do I do?' And in my early career, there's some white men that have a problem with that, a problem with even asking me what to do, and taking my direction and believing that I know what I'm saying, because they have no context for even seeing it. (Ryzik 2018)

This level of transparency of the relationship of her representations to her career experience also sets DuVernay apart as not simply transformative but self-consciously political.

DuVernay is outspoken about the media industry's issues as well. Asked if *Selma* had opened doors to big-budget films, she noted, "It is bit of an improvement for me. But it is not as easy as it would have been had I been a man and certainly not as easy had I been a white man" (Sahani 2015); this stands as a notable divergence from Patty Jenkins's sense of her own position on the heels of *Monster*. As inclusion riders that contractually mandate a certain percentage of women and/or people of color on set became a hot topic after Frances McDormand advocated them at the 2018 Oscars, DuVernay insisted that they or other structural measures toward inclusivity were not responsible for her ability to diversify her set, explicitly refusing them in a response to a question on Twitter: "Nope. Just hired great people of all kinds and colors. xo" (DuVernay 2018a). In fact, that hiring was itself a struggle: "Definitely not organic. If you're not from here, it's hard to explain how rare it is to see women walking around on a set, people of colour—usually it's an all-white male crew. So to make sure it's inclusive took a lot of effort on behalf of my producers and the studio, but they answered my call" (Freeman 2018). DuVernay also founded AFFRM, the African American Film Festival Releasing Movement, "an organisation dedicated to releasing independent work by black film-makers" (Ashley Clark 2015). In all of these ways, then, she directly confronts and pushes against the boundaries of her industry.

Throughout her career, DuVernay has also made a strong use of Twitter as a platform. She's organized twelve-hour Q&A sessions for both Black directors (Ashley Clark 2015) and women filmmakers (Macmedan and Fury 2017). She has also not been shy about using the platform to uplift her colleagues for their accomplishments: "Director @PattyJenks is breaking the box office and making herstory! WONDER WOMAN in theaters now! A triumph! Brava!" (DuVernay 2017b); "For anyone w/ a dream, know how hard the great @LenaWaithe worked for hers. Congrats on your win, Lena. History has its eyes on you! #Emmys" (DuVernay 2017c). She has also been overtly political and unfiltered, such as tweeting, "My sentiments exactly," in relation to pictures of protest signs at the 2017 Tax March saying things like "Roses are red Violets are blue Release your tax returns, motherfucker," addressed to Donald Trump (DuVernay 2017a). Indeed, she has attracted attention from the alt-right publication *Breitbart* for her willingness to address subjects like white privilege boldly and directly on social media, to which she responded: "Sometimes it's hard for white folks to grasp the notion of white privilege. My three posts below are real world, easy examples of how the system we live in favors some and not others. If you'd like to acknowledge Black History Month in some way, recognize this within yourself." (DuVernay 2019). In these ways, DuVernay has politicized her platform, refusing to avoid controversial public statements, despite the reminders in the wake of James Gunn's firing that social media activity can be turned back against the auteur (and likely with more permanent results for those already marginalized within the industry's power structures.)

Ultimately, DuVernay and the Wachowski sisters are emblematic of the best *and* the worst of the contemporary fan auteur moment. They work within the fanboy auteur ecosystem at some moments and strain at its boundaries in others. They have used their visibility to promote their work and stake out some political positions. Yet they have also been victimized, harassed, and threatened as a result of that same visibility.

Breaking the Fanboy Auteur Mold

Throughout this book, we've focused almost entirely on tentpole media. In the contemporary moment, alternative methods of distribution are in theory creating more space for a new type of director—but, in reality, they often amplify familiar franchises across new wavelengths. The recently launched DC Universe streaming platform, which featured as its first original content a dark and brooding version of Robin running a decidedly not family friendly iteration of its previously teen-oriented property, *Titans*, is just the latest in a litany of the familiar. One reviewer notes how the show continues to epitomize a Snyderesque approach to the universe:

> I do truly think every aspect of this show—its tone, its aesthetic, its story, its themes—boil[s] down to the image of Dick Grayson, the original Robin, Boy Wonder, charming vigilante do-gooder, plunging a gardening tool into another man's crotch. Titans is the absolute zenith of the post-Nolan, post-*Dark Knight* era of "mature" comic book storytelling, a show with both the grittiness and enjoyability factor of sandpaper. (Mancuso 2018)

However, in other streaming shows there is hope for changing visions: Hulu's *Runaways* features a diverse cast and prominent lesbian relationship; *Cloak and Dagger*, on Freeform, addresses race and class tension through its hero's dual narratives; and Marvel's 2015–19 *Jessica Jones* at Netflix (with showrunner Melissa Rosenberg) intentionally sought out women to direct the antihero's super battles. Disney's pending streaming service, Disney Plus, offers similar optimism for the future, with planned series projects featuring diverse leads, but no confirmed news on showrunners as of August 2019 (Sorrentino 2019). Yet the reality of the fan influence on these shows is not an easily resolved binary: these showrunners and creators all face other expectations crafted by the fanboy auteur's performance, and particularly by the use of social media. Whether helmed by fangirls or fanboys, these works cannot be easily labeled as reactionary or progressive, and the accountability of franchise runners to their audience often amplifies a responsibility to the canon.

Nowhere is this more visible than in the *Star Wars* franchise, which we've deliberately ignored here because its auteur dynamics could easily fill multiple volumes. *Star Wars* as a transmedia franchise is currently helmed by Kathleen Kennedy, a self-professed fangirl who has been the subject of intense fan scrutiny and hatred, particularly as a result of the new films' more inclusive cast and non-Skywalker-centric narratives. *The Last Jedi* evoked such fan anger that a petition to have the film removed from the canon received over one hundred thousand signatures:

> *Episode VIII* was a travesty. It completely destroyed the legacy of Luke Skywalker and the Jedi. It destroyed the very reasons most of us, as fans, liked *Star Wars*. This can be fixed. Just as you wiped out 30 years of stories, we ask you to wipe out one more, *The Last Jedi*. Remove it from canon, push back *Episode IX* and re-make *Episode VIII* properly to redeem Luke Skywalker's legacy, integrity, and character. (Walsh 2018)[1]

With the final film completed, the resolution of the Skywalker saga has been sealed, but J. J. Abrams (another self-identified fanboy auteur) has been tight-lipped on the likelihood of a reversal of the elements of the plot that provoked the most fan ire. Whether the sequel will prove to meet some common fan demands—performing reparative work on the role of Luke Skywalker, providing Rey with a properly significant father to ensure patriarchal lineage remains the marker of power, and minimizing the role of new women characters such as Rose Tico—remains to be seen as of this writing, with early trailers revealing nothing of significance. But even if the franchise narrative continues on the trajectory set by Rian Johnson, the loud chorus of expectant fans looking to fan auteurs for representation and canon satisfaction is not going away. The fan auteur cannot escape the demands of their audience without losing the credibility the "fan" title provides.

Against this landscape, the potential of progressive narratives arising on alternative platforms can also look like sidelining auteurs who don't fit the mold to the more peripheral, lower stakes texts in transmedia properties, while fanboys continue to reign in the mainstream. The emphasis on women directing in *Jessica Jones* has certainly not translated to the mainstream Marvel cinematic universe, for instance: 2019's *Captain Marvel* was the first of more than twenty films to be directed by a woman. It was also, not coincidentally, the target of such intense review-bombing prior to its release—a coordinated campaign to post negative reviews by people who had not seen the film—that review aggregator Rotten Tomatoes changed its reviewing rules in response. *Captain Marvel*'s success has perhaps paved the way for an increasingly diverse Marvel Cinematic Universe: ComicCon 2019 announcements included a movie centered on Black Widow; the return of Taika Waititi to *Thor*, with Natalie Portman playing Thor; and two Asian American directors attached to new projects with diverse casts (J. Alexander 2019). If the fanboy auteur mold is truly beginning to bend in these major franchises, the process is likely to be slow, and the resistance of fans (and auteurs) to the change is not to be underestimated.

Notes

Introduction

1. Throughout the book, we default to he/him/his pronouns to call attention to the masculinization of authorship as a subject position—which, while formerly hegemonic, is hopefully jarring to the contemporary reader.
2. See early catalogues of negative representations in Jenkins 1992; Jensen 1992; and Lewis 1992.
3. Although, as Martha Woodmansee (1984) notes, this idea of the isolated, individual author-genius was deeply rooted in economics, invented specifically to justify and enable writing as a profession.
4. For a fuller account of performativity in the context of identity, see Judith Butler (1990).
5. In particular, see the work compiled in *A Companion to Media Authorship* (Gray and Johnson 2013).

Chapter 1

1. Thanks to Naomi Jacobs for helping us track down this source.

Chapter 2

1. Interestingly, men who fail to defend their franchises in the perceptions of fans, such as Rick Riordan and Philip Pullman, are viewed as insufficiently aggressive, hinting too at the gendered dimensions of authorship.
2. Given that whether a reuse of someone else's intellectual property has an effect on the market for the initial text is one of the factors courts use to determine whether the use is fair, noncommercial use might actually *be* safer (Tushnet 2007), though, of course, it's only one factor and noncommercial uses can be judged unfair.

Chapter 3

1. This is actually not quite true, since in *Harry Potter and the Prisoner of Azkaban*, Rowling (2001, 401) referred to "Hermione's white face." While in context it refers to paleness as a result of anxiety, it is nevertheless a racialized turn of phrase.

Chapter 4

1. Although, in Scott's (2015, 170) definition, "'fan-ancing' refers to the direct monetary contribution by fans to support the production of a text that would otherwise remain unproduced within the media industries," we expand it here to talk about other alternative funding models where fans serve as the engine.

2. It's also an interesting bit of self-narration that disregards the fact that Smith is an ardent hockey fan.

Chapter 5

1. Founded in 2002 by Caroline van Osten de Boer and Milo Vermeulen, the site is a "community weblog" dedicated to the work of Joss Whedon. The site was named "Whedonesque" after the adjective used to describe works recognizable as having the attributes associated with Whedon's work: strong women characters, quippy dialogue, and teen characters working through their identity in monstrous circumstances.

2. Joss Whedon has a troubling history of issues around childbirth, most notably in his treatment of Charisma Carpenter and her character, Cordelia, on *Angel* following the actress's pregnancy, which resulted in an infamously strange season, followed by the actress being asked to leave the show (Carpenter 2019).

3. The clock is online at: http://hasdcdonesomethingstupidtoday.com. As of September 2019, the all-time record is 127 days without doing something stupid.

4. Scarlet Johansson's endorsement of Whedon's feminism should be placed in context with her similar endorsement of Woody Allen, who has been accused of child molestation (Keegan 2019).

5. While we have cited Whedon's tweets wherever possible, some can't be cited directly due to the deletion of the tweets or the associated account.

Chapter 6

1. All tweet spellings and abbreviations are reproduced as-is, with emendations in brackets as needed for clarity. We acknowledge that our direct quotation means the text of the tweets can be Googled, but by not directly naming users or linking tweets, we are adding a level of protection to avoid exposing individual tweeters to scrutiny they may not have anticipated.

2. To some extent this chapter downplays Deborah Snyder too, though we feel justifiably so since we are discussing Snyder the figure rather than the man.

3. The film was also a notable milestone for another fanboy success story, James Gunn, who wrote the screenplay.

Chapter 7

1. Having scrapped /r/WerthaminAction, one of the Comicsgate subreddits, for another project, a search shows two mentions of Moffat, nine of Snyder, sixteen of Whedon, and three of Jenkins (and zero of anyone else).
2. Her work on Netflix series *Voltron: Legendary Defender* (2016–2018) has attracted more harassment from fans, with one Reddit thread asking fellow fans to "please send positivity to Lauren Montgomery" following an increase in hate and death threats ("R/Voltron—Please Send Positivity to Lauren Montgomery" 2018)
3. Nearly every journalist who provides a ranking of these films has a slightly different one; some of this is attributable to the total gross changing over time and adjusting (or not) for inflation, but even accounting for this, the claims aren't identical.

Conclusion

1. "Wiping out 30 years of stories" refers to the decision to remove the *Star Wars* Expanded Universe material from the canon when Disney acquired the *Star Wars* franchise.

Works Cited

A Potter Head. 2016. "Scorbus No Homo." Tumblr, August 26, 2016. http://a-potter-head.tumblr.com/post/149507844677/scorbus-hugs-cc-writers-no-homo-scorbus/embed.
Abad-Santos, Alex. 2016. "Zack Snyder's Baffling Vision for Superhero Movies, Explained by Zack Snyder." *Vox*, May 2, 2016. https://www.vox.com/2016/5/2/11565932/zack-snyder-justice-league.
Abad-Santos, Alex. 2019. "*Captain Marvel* Is Officially a $1 Billion Box Office Hit." *Vox*, April 3, 2019. https://www.vox.com/culture/2019/4/3/18287032/captain-marvel-box-office-one-billion.
Admin. 2015. "Taika Waititi Chosen to Direct *Thor: Ragnarok*." *Screen Realm*, October 3, 2015. https://screenrealm.com/taika-waititi-chosen-to-direct-thor-ragnarok/.
Admiraal, Christy. 2018. "Taika Waititi, Drew Goddard, and Simon Kinberg Talk Fan Service." Nerdist, October 9, 2018. https://nerdist.com/fan-service-taika-waititi-drew-goddard-simon-kinberg-nycc/.
Advertiser, The. 2012. "Look, It's Superman." December 31, 2012, state edition, sec. Features.
AFP—Relaxnews. 2016. "'Harry Potter and the Cursed Child': No Novel, but You Can Buy the Script." July 19, 2016, English international version edition, sec. Entertainment.
After Hrs Correspondent. 2010. "'I Was a Huge Fan of *Star Wars*'; Acclaimed Film-Maker Zack Snyder, of *300* Fame, Is All Set to Make His an-Imation Debut with the Fantasy Film Based on the Book Guardians of Ga'Hoole." *Daily News & Analysis*, October 28, 2010.
Ahsan, Sadaf. 2016. "Marvel's *Black Panther* Features 90% Black Cast." *National Post* (formerly known as the *Financial Post*), May 20, 2016, all but Toronto edition, sec. News.
Alexander, Al. 2018. "Movie Review: All Pain, No Pleasure in New 'Fifty Shades.'" *Star-News*, February 8, 2018, sec. Entertainment.
Alexander, Bryan, and Andrea Mandell. 2017. "'Wonder'-Filled Highs and Bottomed-out Lows." *USA Today*, December 8, 2017, final edition, sec. Life.
Alexander, Julia. 2017a. "An Obscure App Has Become the Go-to Spot for Exclusive *Justice League* Footage." Polygon, March 25, 2017. https://www.polygon.com/2017/3/25/15060326/justice-league-vero-zack-snyder.
Alexander, Julia. 2017b. "One of *Wonder Woman*'s Best Scenes Was Entirely Improvised." Polygon, June 9, 2017. https://www.polygon.com/2017/6/9/15772134/wonder-woman-improv.

Alexander, Julia. 2018a. "Fans Are Convinced Zack Snyder Is Using an App to Tease *Justice League*'s 'Snyder Cut.'" Polygon, March 6, 2018. https://www.polygon.com/2018/3/6/17086700/zack-snyder-vero-justice-league-snyder-cut.

Alexander, Julia. 2018b. "J. K. Rowling Retconning Harry Potter on Twitter Has Consequences." Polygon, September 26, 2018. https://www.polygon.com/2018/9/26/17906676/nagini-fantastic-beasts-jk-rowling-harry-potter-dumbledore-george-lucas.

Alexander, Julia. 2019. "Marvel Reveals Massive Phase Four Film and Television Plan." *The Verge*, July 20, 2019. https://www.theverge.com/2019/7/20/20702328/marvel-disney-plus-thor-eternals-doctor-strange-wandavision-hawkeye-black-widow-san-diego-comic-con.

Alpha Magazine. 2009. "Watched Man." *Alpha Magazine*, July 22, 2009, first edition, sec. Sport.

Anderson, Jeffrey M. 2006. "'Clerks II:' Cult Classic Is Express Lane for Laughs." *Inside Bay Area*, July 21, 2006, sec. Entertainment.

Anderton, Joe. 2018. "Black Panther Director Reveals Why It 'Terrified' Him." Digital Spy, August 22, 2018. http://www.digitalspy.com/movies/black-panther/news/a864563/black-panther-director-admits-why-he-was-scared-to-take-on-the-film/.

Anelli, Melissa. 2007. "Transcript of Part 1 of PotterCast's JK Rowling Interview." *Leaky Cauldron*, December 23, 2007. http://www.the-leaky-cauldron.org/2007/12/23/transcript-of-part-1-of-pottercast-s-jk-rowling-interview/.

Arpe, Malene. 2007. "Violent Videos Made Me 'Snap': Whedon." thestar.com, May 22, 2007. https://www.thestar.com/entertainment/2007/05/22/violent_videos_made_me_snap_whedon.html.

Arvidsson, Adam. 2005. "Brands: A Critical Perspective." *Journal of Consumer Culture* 5 (2): 235–58. https://doi.org/10.1177/1469540505053093.

Asher-Perrin, Emily. 2016. "Jupiter Ascending Is a Chilling Look at Our Possible Future, in More Ways Than One." tor.com, July 5, 2016. https://www.tor.com/2016/07/05/jupiter-ascending-is-a-chilling-look-at-our-possible-future-in-more-ways-than-one/.

Augustine, Tom. 2018. "No, the *Avengers: Infinity War* Ending Doesn't Suck." *New Zealand Herald*, May 2, 2018, sec. News; General.

Author, Staff. 2005. "Steven Moffat (Writer/ Creator of Coupling)." readjunk.com: Music & Movie News, Reviews & Interviews, February 24, 2005. https://www.readjunk.com/interviews/steven-moffat-writer-creator-of-coupling/.

Author, Staff. 2019. "All Time Worldwide Box Office Grosses." Box Office Mojo, January 29, 2019. https://www.boxofficemojo.com/alltime/world/.

Bahr, Lindsey. 2017. "'Wonder Woman' Director Finds Herself in Rare Summer Role." *St. Louis Post-Dispatch*, May 5, 2017, final edition, sec. Go!

Baim, Tracy. 2016. "Second Wachowski Filmmaker Sibling Comes Out as Trans—Gay Lesbian Bi Trans News Archive." *Windy City Times*, March 8, 2016. http://www.windycitymediagroup.com/lgbt/Second-Wachowski-filmmaker-sibling-comes-out-as-trans-/54509.html.

Baker-Whitelaw, Gavia. 2013. "Why Steven Moffat Rules Tumblr Fandom | The Daily Dot." The Daily Dot, March 29, 2013. https://www.dailydot.com/upstream/steven-moffat-tumblr-fandom-sherlock/.

Baker-Whitelaw, Gavia. 2016. "'Harry Potter and the Cursed Child' Includes Plenty of Fanfic Tropes, but Ignores Queer Representation." The Daily Dot, August 4, 2016. https://www.dailydot.com/parsec/harry-potter-cursed-child-fanfic-albus-scorpius/.

Baker-Whitelaw, Gavia. 2019. "The Cast for Joss Whedon's Show 'The Nevers' Sounds Very Joss Whedon." The Daily Dot, July 31, 2019. https://www.dailydot.com/parsec/joss-whedon-hbo-nevers-cast-sexist/.

Bangkok Post. 2016. "*Batman v Superman* Is a Blast, but Disjointed and Dense." March 25, 2016.

Barker, Meg. 2013. "Consent Is a Grey Area? A Comparison of Understandings of Consent in *Fifty Shades of Grey* and on the BDSM Blogosphere." *Sexualities* 16 (8): 896–914. https://doi.org/10.1177/1363460713508881.

Barnes, Brook. 2018. "'Panther' Changes Game." *New York Times*, February 16, 2018, late final edition, sec. B., Business/Financial.

Barnes, Henry. 2012. "Avengers Assemble—Review." *The Guardian*, April 20, 2012.

Baron, Reuben. 2018. "Why Aquaman Is Basically Jupiter Ascending for Bros (And What Ways It's Better and Worse)." CBR, December 20, 2018. https://www.cbr.com/why-aquaman-better-worse-jupiter-ascending/.

Barrett, Dan. 2016. "*Sherlock* Producer Sue Vertue Adds to Family Legacy." *Mediaweek*, January 24, 2016. https://mediaweek.com.au/sherlock-producer-sue-vertue-adds-family-legacy/.

Barthes, Roland. 1978. "The Death of the Author." In *Image-Music-Text*, translated by Stephen Heath, 142–48. New York: Hill and Wang.

Batley, Sarah. 2010. "How to Reinvent a Classic." *Daily Post*, September 3, 2010, North Wales edition, sec. Features.

Beck, Laura. 2017. "Why It Matters That 'Wonder Woman' Was Directed by a Woman." *Cosmopolitan*, June 1, 2017. https://www.cosmopolitan.com/entertainment/movies/a9953877/wonder-woman-patty-jenkins-woman-directors/.

Beckerman, Jim. 2006. *Bismarck Tribune*, July 21, 2006, sec. Life.

Begley, Chris. 2016. "Over 25 Interesting Details from the 'Batman v Superman' Issue of Empire Magazine." Batman News, January 30, 2016. https://batman-news.com/2016/01/30/batman-v-superman-empire-march-2016/.

Begley, Chris. 2018. "Zack Snyder Will Not Attend San Diego Comic-Con, His Rep Confirms | Batman News." Batman News, July 17, 2018. https://batman-news.com/2018/07/17/zack-snyder-will-not-attend-san-diego-comic-con-his-rep-confirms/.

Belfast Telegraph. 2016. "Stop Donating *Fifty Shades of Grey*, Pleads Oxfam Shop." March 23, 2016, sec. UK.

Belfast Telegraph. 2017. "Doctor Who's Steven Moffat Wishes Peter Capaldi Was Not Leaving the Show." June 29, 2017, online edition, sec. News.

Bell, Crystal. 2018. "Ryan Coogler on the 'Dynamic' Female Energy of *Black Panther*." MTV News, February 15, 2018. http://www.mtv.com/news/3064887/ryan-coogler-black-panther-interview/.

Berardinelli, James. 2007. "Captivity." *Reelviews*, 2007. http://www.reelviews.net/reelviews/captivity.

Bercovici, Jeff. 2013. "The World's Top-Earning Authors: With '50 Shades,' E.L. James Debuts at No. 1." *Forbes*, August 17, 2013. https://www.forbes.com/sites/jeffbercovici/2013/08/12/the-worlds-top-earning-authors-with-50-shades-e-l-james-debuts-at-no-1/.

Berkshire, Geoff. 2015. "Inside the Office of The CW's Mark Pedowitz." *Variety*, June 4, 2015. http://variety.com/2015/tv/awards/mark-pedowitz-office-cw-1201509849/.

Berry, David. 2016. "*Sherlock*'s Influence on TV Profound: Doyle's Detective Seeps into Modern Procedurals." *Vancouver Sun*, January 5, 2016, final edition, sec. Arts & Life.

Betancourt, David. 2017a. "DCs Triumphant Return to Great Storytelling." *Charleston Gazette-Mail*, June 1, 2017, sec. News.

Betancourt, David. 2017b. "More News." *Denver Post*, August 18, 2017, Friday Scene edition, sec. Features.

Bezanidis, Michael. 2019. "Zack Snyder to Produce James Gunn's 'Suicide Squad' Movie." Heroic Hollywood, January 31, 2019. https://heroichollywood.com/zack-snyder-james-gunn-suicide-squad/.

Bishop, Bryan. 2018a. "*Black Panther* is the Grown-up Marvel Movie We've Been Waiting for." *The Verge*, February 6, 2018. https://www.theverge.com/2018/2/6/16977756/black-panther-movie-review-ryan-coogler-marvel-cinematic-universe-chadwick-boseman-michael-b-jordan.

Bishop, Bryan. 2018b. "Jay and Silent Bob Are Coming to Virtual Reality, Whether You're Ready or Not—The Verge." *The Verge*, April 4, 2018. https://www.theverge.com/2018/4/4/17200358/kevin-smith-jay-and-silent-bob-vr-stx-entertainment.

Bizzaca, Caris. 2017. "Taika Waititi: Paying It Forward on *Thor: Ragnarok* | Screen News." Screen Australia, October 17, 2017. https://www.screenaustralia.gov.au/sa/screen-news/2017/10-17-taika-waititi-thor-ragnarok.

Blackwell, Rob. 2015. "Harry Potter Author Names Key Character 'Elizabeth Warren.'" creditunionjournal.com, May 11, 2015, sec. General News.

Blevins, Joe. 2016. "Back in 1999, Kevin Smith Joined the Protests against His Own Film, *Dogma*." *AV Club*, April 29, 2016. https://news.avclub.com/back-in-1999-kevin-smith-joined-the-protests-against-h-1798246714.

Bleznak, Becca. 2019. "Scarlett Johansson on How Joss Whedon Played a Role In Empowering Black Widow." *Showbiz Cheat Sheet*, April 16, 2019. https://www.cheatsheet.com/entertainment/scarlett-johansson-joss-whedon-black-widow.html/.

Boog, Jason. 2012. "The Lost History of *Fifty Shades of Grey*." GalleyCat, November 21, 2012. https://www.adweek.com/galleycat/fifty-shades-of-grey-wayback-machine/50128.

Borgia, Danielle N. 2011. "*Twilight*: The Glamorization of Abuse, Codependency, and White Privilege." *Journal of Popular Culture* 47 (1): 153–73. https://doi.org/10.1111/j.1540-5931.2011.00872.x.

Borrelli, Christopher. 2006. "Kevin Smith Puts His Indie Stamp on Many of His Works." *The Blade*, July 19, 2006, sec. Entertaimnent News.

Bosman, Julie. 2012. "An Erotic Novel, '50 Shades of Grey,' Goes Viral With Women." *New York Times*, March 9, 2012, sec. Media. https://www.nytimes.com/2012/03/10/business/media/an-erotic-novel-50-shades-of-grey-goes-viral-with-women.html.

Bowles, Scott. 2009. "All Eyes on Zack Snyder: Interest Intensifies in 'Watchmen' Director." *USA Today*, February 25, 2009, final edition, sec. Life.

Bowsher, Allison. 2017. "Kevin Smith's Response to the Harvey Weinstein Saga Really Goes above and beyond." The Loop, October 18, 2017. https://www.theloop.ca/kevin-smiths-response-harvey-weinstein-saga-really-goes-beyond/.

Box Office Mojo. n.d. "All Time Worldwide Box Office Grosses." Accessed September 19, 2019. https://www.boxofficemojo.com/alltime/world/.

Braun, Liz. 2017. "Winners and Losers: Missed a Bit of Celebrity Noise This Week? Here's What You Slept Through." *Winnipeg Sun*, June 3, 2017, final edition, sec. Showbiz.

Brownstein, Bill. 2010. "The Puck Stops Here, Says Kevin Smith; Writer-Director's Next Film Will Focus on His Love of Hockey and Fondness for Canada." *Edmonton Journal*, July 8, 2010, final edition, sec. A&E.

Brummitt, Cassie. 2016. "Pottermore: Transmedia Storytelling and Authorship in Harry Potter." *Midwest Quarterly* 58 (1): 112–32.

Buchanan, Kyle. 2016. "Zack Snyder Faces His Haters on the Set of *Justice League*." *Vulture*, June 21, 2016. https://www.vulture.com/2016/06/zack-snyder-set-justice-league.html.

Bulck, Hilde Van den, Nathalie Claessens, and Annebeth Bels. 2014. "'By Working She Means Tweeting': Online Celebrity Gossip Media and Audience Readings of Celebrity Twitter Behaviour." *Celebrity Studies* 5 (4): 514–17. https://doi.org/10.1080/19392397.2014.980655.

Bunch, Sonny. 2018a. "As We Prepare to Celebrate 'Black Panther,' Let's Not Forget 'Blade.'" *Chicago Daily Herald*, February 3, 2018, Web edition, sec. Features.

Bunch, Sonny. 2018b. "End of an Era." *Calgary Sun*, February 22, 2018, final edition, sec. Showbiz.

Burgess, Kaya. 2013. "We Wanted to Kill Off Sherlock before BBC Could Kill the Series." *The Times*, December 28, 2013, 3, national edition, sec. News.

Burgess, Kaya. 2015. "Doctor What? It's All a Bit Complicated." *The Times*, October 31, 2015, 3, national edition, sec. News.

Burlingame, Russ. 2016. "Stan Lee Picks Kevin Smith's *Mallrats* as Favorite Movie He's Been In." comicbook.com, June 16, 2016. http://comicbook.com/marvel/2016/06/19/stan-lee-picks-kevin-smiths-mallrats-as-favorite-movie-hes-been-/.

Burlingame, Russ. 2018. "Kevin Smith Reveals 'Jay And Silent Bob Reboot' Plot Details and Start Date." comicbook.com, May 25, 2018. http://comicbook.com/movies/2018/05/25/jay-silent-bob-reboot-start-date-kevin-smith/.

Burlingame, Russ. 2019. "Kevin Smith Is Rewriting *Clerks 3*, Hopes to Convince Jeff Anderson to Return." comicbook.com, July 21, 2019. https://comicbook.com/movies/2019/07/21/kevin-smith-is-rewriting-clerks-3-hopes-to-convince-jeff-anderso/.

Burrell, Ian. 2011. "Steven Moffat: Storyteller in Chief." *The Independent*, December 17, 2011. https://www.independent.co.uk/news/people/profiles/steven-moffat-storyteller-in-chief-6278307.html.

Burroughs, Alexandra. 2005. "School's In: Not-so-Silent Director Kevin Smith Isn't Shy about Expressing Himself." *Calgary Herald*, February 3, 2005, final edition, sec. Entertainment.

Burt, Stephanie. 2017. "The Promise and Potential of Fan Fiction." *New Yorker*, August 23, 2017. https://www.newyorker.com/books/page-turner/the-promise-and-potential-of-fan-fiction.

Busse, Kristina. 2013. "Geek Hierarchies, Boundary Policing, and the Gendering of the Good Fan." *Participations* 10 (1): 73–91.

Busse, Kristina. 2017. *Framing Fan Fiction: Literary and Social Practices in Fan Fiction Communities*, first edition. Iowa City: University of Iowa Press.

Butler, Eoin. 2009. "Someone to Watch over Them." *Irish Times*, March 6, 2009, sec. the Ticket: Film Features.

Butler, Judith. 1990. *Gender Trouble: Feminism and the Subversion of Identity*. New York: Routledge.

Butler, Karen. 2014. "'Doctor Who' Title Sequence Was Inspired by Fan's Film." UPI, August 23, 2014. https://www.upi.com/Entertainment_News/TV/2014/08/23/Doctor-Who-title-sequence-was-inspired-by-fans-film/3081408126684/.

Byrne-Cristiano, Laura. 2012. "'Doctor Who' Showrunner Steven Moffat Deletes Twitter Account." *Hypable*, September 9, 2012. https://www.hypable.com/doctor-who-showrunner-steven-moffat-deletes-twitter-account/.

Canberra Times. 2011. "Independent Frame of Mind." August 1, 2011, final edition, sec. A.

Canberra Times. 2012. "Smith Swaps Film Fun for Fright." March 13, 2012, final edition, sec. A.

Cardy, Tom. 2006. "The Passion of the *Clerks*." *Dominion Post*, September 1, 2006, sec. Features; Arts.

Carey, Anna. 2003. "Creator of *Buffy* Shows He Is a Hero of the Comic Strip." *Sunday Tribune*, August 31, 2003.

Carpenter, Charisma. 2019. "Charisma Carpenter on Twitter: 'Hey, ☐@screenrant☐ If You'd like to Know the Facts of My Pregnancy / Exit Fr Angel Maybe Call for a Comment Instead of Printing Lies. I NEVER HID My Pregnancy from Production. CLEAR? 9 TV And Movie Pregnancies That Were Real (And 11 That Weren't) Https://T.Co/N7weYUWGAn' / Twitter." Twitter, April 20, 2019. https://twitter.com/allcharisma/status/1119637342455603200.

Cavna, Michael. 2017. "A Look Back at Wonder Woman's Feminist (and Not-so-Feminist) History." *Washington Post*, May 26, 2017. https://www.washingtonpost.com/news/comic-riffs/wp/2017/05/26/a-dive-into-wonder-womans-feminist-and-not-so-feminist-history/?utm_term=.0f53da91d49d.

Chang, Justin. 2009. "*Watchmen*." *Daily Variety*, February 27, 2009, sec. Reviews.

Change.org. n.d. "Warner Bros: Boot Zack Snyder Off of *Justice League*." change.org. Accessed January 13, 2019a. https://www.change.org/p/warner-bros-boot-zack-snyder-off-of-justice-league.

Change.org. n.d. "Warner Bros. : Zack Snyder's Director's and Tom Holkenborg's Score for Home Release." change.org. Accessed January 13, 2019b. https://www.change.org/p/warner-bros-zack-snyder-s-director-s-and-tom-holkenborg-s-score-for-home-release-e90fef07-11c6-4a9a-9ae8-375c7717dafa.

Charles, Ron. 2018. "Perspective | Don't Be so Quick to Dismiss 'Book Club'—or Fans of 'Fifty Shades of Grey.'" *Washington Post*, May 21, 2018, sec. Books Perspective. https://www.washingtonpost.com/entertainment/books/dont-be-so-quick-to-dismiss-book-club—or-fans-of-fifty-shades-of-grey/2018/05/21/8d68d588-5d00-11e8-9ee3-49d6d4814c4c_story.html.

Child, Ben. 2014. "Zack Snyder Defends Jesse Eisenberg's Casting as Lex Luthor." *The Guardian*, March 5, 2014.

Child, Ben. 2015a. "*Monster*'s Patty Jenkins Hired to Direct *Wonder Woman* Movie." *The Guardian*, April 16, 2015, sec. Film.

Child, Ben. 2015b. "Grant Morrison: *Batman v Superman* Denies *Wonder Woman*'s Pacifist Roots." *The Guardian*, July 17, 2015, sec. Film.

Child, Ben. 2015c. "JJ Abrams Touts Ava DuVernay to Direct a *Star Wars* Movie." *The Guardian*, December 11, 2015, sec. Film.

Child, Ben. 2016a. "Is the Biggest *Batman v Superman* Smackdown between Fans and Critics?" *The Guardian*, March 28, 2016, sec. Film.

Child, Ben. 2016b. "Kevin Smith: *Batman v Superman* Shows 'Fundamental Misunderstanding' of Both Superheroes." *The Guardian*, March 30, 2016, sec. Film.

Child, Ben. 2017. "*Wonder Woman*: The Greatest Superhero Flick since *The Dark Knight*?" *The Guardian*, June 2, 2017, sec. Film.

Chin, Bertha, and Matt Hills. 2008. "Restricted Confessions? Blogging, Subcultural Celebrity and the Management of Producer—Fan Proximity." *Social Semiotics* 18 (2): 253–72. https://doi.org/10.1080/10350330802002424.

Chin, Bertha, Bethan Jones, Myles McNutt, and Luke Pebler. 2014. "*Veronica Mars* Kickstarter and Crowd Funding." *Transformative Works and Cultures* 15. https://doi.org/10.3983/twc.2014.0519.

China Daily. 2018. "Diversity Goes Global with 'Black Panther' Leading the Pack." March 22, 2018, US edition.

Clark, Alex. 2015. "Critics Hate *Grey*. So Why Can't Readers Get Enough of the Dark Side of *Fifty Shades*?" *The Observer*, June 27, 2015, sec. Books. http://www.theguardian.com/books/2015/jun/28/what-el-james-grey-success-tells-us-about-future-of-fiction.

Clark, Ashley. 2015. "Ava DuVernay's Rebel-a-Thon Offers Symposium for Black Film-Makers." *The Guardian*, May 28, 2015, sec. Film.

Click, Melissa A., Jennifer Stevens Aubrey, and Elizabeth Behm-Morawitz. 2010. *Bitten by Twilight: Youth Culture, Media, & the Vampire Franchise*. New York: Peter Lang.

Cocca, Carolyn. 2016. *Superwomen: Gender, Power, and Representation*, reprint edition. New York: Bloomsbury Academic.

Cochran, Tanya R. 2012. "'Past the Brink of Tacit Support': Fan Activism and the Whedonverses." *Transformative Works and Cultures* 10. https://doi.org/10.3983/twc.2012.0331.

Cohen, Stanley. 1972. *Folk Devils and Moral Panics*. Abingdon, Oxon, and New York: Routledge.

Colbert, Stephen. 2018a. "Zack Snyder Publicly Thanks Fans for Suicide Prevention Charity and Snyder Cut Banner." Screen Rant, November 19, 2018. https://screenrant.com/justice-league-zack-snyder-publicly-thanks-snyder-cut-fans/.

Colbert, Stephen. 2018b. "Jason Momoa Won't Let Warner Bros. Distance *Aquaman* From Zack Snyder." Screen Rant, December 12, 2018. https://screenrant.com/aquaman-jason-momoa-zack-snyder-warner-bros-distance/.

Colbert, Stephen. 2018c. "5 Ways Warner Bros Can Try to Appease Snyder Cut Fans." Screen Rant, December 15, 2018. https://screenrant.com/snyder-cut-warner-bros-dc-release-options/.

Cole, Kai. 2017. "Joss Whedon Is a 'Hypocrite Preaching Feminist Ideals,' Ex-Wife Kai Cole Says (Guest Blog)." The Wrap, August 20, 2017. https://www.thewrap.com/joss-whedon-feminist-hypocrite-infidelity-affairs-ex-wife-kai-cole-says/.

Colgan, Jenny. 2014. "Is the Monthly Doctor Who Fan Clan Meeting to Be Exterminated?" *The Guardian*, June 12, 2014.

ComingSoon.net. 2008. "SDCC Excl. Interview: Steven Moffat on *Doctor Who*." July 24, 2008. https://www.comingsoon.net/tv/features/47147-sdcc-excl-interview-steven-moffat-on-doctor-who.

Cornet, Roth. 2014. "*Sherlock*: Steven Moffat on the Fake Death, If the Series Has Gone Meta, Character Vs. Mystery-Driven Stories, Doctor Who Crossover—IGN." *IGN*, January 26, 2014. https://www.ign.com/articles/2014/01/26/sherlock-steven-moffat-on-the-fake-death-if-the-series-has-gone-meta-character-vs-mystery-driven-stories-doctor-who-crossover.

"Coupling Steven Moffat." 2004. BBC Press Office, June 16, 2004. http://www.bbc.co.uk/pressoffice/pressreleases/stories/2004/06_june/16/coupling_moffat.shtml.

Cox, Emma. 2017. "The Real Stars of *Sherlock*." *The Sun*, January 8, 2017, 2, national edition, sec. Fabulous; Features.

Coyle, Jake. 2017. "Glutton for Punishment? Then See '50 Shades Darker.'" *Salt Lake Tribune*, February 10, 2017, sec. Features; Movies.

Coyle, Jake. 2018a. "Q&A: Chadwick Boseman on His Personal Wakanda." *Chicago Daily Herald*, February 18, 2018, Web edition, sec. Features.

Coyle, Jake. 2018b. "'Black Panther,' 'Wonder Woman,' 'Get Out' Demonstrate Power of Inclusion at the Box Office." *SHOOTonline*, February 19, 2018. https://www.shootonline.com/news/black-panther-wonder-woman-get-out-demonstrate-power%C2%A0-inclusion-box-office.

Coyle, Jake. 2018c. "*Black Panther* Opens with Bang at Box Office." *Times Colonist*, February 20, 2018, final edition, sec. Arts.

Craft, Dan. 2007. "Clash of the Titans." *The Pantagraph*, March 15, 2007, sec. Go!

Works Cited

Cremen, Christine. 2012. "Steamy Resolve Dissolves in a Proverbial Fumbling of the Literary Bra Straps; Erotica." *Sydney Morning Herald*, June 23, 2012, first edition, sec. Spectrum; Books.

"Cruel & Unusual Motion Picture Company." 2018. Wayback Machine, August 24, 2018. https://web.archive.org/web/20180824005717/http://www.cruelfilms.com/page2.html.

Cummins, Anthony. 2017. "Darker: EL James's Latest *Fifty Shades of Grey* Seems Even More Dubious in a Post-Weinstein World—Review." *The Telegraph*, November 29, 2017. https://www.telegraph.co.uk/books/what-to-read/darker-el-jamess-latest-fifty-shades-grey-seems-even-dubious/.

Daily News of Los Angeles. 2011. "Director Zack Snyder Talks 'Sucker,' 'Superman,'" March 25, 2011, Valley edition, sec. L.A. Life.

Daily Observer. 2016. "Fans Sworn to Secrecy as Harry Potter Play Unveiled." June 9, 2016, final edition, sec. Entertainment.

Daily Times. 2018. "'Black Panther' Sets the Bar for 2018 and Beyond." *Daily Times*, February 20, 2018.

Daniell, Mark. 2017a. "World of Wonder: Patty Jenkins Enters DC's Cinematic Universe with an Origin Story She Hopes Delivers on 'Every Level.'" *Toronto Sun*, April 23, 2017, final edition, sec. Showbiz.

Daniell, Mark. 2017b. "Staking Her Own Ground: Director Patty Jenkins Reflects on *Wonder Woman*'s Success, the Oscars and the DC Cinematic Universe." *London Free Press*, September 19, 2017, final edition, sec. News.

Daswani, Kavita. 2007. "Cut and Thrust." *South China Morning Post*, March 11, 2007, sec. Features.

Daswani, Kavita. 2013. "Role with the Punches." *South China Morning Post*, June 27, 2013, sec. Features.

Davies, Barbara. 2015. "50 Shades of Control FREAK." *Irish Daily Mail*, February 7, 2015, first edition, sec. News.

Davies, Mike. 2004. "Slick Smith Yeans to Get Back to Grunce Cinema." *Birmingham Post*, June 14, 2004, first edition, sec. Features.

Davis, Rick. 2017. "Early Buzz Very Good for *Wonder Woman*." *Kelowna Capital News*, May 30, 2017, final edition, sec. Entertainment.

Day, Felicia. n.d. "The Guild." Accessed February 22, 2019. http://feliciaday.com/project/the-guild/.

DeathIsYourGift. 2009. "GeekU: Joss Whedon—Feminist?" Whedonesque, March 18, 2009. http://whedonesque.com/comments/19548#297786.

Derhy Kurtz, Benjamin W. L. 2014. "Introduction: Transmedia Practices: A Television Branding Revolution." *Networking Knowledge* 7 (1): 1–6.

Desta, Yohana. 2017. "Ben Affleck Won't Be Profiting from His Weinstein Movies Anymore." *Vanity Fair*, November 6, 2017. https://www.vanityfair.com/hollywood/2017/11/ben-affleck-weinstein-movies-charity.

Desta, Yohana. 2018. "Joss Whedon Defends His Controversial *Wonder Woman* Script: 'I Think It's Great.'" *HWD*, April 24, 2018. https://www.vanityfair.com/hollywood/2018/04/joss-whedon-wonder-woman-batgirl.

Di Stefano, Mark. 2018. "JK Rowling's Pottermore Has Just Sacked Loads of Its Editorial Staff." *BuzzFeed News*, March 21, 2018. https://www.buzzfeed.com/markdistefano/potter-less?utm_term=.ojlbvJN5Mx&bftwnews#.hmolPZWwR7.

Dobbs, Sarah. 2012. "Looking Back at the *Buffy the Vampire Slayer* Movie." *Den of Geek*, January 6, 2012. https://www.denofgeek.com/us/go/18561.
Docherty, Gavin. 2010a. "Doctor's Holiday Means a Double Helping of Who." *The Express*, August 30, 2010, first edition, sec. News.
Docherty, Gavin. 2010b. "Who Girl Karen Loses Out to K-9." *Daily Star*, November 16, 2010, first edition, sec. News.
Donn, Emily. 2017. "Arrow Might Not Be in Kevin Smith's Future." Screen Rant, October 18, 2017. https://screenrant.com/kevin-smith-not-allowed-direct-arrow/.
Donnelly, Elisabeth. 2015. "How Amazon and 'Fifty Shades of Grey' Created a Golden Age for Self-Published Romance Authors—and Why It May Already Be Over." *Flavorwire*, February 13, 2015. http://flavorwire.com/504084/how-amazon-and-fifty-shades-of-grey-created-a-golden-age-for-self-published-romance-authors-and-why-it-may-already-be-over.
Dowell, Ben. 2010. "How Will the Doctor Get out of This One?" *The Guardian*, July 12, 2010, sec. Guardian Media Pages.
Duggan, Jennifer. 2017. "Revising Hegemonic Masculinity: Homosexuality, Masculinity, and Youth-Authored Harry Potter Fanfiction." *Bookbird: A Journal of International Children's Literature* 55 (2): 38–45. https://doi.org/10.1353/bkb.2017.0022.
Dumarog, Ana. 2018. "Zack Snyder Gave James Wan His Blessing for *Aquaman*." Screen Rant, December 31, 2018. https://screenrant.com/aquaman-zack-snyder-james-wan/.
Duran, Nidoran. 2016. "Things My Immortal Does Better than *The Cursed Child*." Tumblr, September 24, 2016. https://web.archive.org/web/20160924174709/http://nidoranduran.tumblr.com/post/145784773083/things-my-immortal-does-better-than-the-cursed.
Duritz, Clinton, and Kevin Smith. 1996. "A Conversation with Writer and Director Kevin Smith." *Film History* 8 (2): 237–48.
DuVernay, Ava. 2017a. "My Sentiments Exactly. #TaxMarchpic.Twitter.Com/KuMwKZ5NgS." Tweet. @*ava*, April 15, 2017. https://twitter.com/ava/status/853305641850486784?lang=en.
DuVernay, Ava. 2017b. "Director @PattyJenks Is Breaking the Box Office and Making Herstory! WONDER WOMAN in Theaters Now! A Triumph! Brava!Pic.Twitter.Com/UWPdoaNS4a." Tweet. @*ava*, June 2, 2017. https://twitter.com/ava/status/870859101089054722?lang=en.
DuVernay, Ava. 2017c. "For Anyone w/ a Dream, Know How Hard the Great @LenaWaithe Worked for Hers. Congrats on Your Win, Lena. History Has Its Eyes on You! #Emmyspic.Twitter.Com/Dt6WC3waMr." Tweet. @*ava*, September 17, 2017. https://twitter.com/ava/status/909600411593490433?lang=en.
DuVernay, Ava. 2018a. "Nope. Just Hired Great People of All Kinds and Colors. Xo. . . ." Twitter, March 12, 2018. https://twitter.com/ava/status/973168950136762368?ref_src=twsrc%5Etfw.
DuVernay, Ava. 2018b. "I Actually Said: 'Hey Guys, I Wanna Make a New Gods Movie.' Then Someone Said Ok. #AskAvahttps://Twitter.Com/Landonoleary/Status/1003352999647903744. . . ." Tweet. @*ava*, June 3, 2018. https://twitter.com/ava/status/1003355460416692224?ref_src=twsrc%5Etfw%7Ctwcamp%5Etweetembed%7Ctwterm%5E1003355460416692224&ref_url=https%3A%2F%2Fscreenrant.com%2Fava-duvernay-asked-dc-films-direct-new-gods%2F.
DuVernay, Ava. 2018c. "Lovely Room to Be in. But Can't Wait for More Sisters to Be Here Too. #Onwardhttps://Twitter.Com/Blackfilm/Status/1008748807859908608. . . ." Tweet. @*ava*, June 18, 2018. https://twitter.com/ava/status/1008836184649412608?ref_src=

twsrc%5Etfw%7Ctwcamp%5Etweetembed%7Ctwterm%5E1008836184649412608&ref_url=https%3A%2F%2Fwww.fastcompany.com%2F40587453%2Fava-duvernay-becomes-the-first-black-woman-to-direct-a-100-million-grossing-film.

DuVernay, Ava. 2019. "Sometimes It's Hard for White Folks to Grasp the Notion of White Privilege. My Three Posts below Are Real World, Easy Examples of How the System We Live in Favors Some and Not Others. If You'd like to Acknowledge Black History Month in Some Way, Recognize This within Yourself." Tweet. @ava, February 5, 2019. https://twitter.com/ava/status/1092823940232179714?ref_src=twsrc%5Etfw%7Ctwcamp%5Etweetembed%7Ctwterm%5E1092823940232179714&ref_url=https%3A%2F%2Fwww.breitbart.com%2Fentertainment%2F2019%2F02%2F05%2Fdirector-ava-duvernay-smears-melania-trump-in-unhinged-rant-about-white-privilege%2F.

Eakin, Marah. 2015. "Holy Crow! *Fifty Shades of Grey* Is Crazy Similar to Its *Twilight* Origin Story." *AV Club*, February 12, 2015. https://news.avclub.com/holy-crow-fifty-shades-of-grey-is-crazy-similar-to-its-1798276528.

Earl, William. 2017. "Zack Snyder's Favorite Films, From 'A Clockwork Orange' to 'Blue Velvet.'" *IndieWire*, November 15, 2017. https://www.indiewire.com/gallery/zack-snyder-favorite-films/.

Ebert, Roger. 1995. "*Mallrats* Movie Review & Film Summary (1995)." rogerebert.com, October 20, 1995. https://www.rogerebert.com/reviews/mallrats-1995.

Ebert, Roger. 1997. "*Chasing Amy* Movie Review & Film Summary (1997)." rogerebert.com, April 18, 1997. https://www.rogerebert.com/reviews/chasing-amy-1997.

Ebert, Roger. 1999. "*Dogma* Movie Review & Film Summary (1999)." rogerebert.com, November 12, 1999. https://www.rogerebert.com/reviews/dogma-1999.

Edelstein, David. 2006. "Now Playing at Your Local Multiplex: Torture Porn." *New York*, February 6, 2006. http://nymag.com/movies/features/15622/index.html.

Edidin, Rachel. 2013. "Grim, Violent *Man of Steel* Sells *Superman*'s Soul for Spectacle | WIRED." *Wired*, June 13, 2013. https://www.wired.com/2013/06/man-of-steel-movie-review/.

Edwards, Chandler. 2018. "Marvel: Re-Hire James Gunn." change.org, August 2018. https://www.change.org/p/marvel-re-hire-james-gunn.

EdwardTLC. 2007. "J. K. Rowling at Carnegie Hall Reveals Dumbledore Is Gay; Neville Marries Hannah Abbott, and Much More." *The-Leaky-Cauldron.org*, October 20, 2007. http://www.the-leaky-cauldron.org/2007/10/20/j-k-rowling-at-carnegie-hall-reveals-dumbledore-is-gay-neville-marries-hannah-abbott-and-scores-more/.

Ehrlich, David. 2018. "'Black Panther' Review: Ryan Coogler Delivers the Best Marvel Movie So Far." *IndieWire*, February 6, 2018. https://www.indiewire.com/2018/02/black-panther-review-ryan-coogler-1201925524/.

Ellis, David. 2015. "*Harry Potter and the Cursed Child* Play to Open in London 2016, Says J. K. Rowling." *London Evening Standard*, June 26, 2015, sec. Home.

Ellis, David. 2017. "*Wonder Woman* Review of Reviews: Critics Praise 'Endlessly Watchable' Gal Gadot but Question Gender Politics." *London Evening Standard*, May 30, 2017, sec. Film.

Ellis, Warren. 2019. "My Kevin Smith Story." Warren Ellis LTD, August 8, 2019. https://warrenellis.ltd/jot/my-kevin-smith-story/.

Ellis-Petersen, Hannah. 2015. "*Fifty Shades of Grey*: The Series That Tied Publishing up in Knots." *The Guardian*, June 18, 2015, sec. Books. http://www.theguardian.com/books/2015/jun/18/fifty-shades-of-grey-the-series-that-tied-publishing-up-in-knots.

Espino, Joe. 2016. "Hero Complex: Zack Snyder's Simple, Flawed Film Formula." *Young Folks*, March 25, 2016. https://www.theyoungfolks.com/film/75438/hero-complex-zack-snyders-simple-flawed-film-formula/.
Express Web Desk. 2018. "*Black Panther* Box Office Collection: The Marvel Film's Winning Streak Continues, Becomes Second Highest Four-Day Grosser in US." *Indian Express*, February 21, 2018.
Fairchild, Phaylen. 2019. "JK Rowling Confirms Stance Against Transgender Women." Medium, June 26, 2019. https://medium.com/@Phaylen/jk-rowling-confirms-stance-against-transgender-women-9bd83f7ca623.
Fallon, Claire. 2016. "The New 'Harry Potter' Book Seems Like Fan Fiction Because It Basically Is." *Huffington Post*, August 16, 2016, sec. Culture & Arts. https://www.huffingtonpost.com/entry/new-harry-potter-book-cursed-child_us_57b21d7be4b07184041265a7.
Fathallah, Judith. 2015. "Moriarty's Ghost: Or the Queer Disruption of the BBC's *Sherlock*." *Television & New Media* 16 (5): 490–500. https://doi.org/10.1177/1527476414543528.
Ferguson, Brian. 2010. "Doctor Who Fans Promised Best-Ever Cliffhanger—and Double Finale." *The Scotsman*, August 30, 2010.
Fleming, Jr., Mike. 2018. "James Gunn Fired From 'Guardians of the Galaxy' Franchise Over Offensive Tweets." *Deadline*, July 20, 2018. https://deadline.com/2018/07/james-gunn-fired-guardians-of-the-galaxy-disney-offensive-tweets-1202430392/.
Fleming, Jr., Mike. 2019. "Disney Reinstates Director James Gunn for 'Guardians of the Galaxy 3.'" *Deadline*, March 15, 2019. https://deadline.com/2019/03/james-gunn-reinstated-guardians-of-the-galaxy-3-disney-suicide-squad-2-indefensible-social-media-messages-1202576444/.
Flood, Alison. 2017. "*Fifty Shades* Sequel Tops Bestseller Lists but Whips up Little Enthusiasm." *The Guardian*, December 7, 2017, sec. Books. http://www.theguardian.com/books/2017/dec/07/fifty-shades-sequel-darker-tops-bestseller-lists-sales-el-james.
Flood, Alison. 2019. "EL James's New Romance Whipped by Critics, but Still Romps to No 1." *The Guardian*, April 24, 2019, sec. Books. https://www.theguardian.com/books/2019/apr/24/el-james-new-romance-thrashed-critics-no-1-the-mister-fifty-shades.
Foster, Alastair. 2011. "Dr Who Boss Would Exterminate Leakers." *Evening Standard*, May 11, 2011.
Foucault, Michel. 1980. "What Is an Author?" In *Language, Counter-Memory, Practice: Selected Essays and Interviews*, 113–38. Ithaca, NY: Cornell University Press.
Francisco, Eric. 2017. "New Jersey Still Idolizes Kevin Smith." Inverse, August 11, 2017. https://www.inverse.com/article/35417-kevin-smith-new-jersey-jay-silent-bob-cosplay-world-record.
Freeman, Hadley. 2018. "'You Are Not Expecting This': Oprah on *A Wrinkle in Time*." *The Guardian*, March 15, 2018, first edition, sec. Film.
Frishberg, Hannah. 2019. "Kevin Smith Is Bringing 'Masters of the Universe' Series to Netflix." *New York Post*, August 19, 2019. https://nypost.com/2019/08/19/kevin-smith-is-bringing-masters-of-the-universe-series-to-netflix/.
Frost, Vicky. 2012. "*Sherlock* Series Three: Creators Give Clues about Episodes." *The Guardian*, August 24, 2012.
Fullerton, Huw. 2019. "Dracula Will Be 'the Hero of His Own Story' in Radical Reinterpretation by *Sherlock* Creators." *Radio Times*, April 30, 2019. https://www.radiotimes.com/news/tv/2019-04-30/dracula-will-be-the-hero-of-his-own-story-in-radical-reinterpretation-by-sherlock-creators/.

Gardner, Kate. 2019. "There Are Three Snyder Cut Billboards Outside San Diego Comic Con, and No, This Is Not a Joke." *The Mary Sue*, July 16, 2019. https://www.themarysue.com/snyder-cut-billboards-justice-league-san-diego-comic-con/.

Gibson, Caitlin. 2017. "Trump Blocked Stephen King on Twitter—but J. K. Rowling Came to the Rescue." *Washington Post*, June 13, 2017. https://www.washingtonpost.com/news/arts-and-entertainment/wp/2017/06/13/trump-blocked-stephen-king-on-twitter-but-j-k-rowling-came-to-the-rescue/.

Gilbert, Sophie. 2019. "The Indelible Awfulness of E. L. James's 'The Mister.'" *The Atlantic*, April 18, 2019. https://www.theatlantic.com/entertainment/archive/2019/04/e-l-james-the-mister-review/587515/.

Goddard, Peter. 1997. "Mr. Smith Goes to Church, or a Boy and His *Dogma*: Next Film for *Chasing Amy*'s Writer/Director Satirizes Religion." *Toronto Star*, April 25, 1997, final edition, sec. Entertainment.

Godfrey, Alex. 2011. "We Need to Talk about Kevin." *The Guardian*, September 24, 2011, final edition, sec. the Guide.

Gold Coast Sun. 2009. "High Ambition Pays Off." March 18, 2009, sec. Scene.

Goldberg, Lesley. 2018. "Joss Whedon Sci-Fi Drama Ordered Straight to Series at HBO." *Hollywood Reporter*, July 13, 2018. https://www.hollywoodreporter.com/live-feed/joss-whedon-sci-fi-drama-nevers-ordered-straight-series-at-hbo-1126951.

Gonzalez, Umberto. 2018. "'Birds of Prey' Screenwriter on Post-#MeToo Climate: 'Now Everything Has Shifted.'" The Wrap, July 21, 2018. https://www.thewrap.com/birds-of-prey-screenwriter-christina-hodson-post-metoo-optimism/.

Goodman, Lee-Anne. 2006. "Kevin Smith Inspired by Degrassi." *Prince George Citizen*, November 28, 2006, final edition, sec. Entertainment.

Grant, Drew. 2012. "Kevin Smith on Lack of Women on AMC Comic Book Show: 'That's Reality.'" *Observer*, February 7, 2012. http://observer.com/2012/02/kevin-smith-on-lack-of-women-in-comic-book-reality-show-thats-not-reality/.

Gray, Jonathan. 2010. *Show Sold Separately: Promos, Spoilers, and Other Media Paratexts*. New York: New York University Press.

Gray, Jonathan. 2013. "When Is the Author?" In *A Companion to Media Authorship*, edited by Jonathan Gray and Derek Johnson, 88–111. New York: John Wiley & Sons.

Gray, Jonathan, and Derek Johnson. 2013. *A Companion to Media Authorship*. Malden, MA: John Wiley & Sons.

Green, Shoshanna, Cynthia Jenkins, and Henry Jenkins. 1998. "Normal Female Interest in Men Bonking: Selections from the Terra Nostra Underground and Strange Bedfellows." In *Theorizing Fandom: Fans, Subculture and Identity*, edited by Cheryl Harris and Alison Alexander, 9–38. Creskill, NJ: Hampton Press.

Greene, David. 2018. "Director Ryan Coogler Says 'Black Panther' Brought Him Closer to His Roots." npr.org, February 15, 2018. https://www.npr.org/2018/02/15/585702642/director-ryan-coogler-says-black-panther-brought-him-closer-to-his-roots.

Greenwood, Carl. 2015. "Doctor Who: Maisie Williams Will NOT Play a Returning Character—Unless Steven Moffat's Lying." *Irish Mirror*, August 1, 2015.

Gregory, Nina. 2012. "Original Fiction in All the 'Shades' of Fandom." npr.org, July 13, 2012. https://www.npr.org/2012/07/13/156681365/original-fiction-in-all-the-shades-of-fandom.

Griffin, Susan. 2015. "Look Who's Back!" *Sunday Life*, December 20, 2015, 1, national edition, sec. Christmas TV; Features.

Gross, Joe. 2016. "In 'Batman v Superman,' Audience Is Biggest Loser." *American-Statesman Austin*, March 25, 2016, sec. A360.
Guardian staff. 2017. "'Game of Thrones' Star Jason Momoa Joked about Raping 'Beautiful Women' on Show." *The Guardian*, October 13, 2017, sec. Television & radio. https://www.theguardian.com/tv-and-radio/2017/oct/12/jason-momoa-game-of-thrones-raping-beautiful-women.
Guerrasio, Jason. 2017. "'Justice League' is Agonizing to Watch—and Zack Snyder Is to Blame." *Business Insider*, November 15, 2017. https://www.businessinsider.com/justice-league-review-agonizing-to-watch-2017-11.
Gunn, James. 2018. "2. It's Not to Say I'm Better, but I Am Very, Very Different than I Was a Few Years Ago; Today I Try to Root My Work in Love and Connection and Less in Anger. My Days Saying Something Just Because It's Shocking and Trying to Get a Reaction Are over." Tweet. @*JamesGunn*, July 19, 2018. https://twitter.com/JamesGunn/status/1020154777525575682.
Hadsall, Joe. 2017. "Joe Hadsall Column." *Joplin Globe*, June 18, 2017, sec. Lifestyle.
Hale-Stern, Kaila. 2015. "When Twitter Q&As Backfire Disastrously." Gizmodo, July 1, 2015. https://gizmodo.com/when-twitter-q-as-backfire-disastrously-1715201128.
Hall, Ellie. 2013. "'Firefly' Hat Triggers Corporate Crackdown." *BuzzFeed News*, April 9, 2013. https://www.buzzfeednews.com/article/ellievhall/firefly-hat-triggers-corporate-crackdown.
Halliday, Josh, and Lisa O'Carroll. 2011. "JK Rowling 'Felt Invaded' at Note Put by Press in Daughter's Schoolbag." *The Guardian*, November 24, 2011, sec. Media. https://www.theguardian.com/media/2011/nov/24/jk-rowling-invaded-press.
Hank, All Rights. 2016. "Kevin Smith Talks Batman, Comic Book Men and the Meaning of Life—Canada.Com." o.canada.com, February 11, 2016. http://o.canada.com/entertainment/television/kevin-smith-talks-batman-comic-book-men-and-the-meaning-of-life.
Harman, Sarah, and Bethan Jones. 2013. "Fifty Shades of Ghey: Snark Fandom and the Figure of the Anti-Fan." *Sexualities* 16 (8): 951–68. https://doi.org/10.1177/1363460713508887.
Harold, Theresa. 2017. "Why *Wonder Woman* Isn't the Feminist Fantasy We've Been Told It Is." *Metro*, June 24, 2017. https://metro.co.uk/2017/06/24/why-wonder-woman-isnt-the-feminist-fantasy-weve-been-told-it-is-6731062/.
Harrington, Donnia. 2019. "EXCLUSIVE: An Interview with Zack Snyder." ComicBook Debate, May 20, 2019. https://comicbookdebate.com/2019/05/20/exclusive-an-interview-with-zack-snyder/.
Harrington, Ellen Burton. 2014. "*Sherlock*'s Epistemological Economy and the Value of 'Fan' Knowledge: How Producer-Fans Play the (Great) Game of Fandom." In *Sherlock and Transmedia Fandom: Essays on the BBC Series*, edited by Louisa Ellen Stein and Kristina Busse, 70–84. Jefferson, NC: McFarland.
Harrison, Andrew. 2013. "When Worlds Collide: Doctor Who's 50th Anniversary Episode Is BBC Drama's Biggest Event Ever." *The Guardian*, November 19, 2013, final edition, sec. Guardian Features.
Harrison, Ellie. 2019. "Former Doctor Who Showrunner Steven Moffat Defends Jodie Whittaker from Online Trolls." *Radio Times*, February 21, 2019. https://www.radiotimes.com/news/tv/2019-02-21/steven-moffat-responds-doctor-who-jodie-whittaker-trolls/.
Harrison, Mark. 2017. "*Clerks*—An Unlikely Multimedia Franchise." *Den of Geek*, September 28, 2017. http://www.denofgeek.com/us/go/267844.

Hartley, John. 2013. "Authorship and the Narrative of the Self." In *A Companion to Media Authorship*, edited by Jonathan Gray and Derek Johnson, 23–47. New York: John Wiley & Sons.

Havens, Candace. 2003. *Joss Whedon: The Genius Behind Buffy*, first edition. Dallas and Chicago: BenBella Books.

Hellekson, Karen. 2009. "A Fannish Field of Value: Online Fan Gift Culture." *Cinema Journal* 48 (4): 113–18. https://doi.org/10.1353/cj.0.0140.

Hemon, Aleksandar. 2012. "Beyond the Matrix." *New Yorker*, September 3, 2012. https://www.newyorker.com/magazine/2012/09/10/beyond-the-matrix.

Henry, Evan. 2017. "Zack Snyder's *Watchmen* and the Authoritarian Aesthetic." Black Ship Books, March 28, 2017. http://www.blackshipbooks.com/zack-snyders-watchmen-and-the-authoritarian-aesthetic/.

Herman, Edward S., and Noam Chomsky. 1988. *Manufacturing Consent: The Political Economy of the Mass Media*. New York: Pantheon Books.

Hertz, Arry. 2017. "Summer Nights." *Globe and Mail*, April 7, 2017, Ontario edition, sec. Film.

Hetherington, Thomas. 2017. "Kevin Smith, Self-Distribution, and the Future of Cinema." *Den of Geek*, August 9, 2017. http://www.denofgeek.com/uk/go/50968.

Hewitt, With Sean. 2017. "*Sherlock*: We Name the Guilty Men." *Nottingham Post*, January 20, 2017, sec. News: Other.

Heyman, Stephen. 2014. "A Conversation with Steven Moffat, a 'Sherlock' Co-Creator." *International New York Times*, January 21, 2014, sec. Leisure.

Heyman, Taylor. 2018. "A Fan Cosplayed as Patty Jenkins—and the *Wonder Woman* Director Loved It." *The Independent*, November 13, 2018. https://www.independent.ie/entertainment/movies/a-fan-cosplayed-as-patty-jenkins-and-the-wonder-woman-director-loved-it-36797128.html.

Hibberd, James. 2013a. "Joss Whedon Takes on 'Empire Strikes Back,' 'Twilight.'" ew.com, August 22, 2013. https://ew.com/article/2013/08/22/joss-whedon-empire-strikes-back-twilight/.

Hibberd, James. 2013b. "Joss Whedon: The Definitive EW Interview." ew.com, September 24, 2013. https://ew.com/article/2013/09/24/joss-whedon-interview/.

Hibberd, James. 2018. "Former DC Boss Deletes Twitter after Zack Snyder Fans Attack Her 'Joker' Praise." ew.com, September 24, 2018. https://ew.com/movies/2018/09/24/dc-boss-twitter-joker-zack-snyder-fans/.

Hills, Matt. 2006. "Not Just Another Powerless Elite?: When Media Fans Become Subcultural Celebrities." In *Framing Celebrity: New Directions in Celebrity Culture*, edited by Su Holmes and Sean Redmond, 101–118. Abingdon, Oxon, and New York: Routledge.

Hills, Matt. 2010. "Subcultural Celebrity." In *The Cult TV Book*, edited by Stacey Abbott, 233–38. London: I. B. Tauris.

Hills, Matt. 2014. "*Sherlock*'s Epistemological Economy and the Value of 'Fan' Knowledge: How Producer-Fans Play the (Great) Game of Fandom." In *Sherlock and Transmedia Fandom: Essays on the BBC Series*, edited by Louisa Ellen Stein and Kristina Busse, 27–40. Jefferson, NC: McFarland.

Hills, Matt. 2015a. "Veronica Mars, Fandom, and the 'Affective Economics' of Crowdfunding Poachers." *New Media & Society* 17 (2): 183–97. https://doi.org/10.1177/1461444814558909.

Hills, Matt. 2015b. "The Expertise of Digital Fandom as a 'Community of Practice': Exploring the Narrative Universe of *Doctor Who*." *Convergence* 21 (3): 360–74. https://doi.org/10.1177/1354856515579844.

Hoby, Hermione. 2017a. "*Wonder Woman* Director Patty Jenkins: 'People Really Thought That Only Men Loved Action Movies.'" *The Guardian*, May 26, 2017, sec. Film. https://www.theguardian.com/film/2017/may/26/wonder-woman-director-patty-jenkins-people-really-thought-that-only-men-loved-action-movies.

Hoby, Hermione. 2017b. "Meet 'Wonder Woman' Director Patty Jenkins." *Gulf News*, May 28, 2017.

Holl, Jennifer. 2017. "Shakespeare Fanboys and Fangirls and the Work of Play." In *The Shakespeare User*, 109–27. Cham, CH: Palgrave Macmillan. https://doi.org/10.1007/978-3-319-61015-3_6.

Holmes, Adam. 2019. "Kevin Smith's Emotional Reason for Bringing Jay and Silent Bob Out of Retirement." CinemaBlend, August 2, 2019. https://www.cinemablend.com/news/2477533/kevin-smiths-emotional-reason-for-bringing-jay-and-silent-bob-out-of-retirement.

Hoobs, Belinda. 2006. "HPL: Guide to Jkrowling.Com—Extra Stuff—Bulletin Board." HP Lexicon, July 1, 2006. https://legacy.hp-lexicon.org/about/sources/jkr.com/jkr-com-bboard2.html.

Hood, Copper. 2018. "Zack Snyder Reveals Deleted Lois Lane Scene from *Justice League*." Screen Rant, December 5, 2018. https://screenrant.com/justice-league-zack-snyder-lois-lane-deleted-scene/.

Hornaday, Ann. 2016. "Studios as Auteurs." *Washington Post*, August 28, 2016, sec. Sunday Arts.

Horton, Robert. 1999. "Snoochie Boochies: The Gospel According to Kevin Smith." *Film Comment* 35 (6): 60–65.

Hough, Andrew. 2012. "*Fifty Shades of Grey*: EL James's 'Mummy Porn' Sets 1m Kindle Record." *The Telegraph*, June 26, 2012, sec. Culture. https://www.telegraph.co.uk/culture/books/booknews/9356803/Fifty-Shades-of-Grey-EL-Jamess-Mummy-porn-sets-1m-Kindle-record.html?utm_source=&utm_medium=&utm_campaign=.

Howarth, Angus. 2017. "Steven Moffat Blasts *Dr. Who* Fans over Jodie Whittaker Backlash." *The Scotsman*, July 24, 2017.

Howell, Charlotte E. 2015. "'Tricky' Connotations: *Wonder Woman* as DC's Brand Disruptor." *Cinema Journal* 55 (1): 141–49. https://doi.org/10.1353/cj.2015.0072.

Howell, Peter. 1999. "Yes *Dogma* Is Insulting, but Only to Blasphemy." *Toronto Star*, November 12, 1999, first edition, sec. Entertainment.

Hoyle, Ben. 2017. "How to Create Box Office Wonder: Give All the Top Jobs to Women." *The Times*, July 25, 2017, Scotland edition, sec. News.

Huddleston, Tom. 2015. "The Wachowskis on Egos, Identity and Their Epic New Sci-Fi Movie 'Jupiter Ascending.'" *Time Out London*, February 2, 2015. https://www.timeout.com/london/film/the-wachowskis-on-egos-identity-and-their-epic-new-sci-fi-movie-jupiter-ascending.

Hudson, Tim. 2015. "The Legacy of Dr. Horrible: Potential Research into SecondScreen Intrusion, Coordination, and Influence." In *Digital Technology and the Future of Broadcasting: Global Perspectives*, edited by John V. Pavlik, first edition, 194–201. New York: Routledge.

Hughes, Mark. 2018. "What Zack Snyder's DCEU Was Really All About, And Why So Many People Rejected It." *Forbes*, January 30, 2018. https://www.forbes.com/sites/markhughes/2018/01/30/what-zack-snyders-dceu-was-really-all-about-and-why-so-many-people-rejected-it/.

Hughes, William. 2016. "Joss Whedon Finally Explains Black Widow's 'Monster' Line from *Age of Ultron*." *AV Club*, September 8, 2016. https://news.avclub.com/joss-whedon-finally-explains-black-widow-s-monster-li-1798254111.

Hull Daily Mail. 2016. "Crime-Fighters Battle It Out in Cacophony of Slam and Bang." March 26, 2016, sec. News: Other.

Hull, Gloria T., Patricia Bell Scott, and Barbara Smith. 1993. *But Some of Us Are Brave: All the Women Are White, All the Blacks Are Men: Black Women's Studies*. New York: Feminist Press at CUNY.

Ingram, Noble. 2018. "Beyond Ticket Sales: 'Black Panther' Wields Cultural Punch." *Christian Science Monitor*, February 15, 2018, sec. the Culture.

Irish Times. 2006. "Counter Culture." September 22, 2006, sec. the Ticket.

Itzkoff, Dave. 2011. "A To-Do About a Surprise 'Much Ado' From Joss Whedon." *ArtsBeat*, October 24, 2011. https://artsbeat.blogs.nytimes.com/2011/10/24/a-to-do-about-a-surprise-much-ado-from-joss-whedon/.

James, Caryn. 2006. "A New Jersey Boy and His Humor Grow up a Little." *International Herald Tribune*, June 23, 2006.

James, E L. 2018. "About Me." E L James: Provocative Romance, 2018. https://www.eljamesauthor.com/about-me/.

Jamison, Anne. 2013a. "Snowqueens Icedragon (E.L. James) and Sebastien Robichaurd (Sylvain Reynard): A Fandom Exchange." In *Fic: Why Fanfiction Is Taking Over the World*. Dallas: BenBella Books.

Jamison, Anne. 2013b. "When Fifty Was Fic." In *Fic: Why Fanfiction Is Taking Over the World*, 310–21. Dallas: BenBella Books.

Jeffries, Stuart. 2012. "Viewers' Elementary Failure to Crack *Sherlock* Case." *The Guardian*, January 21, 2012, final edition, sec. Guardian Home Pages.

Jenkins, David. 2016. "It's Time to Take a Serious Look at Zack Snyder." Little White Lies, March 23, 2016. https://lwlies.com/articles/a-serious-look-at-zack-snyder-batman-v-superman/.

Jenkins, Henry. 1992. *Textual Poachers: Television Fans & Participatory Culture*. New York: Routledge.

Jenkins, Henry. 1995. "'Infinite Diversity in Infinite Combinations': Genre and Authorship in Star Trek." In *Science Fiction Audiences: Watching Star Trek and Doctor Who*, edited by John Tulloch and Henry Jenkins, 173–93. London and New York: Routledge.

Jenkins, Henry. 2004. "Quentin Tarantino's *Star Wars*? Digital Cinema, Media Convergence, and Participatory Culture." In *Rethinking Media Change: The Aesthetics of Transition*, 281–312. Cambridge, MA: MIT Press.

Jenkins, Henry. 2006a. *Convergence Culture: Where Old and New Media Collide*. New York: New York University Press.

Jenkins, Henry. 2006b. "Interactive Audiences?: The 'Collective Intelligence' of Media Fans." In *Fans, Bloggers, and Gamers: Exploring Participatory Culture*, 134–51. New York: New York University Press.

Jenkins, Henry. 2013. "Joss Whedon, The Browncoats, and Dr. Horrible." In *Spreadable Media: Creating Value and Meaning in a Networked Culture*, edited by Henry Jenkins, Sam Ford, and Joshua Green. New York: New York University Press. http://spreadablemedia.org/essays/jenkins1/#.UbSjq5zqOZQ.

Jenkins, Henry, and Sangita Shresthova. 2012. "Up, Up, and Away!: The Power and Potential of Fan Activism." *Transformative Works and Cultures* 10: n.p.

Jenkins, Henry, Sam Ford, and Joshua Green. 2013. *Spreadable Media: Creating Value and Meaning in a Networked Culture*. New York: New York University Press.

Jenkins, Patty. 2016. "Real Lasso of Truth, Time, Will Reveal That Letter to Be False Soon Enough. But Lame Something so Transparent in Its Agenda Gets Traction." Tweet. @pattyjenks, August 12, 2016. https://twitter.com/pattyjenks/status/764248159996420096.

Jenkins, Patty. 2017. "pic.twitter.com/8zkJXHLCJW." Tweet. *@PattyJenks*, August 24, 2017. https://twitter.com/PattyJenks/status/900917648015405062?ref_src=twsrc%5Etfw%7Ctwcamp%5Etweetembed%7Ctwterm%5E900917648015405062&ref_url=https%3A%2F%2Fabcnews.go.com%2FEntertainment%2Fjames-cameron-calls-woman-step-backwards%2Fstory%3Fid%3D49407670.

Jenkins, Patty. 2018. "Can't Express How Totally Mind Blowing and Delightful It Is to Have Your Childhood Favorite Resemble You!! Thank You @Barbie, for This Incredible Honor, and for Celebrating All Kinds of Women, Everywhere. What a Great Way to Inspire the Girls of Tomorrow!Pic.Twitter.Com/X5FteJQltn." Tweet. *@pattyjenks*, March 6, 2018. https://twitter.com/pattyjenks/status/971109371353681926?lang=en.

Jenkins, Patty, and Rebecca Ford. 2016. "'Wonder Woman' Director Patty Jenkins: How to Make a Female Heroine 'Vulnerable,' But Not 'Lesser in Any Way.'" *Hollywood Reporter*, December 9, 2016. https://www.hollywoodreporter.com/heat-vision/wonder-woman-director-patty-jenkins-how-make-a-female-heroine-vulnerable-but-not-lesser-any-w.

Jensen, Jeff. 2000. "'Fire' Storm." *Entertainment Weekly*, September 7, 2000. http://www.accio-quote.org/articles/2000/0900-ew-jensen.htm.

Jensen, Jeff. 2008. "'Watchmen': A Chat with Director Zack Snyder." ew.com, July 17, 2008. https://ew.com/article/2008/07/17/watchmen-chat-director-zack-snyder/.

Jensen, Joli. 1992. "Fandom as Pathology: The Consequences of Characterization." In *The Adoring Audience: Fan Culture and Popular Media*, edited by Lisa A. Lewis, 9–29. London: Routledge.

Jirak, Jamie. 2019. "Kevin Smith Scores *Wonder Woman* Book and Record Set in *Jay and Silent Bob* Reboot Ticket Trade." DC, August 15, 2019. https://comicbook.com/dc/2019/08/15/kevin-smith-wonder-woman-book-record-set-jay-silent-bob-reboot-ticket-trade/.

John, Emma. 2013. "Joss Whedon: 'I Kept Telling My Mum Reading Comics Would Pay Off.'" *The Observer*, June 2, 2013, sec. Culture. https://www.theguardian.com/culture/2013/jun/02/joss-whedon-reading-comics-pay-off.

Johnson, Derek. 2013. *Media Franchising*. New York: New York University Press.

Johnson, Derek, and Jonathan Gray. 2013. "Introduction: The Problem of Media Authorship." In *A Companion to Media Authorship*, edited by Jonathan Gray and Derek Johnson, 1–19. New York: John Wiley & Sons.

Johnson, Jay. 2016. "Kevin Smith Says His Supergirl Episode Is Bigger Than Anything He's Directed Before." DC, October 16, 2016. http://comicbook.com/dc/2016/10/16/kevin-smith-says-his-supergirl-episode-is-bigger-than-anything-h/.

Jones, Bethan. 2014. "Fifty Shades of Fan Labor: Exploitation and *Fifty Shades of Grey*." *Transformative Works & Cultures* 15. https://doi.org/10.3983/twc.v15i0.501.

Jones, Bethan. 2018. "#AskELJames, Ghostbusters, and #Gamergate: Digital Dislike and Damage Control." In *A Companion to Fandom and Fan Studies*, edited by Paul Booth, 415–30. Oxford, UK: Wiley-Blackwell.

Jones, Nate. 2016. "Zack Snyder on *Batman v Superman*'s Terrible Reviews: 'It Is What It Is.'" *Vulture*, March 24, 2016. https://www.vulture.com/2016/03/zack-snyder-batman-v-superman-reviews.html.

Jordan, Tina. 2018. "J. K. Rowling's Friend Robert Galbraith Has Something to Say." *New York Times*, September 16, 2018. https://www.nytimes.com/2018/09/16/books/robert-galbraith-jk-rowling.html.

"Jossed." n.d. TV Tropes. Accessed February 24, 2019. https://tvtropes.org/pmwiki/pmwiki.php/Main/Jossed.

Jusino, Teresa. 2017a. "Joss Whedon and the Terrible, Horrible, No-Good, Very Bad Script: A Wonder Woman Story." *The Mary Sue*, June 16, 2017. https://www.themarysue.com/joss-whedon-and-the-terrible-horrible-no-good-very-bad-script/.

Jusino, Teresa. 2017b. "Whedonesque Shuts Down after Fifteen Years Following News of Joss Whedon's Infidelity." *The Mary Sue*, August 21, 2017. https://www.themarysue.com/whedonesque-shut-down/.

Kanjilal, Pratik. 2012. "Grey Without Matter." *Indian Express*, June 23, 2012.

Karim, Anhar. 2018. "James Gunn's Firing Is What Happens When We Outsource Morality to Capitalism." *Forbes*, September 16, 2018. https://www.forbes.com/sites/anharkarim/2018/09/16/james-gunns-firing-is-what-happens-when-we-outsource-morality-to-capitalism/.

Karpel, Ari. 2010. "Elvis Has Left the Chapel." *New York Times*, December 12, 2010, late edition, sec. ST.

Katy. 2013. "Crazy Cat Lady Diaries: Sexism Is a Form of Hate Speech." *Crazy Cat Lady Diaries*, December 30, 2013. http://scottishcrazycatlady.blogspot.com/2013/12/sexism-is-form-of-hate-speech.html.

Katz, Brandon. 2018. "What We Can Learn From the 7 Biggest Box Office Opening Weekends of 2018 So Far." *New York Observer*, June 18, 2018.

Kearney, Christine. 2008. "Legal Fight Hindered Progress on New Book, J. K. Rowling Says." *Vancouver Sun*, April 15, 2008, final edition, sec. News.

Keegan, Rebecca. 2016. "With 'A Wrinkle In Time,' Ava DuVernay Will Pass a Milestone." latimes.com, August 30, 2016. https://www.latimes.com/entertainment/movies/la-et-mn-wrinkle-budget-20160803-snap-story.html.

Keegan, Rebecca. 2018. "Yes, Disney Thinks *Black Panther* is Best Picture-Worthy." *Vanity Fair*, September 2018. https://www.vanityfair.com/hollywood/2018/07/disney-thinks-black-panther-is-best-picture-worthy.

Keegan, Rebecca. 2019. "The Season of Scarlett Johansson: Two Hot Films, Her Marvel Future, Woody Allen and a Pick for President." *Hollywood Reporter*, September 4, 2019. https://www.hollywoodreporter.com/features/scarlett-johansson-talks-woody-allen-elizabeth-warren-black-widow-1235618.

Kegu, Jessica. 2017. "Director Patty Jenkins on How 'Wonder Woman' Differs from Other Comic Book Movies." CBS News, June 1, 2017. https://www.cbsnews.com/news/patty-jenkins-director-wonder-woman/.

Kelley, Seth. 2017. "Razzie Awards 2017 Winners List: 'Hillary's America,' 'Batman v Superman' Dominate." *Variety*, February 25, 2017. https://variety.com/2017/film/news/razzies-2017-winners-list-hillarys-america-batman-v-superman-1201996446/.

Kelley, Sonaiya. 2018. "'Black Panther' Flexes Its Might in Los Angeles: Fans Help Afrocentric Superhero Film Break Record." *Los Angeles Times*, February 19, 2018, home edition, sec. Home News; Entertainment Desk.

Kelly, Stephen. 2017. "Steven Moffat and the Doctor Who Fans: Their Messy Relationship." *The Telegraph*, April 15, 2017. https://www.telegraph.co.uk/tv/0/steven-moffatt-doctor-fans-messy-relationship/.

Kenney, David. 2006. "Krak! Whomp! Thok! Fwam!: Kevin Smith Runs Amok in Comic-Dom—and This Weekend in Calgary." *Calgary Herald*, February 3, 2006, final edition, sec. Swerve.

Kestler-D'Amours, Jillian. 2015. "Harry Potter Stage Cast Features Black Hermione." *Toronto Star*, December 22, 2015, sec. Entertainment.

Khosla, Proma. 2017. "How J. K. Rowling, the 'Harry Potter' Fandom, and Technology All Grew up Together." Mashable, June 26, 2017. https://mashable.com/2017/06/26/j-k-rowling-harry-potter-fandom-anniversary/.

Kim, Dorothy. 2019. "White Supremacists Have Weaponized an Imaginary Viking Past. It's Time to Reclaim the Real History." *Time*, April 15, 2019. https://time.com/5569399/viking-history-white-nationalists/.

Klink, Flourish, and Elizabeth Minkel. 2017. "Is 'Harry Potter and the Cursed Child' Fanfiction?" Fansplaining, July 8, 2017. http://fansplaining.com/post/162751398750/is-harry-potter-and-the-cursed-child-fanfiction.

Kloer, Phil. 2009. "*Watchmen*: Gory Twist on Superhero Flicks Isn't for Kids." *Atlanta Journal-Constitution*, March 4, 2009, main edition, sec. Living.

Knight, Chris. 2010. "Don't Give a Hoot: 'Legend of the Guardians' Fails to Soar." *Nanaimo Daily News*, September 24, 2010, sec. Entertainment.

Kornblum, Janet. 2001. "Director Not so Silent on 'Strike Back' Site." *USA Today*, August 23, 2001, final edition, sec. Life.

Kristian, Bonnie. 2017. "SNL's Shipwrecked Lesbian Friends Are Super Disappointed with *Wonder Woman*'s All-Female Island." *The Week*, October 8, 2017. https://theweek.com/speedreads/729633/snls-shipwrecked-lesbian-friends-are-super-disappointed-wonder-womans-allfemale-island.

Kroll, Justin. 2019. "'Matrix 4' Officially a Go With Keanu Reeves, Carrie-Anne Moss and Lana Wachowski (EXCLUSIVE)." *Variety*, August 20, 2019. https://variety.com/2019/film/news/matrix-4-keanu-reeves-carrie-anne-moss-lana-wachowski-1203307955/.

Lacey, Liam. 2004. "Kevin Smith, Uncensored; When the Director of Jersey Girl Does His Popular Q&A Sessions on College Campuses, He Gets Asked Why He Cast Jennifer Lopez after Seeing Gigli." *Globe and Mail*, March 25, 2004, sec. the Globe Review.

Lamberson, Carolyn. 2018. "Glowing Reviews Roll in for 'Black Panther.'" *Spokesman Review*, February 9, 2018, main edition, sec. E.

Larson, Chris. 2018. "What Gig Workers Can Learn from Romance Writers." *BBC Capital*, January 22, 2018. http://www.bbc.com/capital/story/20180119-what-gig-workers-can-learn-from-romance-writers.

Lau, Melody. 2017. "5 Reasons You Need to Know *Thor: Ragnarok* Director Taika Waititi | CBC Radio." CBC, November 1, 2017. https://www.cbc.ca/radio/q/blog/5-reasons-you-need-to-know-thor-ragnarok-director-taika-waititi-1.4380350.

Lavery, David. 2002. "'Emotional Resonance and Rocket Launchers': Joss Whedon's Commentaries on the Buffy the Vampire Slayer DVDs." *Slayage* 2 (2 [6]).

Law, John. 2016. "An Evening with Kevin Smith." *St. Catherine's Standard*, June 3, 2016, final edition, sec. Life.

Lawless, Jill. 2016. "Wizard Magic: J. K. Rowling Hopes 'Harry Potter' Play Goes Global." *Chicago Daily Herald*, August 6, 2016, sec. Features.

Laws, Roz. 2014. "Meet the New Hit TV Darling but Ssshhh, It's a Secret." *Birmingham Post*, August 21, 2014, 1, national edition, sec. Life; Features.

Lawson, Mark. 2014. "*Sherlock* and *Doctor Who*: Beware of Fans Influencing the TV They Love." *The Guardian*, January 3, 2014, sec. Television & Radio. https://www.theguardian.com/tv-and-radio/tvandradioblog/2014/jan/03/sherlock-doctor-who-fans-influencing-tv.

Lawson, Mark. 2016. "Jack Thorne: Go-to Guy Trusted by JK Rowling to Magic up Theatre Gold." *The Guardian*, June 11, 2016, sec. Stage. https://www.theguardian.com/stage/2016/jun/11/jack-thorne-trusted-jk-rowling-theatre-scriptwriter-harry-potter-play.

Lawson, Terry. 2001. "Kevin Smith Continues to Strike Back." *Hamilton Spectator*, August 22, 2001, final edition, sec. Entertainment.

Leaver, Tama. 2013. "Joss Whedon, Dr. Horrible, and the Future of Web Media." *Popular Communication* 11 (2): 160–73. https://doi.org/10.1080/15405702.2013.779510.

Leigh, Rob. 2013. "Steven Moffat Says *Doctor Who* Fan Peter Capaldi Will Have No Problem in Time Lord Starring Role." *Irish Mirror*, December 25, 2013, sec. TV; TV News.

Lejeune, Tristan. 2019. "Pelosi, JK Rowling among This Year's Robert F. Kennedy Human Rights Award Recipients." TheHill, August 13, 2019. https://thehill.com/blogs/in-the-know/in-the-know/457257-pelosi-jk-rowling-among-this-years-robert-f-kennedy-human.

Lengel, Kerry. 2019. "'Fifty Shades' Author E. L. James on 'The Mister': 'Women like a Good Romantic Story.'" *Azcentral*, April 30, 2019. https://www.azcentral.com/story/entertainment/arts/2019/04/30/el-james-on-the-mister-christian-grey-50-shades-of-grey-and-haters/3624581002/.

Leonard, Devin. 2016. "Zack Snyder's Superhero Life." bloomberg.com, March 1, 2016. http://www.bloomberg.com/features/2016-zack-snyder-profile/.

Levin, Sam. 2018. "*Black Panther*'s Legacy: Will the Record Breaker Finally Smash Hollywood Bi-As?" *The Guardian*, March 24, 2018, sec. Film.

Lewis, Lisa A. 1992. "'Something More than Love': Fan Stories on Film." In *The Adoring Audience: Fan Culture and Popular Media*, edited by Lisa A. Lewis, 135–59. London, UK: Routledge.

Lim, Thea. 2010. "Genderlicious: Zack Snyder and Sucker Punch." Bitch Media, August 9, 2010. https://www.bitchmedia.org/post/genderlicious-zack-snyder-filmmaking-and-sucker-punch.

Littleton, Cynthia. 2015. "Joss Whedon Says He Made More Money From 'Dr. Horrible' Than The First 'Avengers' Movie." *Variety*, October 11, 2015. https://variety.com/2015/tv/news/dr-horribles-sing-along-blog-joss-whedon-avengers-paleyfest-1201615455/.

Liverpool Echo. 2015. "Who's the Biggest Doctor Fan?" August 30, 2015, 1, national edition, sec. News.

lolcoholic. 2008. "The Steven Moffat OG Quote Post." Doctorwho—LiveJournal, June 5, 2008. https://doctorwho.livejournal.com/3086519.html.

London Free Press. 2017. "Hollywood Sticks to Its Big Guns: J. J. Abrams Returns to *Star Wars*, Patty Jen-Kins Gets *Wonder Woman* Sequel." September 13, 2017, final edition, sec. Entertainment.

Longino, Bob. 2001. "Jay and Silent Bob: Their Last Picture Show." *Atlanta Journal-Constitution*, August 23, 2001, home edition, sec. Features.

Lost, Little Geek. 2018. "37 In a Row." *Little Geek Lost*, May 21, 2018. http://www.littlegeeklost.com/blog/37-in-a-row/.

Lothian, Alexis. 2009. "Living in a Den of Thieves: Fan Video and Digital Challenges to Ownership." *Cinema Journal* 48 (4): 130–36. https://doi.org/10.1353/cj.0.0152.

Lury, Celia. 2004. *Brands: The Logos of the Global Economy*, first edition. London and New York: Routledge.

Luscombe, Belinda, Diane Tsai, and Gillian Laub. n.d. "Then and Now: Two Interviews With *Fifty Shades of Grey* Author E. L. James." *Time*. Accessed June 16, 2018. http://time.com/3697185/fifty-shades-of-grey-e-l-james-interview/.

Lyall, Sarah. 2015. "'Fifty Shades of Grey,' the Movie, as a Fairy Tale." *New York Times*, February 11, 2015, sec. Movies. https://www.nytimes.com/2015/02/15/movies/fifty-shades-of-grey-the-movie-as-a-fairy-tale.html.

Macdonald, Neil. 2013. "Doctor's Anniversary a Treat for Whoniverse." *Aberdeen Evening Express*, November 30, 2013, sec. Features; Hobbies; TV/Video.

Machosky, Michael. 2012. "Kevin Smith Brings Humor, Introspection to Music Hall Show." *Pittsburgh Tribune Review*, November 22, 2012.

Macmedan, Dan, and Rich Fury. 2017. "Lifeline." *Dayton Daily News*, March 2, 2017.

Maddox, Garry. 2018. "Out of Africa: With *Black Panther*, Director Ryan Coogler Has Turned the Superhero Genre on Its Head." *Sun Herald*, February 4, 2018, sec. S.

Maggs, Sam. 2015. "Review: *Jupiter Ascending* is the Worst Movie Ever Go See It Immediately." *The Mary Sue*, February 9, 2015. https://www.themarysue.com/review-jupiter-ascending-the-worst/.

Maidy, Alex. 2019. "Kevin Smith Makes an Emotional Return for His Comic Con Panel in Hall H." JoBlo.com, July 21, 2019. https://www.joblo.com/movie-news/kevin-smith-makes-an-emotional-return-for-his-comic-con-panel-in-hall-h.

Mallenbaum, Carly. 2019. "'Fifty Shades of Grey' to 'The Mister': E. L. James' New Book Has Tamer Sex, Social Awareness." *USA Today*, April 15, 2019. https://www.usatoday.com/story/life/books/2019/04/15/fifty-shades-of-grey-el-james-new-book-the-mister-50-shades-of-grey/3455102002/.

Malloy, Steve. 2011. "Smith's Red State Finally Hits Home." *Times & Transcript*, October 21, 2011, sec. Entertainment.

Mancuso, Vince. 2018. "'Titans' Review: Teen Titans, No." *Collider*, October 4, 2018. http://collider.com/titans-review/.

Mandell, Andrea. 2018. "'Fifty Shades Freed' Is My Personal Bad Place." *USA Today*, February 8, 2018. https://www.usatoday.com/story/life/movies/2018/02/08/fifty-shades-freed-my-personal-bad-place/313851002/.

Mansuri, Nasim. 2018. "The Problem with Pottermore: How the Platform Failed to Keep up with Fandom." *Hypable*, March 24, 2018. https://www.hypable.com/the-problem-with-pottermore/.

Marr, Bernard. 2016. *Big Data in Practice: How 45 Successful Companies Used Big Data Analytics to Deliver Extraordinary Results*, first edition. Chichester, West Sussex: Wiley.

Martin, Dan. 2010. "*Doctor Who*: Is Steven Moffat's Who Living up to Expectations?" *The Guardian*, May 13, 2010.

Marwick, Alice E. 2008. "To Catch a Predator? The MySpace Moral Panic." *First Monday* 13 (6). http://www.firstmonday.dk/ojs/index.php/fm/article/view/2152.

Marwick, Alice E., and danah boyd. 2011. "I Tweet Honestly, I Tweet Passionately: Twitter Users, Context Collapse, and the Imagined Audience." *New Media & Society* 13 (1): 114–33. https://doi.org/10.1177/1461444810365313.

Matadeen, Renaldo. 2018. "With *Aquaman*, the DCEU Learns from the Mistakes of the Snyder Era." CBR, December 23, 2018. https://www.cbr.com/aquaman-dceu-learned-from-zack-snyder-mistakes/.

Mayer-Schonberger, Viktor, and Lena Wong. 2013. "Fan or Foe: Fan Fiction, Authorship, and the Fight for Control." *IDEA: The Intellectual Property Law Review* 54: 1.

McCarthy, Simone. 2016. "Harry Potter Play Previews in London: Will J. K. Rowling's Magic Endure?" *Christian Science Monitor*, June 8, 2016, sec. the Culture.

McClatchy Newspapers. 2010. "Nothing Off Limits with Kevin Smith." *Star Phoenix*, March 26, 2010, final edition, sec. Arts & Life.

McClintock, Pamela. 2015. "Warner Bros. Film Chief on 'Wonder Woman,' J. K. Rowling's 'Fantastic Beasts' Script and How DC Will Compete With Marvel." *Hollywood Reporter*, June 3, 2015, sec. News.

McCloud, Scott. 1994. *Understanding Comics*. New York: Harper Collins.

McEwan, Cameron K. 2017. "Steven Moffat Reveals the 'Absolute, Ultimate Boss' Behind 'Sherlock.'" *New York Observer*, January 16, 2017.

McGeorge, Alistair. 2016. "J. K. Rowling Reveals New Wizarding Schools to Rival Hogwarts as Harry Potter World Keeps Growing." *Irish Mirror*, January 30, 2016, sec. Showbiz; Celebrity News.

McLean, Ralph. 2018. "Black Magic: Amazing Adaptation Will Have Hero Fans Purring like a Kitten." *Sunday Life*, February 18, 2018, 1, national edition, sec. Features.

McLeod, Dion, and Travis Holland. 2017. "The Ghost of J. K. Rowling: Harry Potter and the Ur-Fan." *Media, Film, and Commnication Otago Working Papers Series* 3: 1–20.

McNary, Dave. 2018. "'Black Panther' Passes 'Wonder Woman,' 'Toy Story 3' at U.S. Box Office." *Variety*, February 28, 2018. https://variety.com/2018/film/news/black-panther-box-office-passes-wonder-woman-1202713001/.

McRobbie, Angela, and Sarah L. Thornton. 1995. "Rethinking 'Moral Panic' for Multi-Mediated Social Worlds." *British Journal of Sociology* 46 (4): 559–74. https://doi.org/10.2307/591571.

McWeeny, Drew. 2015. "Review: The Wachowskis Bring Mad Style to the YA Genre in 'Jupiter Ascending.'" *Uproxx*, February 2, 2015. https://uproxx.com/hitfix/review-the-wachowskis-bring-mad-style-to-the-ya-genre-in-jupiter-ascending/.

Mellor, Louisa. 2014. "*Doctor Who*: Steven Moffat on Series 8, Missy, Lies and Leaks." *Den of Geek*, November 13, 2014. https://www.denofgeek.com/tv/doctor-who/32928/doctor-who-steven-moffat-on-series-8-missy-lies-and-leaks.

Mendelson, Scott. 2018a. "'Fantastic Beasts' Can't Afford a Gay Dumbledore Thanks to Overseas Box Office." *Forbes*, February 1, 2018. https://www.forbes.com/sites/scottmendelson/2018/02/01/fantastic-beasts-warner-bros-cant-afford-a-gay-dumbledore/.

Mendelson, Scott. 2018b. "One Key Reason 'Black Panther' Made Box Office History." *Forbes*, April 19, 2018. https://www.forbes.com/sites/scottmendelson/2018/04/19/box-office-one-huge-reason-why-black-panther-was-such-a-big-hit/.

Mendelson, Scott. 2018c. "Box Office: 'Captain Marvel' Is Being Set up to Fail." *Forbes*, September 25, 2018. https://www.forbes.com/sites/scottmendelson/2018/09/25/box-office-captain-marvel-is-being-set-up-to-fail/.

Merry, Stephanie. 2018. "The Surprising Lessons We Learned from the 'Fifty Shades' Trilogy (Yes, Really)." *Chicago Tribune*, February 9, 2018. http://www.chicagotribune.com/entertainment/movies/ct-fifty-shades-lessons-20180209-story.html.

Mihm, Lance. 2016. "Locals Say 'Superman V Batman' Delivers." *Lima News*, March 26, 2016.

Miller, Gregory E. 2015. "Fan Fiction Writers Speak out against 'Fifty Shades of Grey.'" *New York Post*, February 8, 2015. https://nypost.com/2015/02/07/fan-fiction-writers-speak-out-against-50-shades-of-grey/.

Mitra, Mili. 2018. "Latest Harry Potter Controversy Reveals Truth about JK Rowling." *Sydney Morning Herald*, October 3, 2018. https://www.smh.com.au/entertainment/movies/latest-harry-potter-controversy-reveals-truth-about-jk-rowling-20181003-p507j4.html.

Mohanty, Chandra Talpade. 1984. "Under Western Eyes: Feminist Scholarship and Colonial Discourses." *Boundary 2* 12/13: 333–58. https://doi.org/10.2307/302821.

Monetti, Sandro. 2008. "BBC Spoilsport Kills Off Daleks." express.co.uk, July 27, 2008. https://www.express.co.uk/news/uk/54182/BBC-spoilsport-kills-off-Daleks.

Montagne, Renee. 2015. "J. K. Rowling on Her Nom De Plume Robert Galbraith." npr.org, November 2, 2015. https://www.npr.org/2015/11/02/453885684/j-k-rolling-on-her-nom-de-plume-robert-galbraith.

Monterey County Herald. 2007. "Rowling to Fans: Don't Spoil It." May 20, 2007, sec. Z_Commentary.

Moon, Rachael. 2016. "J. K. Rowling Urges Fans Not to Give Spoilers as *Cursed Child* Debuts." *Mirror*, June 6, 2016. http://www.mirror.co.uk/3am/celebrity-news/jk-rowling-insists-keepthesecrets-isnt-8124529.

Moore, Roger. 2001. "Kevin Smith Strikes Back." *Toronto Star*, August 25, 2001, Saturday Ontario edition, sec. Arts.

Moran, Lee. 2018. "J. K. Rowling Taunts Donald Trump With Lewis Carroll Tweedledee Quote." *Huffington Post*, August 1, 2018, sec. Culture & Arts. https://www.huffingtonpost.com/entry/jk-rowling-donald-trump-lewis-carroll_us_5b614fc1e4b0de86f49c0627.

Morris, Linda. 2012. "*Fifty Shades*—A Lustful Force of Social Media." *Canberra Times*, August 25, 2012, final edition, sec. A.

Mukherjee, Tatsam. 2018. "*Black Panther*'s Purple Carpet Premiere Is a Whole Lot of YAAAAS." *Indian Express*, January 31, 2018.

Muntean, Nick, and Anne Helen Petersen. 2009. "Celebrity Twitter: Strategies of Intrusion and Disclosure in the Age of Technoculture." *M/C Journal* 12 (5). http://journal.media-culture.org.au/index.php/mcjournal/article/view/194.

Murray, Noel. 2018. "A Standout in Marvel's Universe." *Los Angeles Times*, May 13, 2018, home edition, sec. Home Theater; New Releases; Sunday Calendar; Calendar Desk.

Nair, Sharika. 2017. "Blame It on Your Male Privilege if You Canat Understand Why *Wonder Woman* is Amazing." yourstory.in, June 15, 2017.

Nakagawa, Chiho. 2011. "Safe Sex with Defanged Vampires: New Vampire Heroes in *Twilight* and the Southern Vampire Mysteries." *Journal of Popular Romance Studies* 2 (1). http://jprstudies.org/wp-content/uploads/2011/10/JPRS2.1_Nakagawa_DefangedVampires.pdf.

Nation, The. 2017. "From Superwoman to *Wonder Woman*." June 2, 2017.

Navar-Gill, Annemarie. 2018. "From Strategic Retweets to Group Hangs: Writers' Room Twitter Accounts and the Productive Ecosystem of TV Social Media Fans." *Television & New Media* 19 (5): 415–30. https://doi.org/10.1177/1527476417728376.

Navar-Gill, Annemarie, and Mel Stanfill. 2018. "'We Shouldn't Have to Trend to Make You Listen': Queer Fan Hashtag Campaigns as Production Interventions." *Journal of Film and Video* 70 (3–4): 85–100.

New Zealand Herald. 2011. "Born in the Who-S-A!" May 12, 2011, sec. News; General.

New Zealand Herald. 2012. "'Mummy Porn' Book Hits Spot for Women." April 14, 2012, sec. Entertainment; General.

News International. 2017. "Deconstructing the *Wonder Woman* Juggernaut." June 1, 2017.

News International. 2018. "*Black Panther* Director Pens Letter of Gratitude." February 22, 2018.

Newton, Casey. 2018. "As Controversy Swirls, Social Network Vero Is Closing in on 3 Million Users." *The Verge*, March 2, 2018. https://www.theverge.com/2018/3/2/17067610/vero-social-media-ayman-hariri-downloads.

Ng, Eve. 2017. "Between Text, Paratext, and Context: Queerbaiting and the Contemporary Media Landscape." *Transformative Works and Cultures* 24. http://journal.transformativeworks.org/index.php/twc/article/view/917.

Nicholson, Amy. 2017. "How Tessa Thompson Went From Indie Actor to 'Thor: Ragnarok' Badass." *Rolling Stone*, October 31, 2017. https://www.rollingstone.com/movies/movie-features/how-tessa-thompson-went-from-indie-actor-to-thor-ragnarok-badass-116635/.

Northover, Kylie. 2015. "All Talk." *The Age*, September 5, 2015, first edition, sec. Arts.

Nussbaum, Emily. 2002. "Must-See Metaphysics." *New York Times*, September 22, 2002, sec. Magazine. https://www.nytimes.com/2002/09/22/magazine/must-see-metaphysics.html.

obsession_inc. 2009. "Affirmational Fandom vs. Transformational Fandom." June 1, 2009. https://obsession-inc.dreamwidth.org/82589.html.

Office, Press. 2004. "BBC—Press Office—Coupling Steven Moffat." BBC, June 16, 2004. http://www.bbc.co.uk/pressoffice/pressreleases/stories/2004/06_june/16/coupling_moffat.shtml.

Ohlheiser, Abby. 2016. "Fans Make Harry Potter Universe into Their Own." *Leader-Post*, August 24, 2016, early edition, sec. You.

Olding, Rachel. 2010. "Akira V. Regurgitator." *Sydney Morning Herald*, August 6, 2010, first edition, sec. Metro.

Oleksinski, Johnny. 2016. "We've Been Tricked! Harry Potter's Publisher Promises a New Book, but Delivers a London Play Cloaked in Wizardry." *New York Post*, August 5, 2016.

Osterheldt, Jenee. 2012. "Sexy or Sick?; *Twilight* Fan Scores Huge with *Fifty Shades* Trilogy." *Ottawa Citizen*, April 1, 2012, final edition, sec. News.

Outlaw, Kofi. 2017. "*Wonder Woman*'s Patty Jenkins Would Love to Direct a Superman Movie." DC, June 9, 2017. https://comicbook.com/dc/2017/06/10/wonder-woman-patty-jenkins-superman-movie/.

Outlaw, Kofi. 2018a. "Zack Snyder Reveals 'Justice League' Original Ending." DC, October 25, 2018. https://comicbook.com/dc/2018/10/25/justice-league-original-alternate-ending-zack-snyder/.

Outlaw, Kofi. 2018b. "Zack Snyder Responds to Question About 'Man of Steel's NSFW Pod Shapes." DC, December 10, 2018. https://comicbook.com/dc/2018/12/10/man-steel-movie-penis-pods-rockets-zack-snyder/.

Outlaw, Kofi. 2019. "Zack Snyder Announces New Production Company." DC, January 7, 2019. https://comicbook.com/dc/2019/01/07/zack-snyder-stone-quarry-production-company-cruel-unusual-films/.

Owen, Cathy. 2014. "*Sherlock* Season 3: Your Reviews of the Return of the Super-Sleuth." *Wales Online*, January 2, 2014, sec. What's On.

Paige, Rachel. 2018. "'Harry Potter' Is Actively Trying to Destroy the Legacy of 'Harry Potter'—HelloGiggles." Hello Giggles, February 1, 2018. https://hellogiggles.com/news/harry-potter-legacy-twitter/.

Pantozzi, Jill. 2012. "Hey, That's My Cape!—Why No Women in COMIC BOOK MEN?" Newsarama, January 5, 2012. https://www.newsarama.com/8902-hey-that-s-my-cape-why-no-women-in-comic-book-men.html.

Pappademas, Alex. 2011. "Hollywood's Leading Geek." *New York Times Magazine*, March 18, 2011. https://www.nytimes.com/2011/03/20/magazine/mag-20Snyder-t.html.

Parham, Jason. 2018. "The Ryan Coogler Effect: What the Success of 'Black Panther' Means for Black Directors." *Wired*, March 23, 2018. https://www.wired.com/story/black-panther-the-ryan-coogler-effect/.

Parker, Ian. 2012. "J. K. Rowling's Novel for Adults." *New Yorker*, September 24, 2012. https://www.newyorker.com/magazine/2012/10/01/mugglemarch.

Patrizio, Andy. 2004. "An Interview with Patty Jenkins." *IGN*, May 28, 2004. https://www.ign.com/articles/2004/05/28/an-interview-with-patty-jenkins?page=3.

per-mare-ad-astra. 2012. "Doctor Who?" Tumblr, October 1, 2012. http://per-mare-ad-astra.tumblr.com/post/32671238866.

Phegley, Kiel. 2010. "Kevin Smith's *Green Hornet* Goodbye." CBR, November 24, 2010. https://www.cbr.com/kevin-smiths-green-hornet-goodbye/.

Philippines Daily Inquirer. 2017. "Director Christopher Nolan Says DC Should Not Rush Superhero Films." *Philippines Daily Inquirer*, December 6, 2017.

Philippines Daily Inquirer. 2018. "Ryan Coogler Suddenly Finds Himself at the Center of Marvel Cinematic Uni-Verse." February 23, 2018.

Phillips, Mark. 2017. "Extended Transcript: J. K. Rowling and the Creative Team Behind 'Cursed Child.'" CBS News, September 24, 2017. https://www.cbsnews.com/news/extended-transcript-j-k-rowling-and-the-creative-team-behind-harry-potter-and-the-cursed-child/.

Phillips, Tom. 2011. "When Film Fans Become Fan Family: Kevin Smith Fandom and Communal Experience." *Participations* 8 (2): 478–96.

Phillips, Tom. 2012. "Too Fat to Fly: A Case Study of Unsuccessful Fan Mobilization." *Transformative Works and Cultures* 10. https://doi.org/10.3983/twc.2012.0330.

Phillips, Whitney. 2015. *This Is Why We Can't Have Nice Things: Mapping the Relationship between Online Trolling and Mainstream Culture*. Cambridge, MA: MIT Press.

Plaugic, Lizzie. 2017. "Joss Whedon Fan Site Whedonesque Shuts Down after 15 Years." *The Verge*, August 21, 2017. https://www.theverge.com/2017/8/21/16179080/joss-whedon-fan-site-whedonesque-shut-down.

Plunkett, John. 2016. "We Nearly Appointed a Black Doctor, Says *Doctor Who* Showrunner." *The Guardian*, June 2, 2016, sec. Television & Radio. https://www.theguardian.com/tv-and-radio/2016/jun/02/steven-moffat-there-was-going-to-be-a-black-doctor-who.

Pocklington, Rebecca. 2015. "*Fifty Shades of Grey* Author E. L. James' Twitter Q&A Majorly Backfires as it's Taken Over by Haters." *Irish Mirror*, June 30, 2015, sec. Showbiz, Celebrity News.

Poniewozik, James. 2015. "Casting Black Hermione Granger Reinforces a 'Harry Potter' Theme." *International New York Times*, December 24, 2015, sec. Leisure.

Portman, Jamie. 2001. "*Dogma* Director Returns to Safer Characters: Kevin Smith Hopes His New Comedy Will Dodge the Intense Controversy That Dogged His Last Feature." *Vancouver Sun*, August 14, 2001, final edition, sec. Entertainment.

Portman, Jamie. 2004. "How *Gigli* Nearly Sank Jersey Girl: Director Kevin Smith Thought He Had a Hit on His Hands. But That Was before He Was Blindsided by the Jen and Ben Sideshow." *Ottawa Citizen*, March 16, 2004, final edition, sec. Arts.

Potton, Ed. 2004. "Not-so-Silent Bob." *The Times*, June 26, 2004, sec. Features.

Powell, Emma. 2015. "JK Rowling Finally Reveals Why She Named Harry Potter's Son after Professor Snape; The Decison to Name Albus Severus after the Slytherin Head Has Confused Fans for Years." *London Evening Standard*, November 27, 2015.

PR Script Managers. 2017. "Time for a Change." *Eastern Daily Press*, February 9, 2017, sec. FET.

Pulliam-Moore, Charles. 2018. "GLAAD Calls Out Marvel and WB for Not Acknowledging Their LGBTQ Movie Characters." I09, May 22, 2018. https://io9.gizmodo.com/glaad-calls-out-marvel-and-wb-for-not-acknowledging-the-1826230143.

Purdom, Clayton. 2017. "Zack Snyder's Dawn of the Dead Sure was a Zack Snyder Movie." *AV Club*, August 22, 2017. https://news.avclub.com/zack-snyder-s-dawn-of-the-dead-sure-was-a-zack-snyder-m-1798346278.

Quine, Oscar. 2018. "*Doctor Who* Stars Reject Claim the Show Has Become Too PC." *The Telegraph*, December 3, 2018. https://www.telegraph.co.uk/news/2018/12/03/doctor-stars-reject-claim-show-has-become-pc/.

Rahman, Abid. 2015. "J. K. Rowling Drops Hints of an 'American Hogwarts' on Twitter." *Hollywood Reporter*, June 9, 2015, sec. News.

Ramos, Dino-Ray. 2018. "'Thor: Ragnarok' Director Taika Waititi Describes New Zealand as 'A Racist Place.'" *Deadline*, April 9, 2018. https://deadline.com/2018/04/thor-ragnarok-director-taika-waititi-racism-maori-new-zealand-racism-1202361085/.

Rampton, James. 2004. "Whatever Do They See in Each Other?" *The Independent*, June 29, 2004, first edition, sec. Arts; Features.

Recode Staff. 2017. "Full Transcript: Shondaland CEO and TV Producer Shonda Rhimes on Recode Decode." Recode, October 25, 2017. https://www.recode.net/2017/10/25/16548558/transcript-shonda-rhimes-shondaland-greys-anatomy-television-recode-decode.

Reuters. 2011. "J. K. Rowling Fills Harry Potter Void with Mysterious New Website." *National Post (Financial Post)*, June 17, 2011, national edition, sec. Arts & Life.

Rich, Adrienne. 1980. "Compulsory Heterosexuality and Lesbian Existence." *Signs* 5 (4): 631–60.

Rich, Motoko. 2008. "Rowling Hopes to Draw Magic Circle Around Potter." *International Herald Tribune*, April 15, 2008, sec. Finance.

Riesman, Abraham. 2017. "How Kevin Smith Makes Big Business Out of Niche Audiences." *Vulture*, September 5, 2017. http://www.vulture.com/2017/09/kevin-smith-red-state.html.

Riesman, Abraham. 2018. "Comicsgate, a Comic-Book Harassment Campaign, Is Growing." *Vulture*, August 29, 2018. https://www.vulture.com/2018/08/comicsgate-a-comic-book-harassment-campaign-is-growing.html.

Rigler, Natasha. 2017. "Hell for Leather: *Wonder Woman* Fans Furious After Amazons Wear 'Tiny Leather Bikinis' in New *Justice League* Movie." *The Sun*, November 14, 2017, sec. Film.

"R/Movies—Why Hasn't Patty Jenkins Directed a Feature Film in 14 Years until *Wonder Woman*?" 2017. Reddit, May 22, 2017. https://www.reddit.com/r/movies/comments/6clfth/why_hasnt_patty_jenkins_directed_a_feature_film/.

Roach, Vicky. 2015. "As Long as Fans Are Titillated, I'm Happy." *Daily Telegraph*, February 15, 2015, sec. Lifestyle.

Robey, Tim. 2017. "Too Big for Their Boots: Tim Robey Explores Whether We've Had Enough of All These Superheroes." *Calgary Herald*, November 24, 2017, early edition, sec. Movies.

Robinson, Joanna. 2015. "Can the Man Behind *Sherlock* and *Doctor Who* Be Saved from Himself?" *Vanity Fair*, July 10, 2015. https://www.vanityfair.com/hollywood/2015/07/sherlock-doctor-who-steven-moffat-comic-con.

Rogers, Adam. 2012. "Joss Whedon on Comic Books, Abusing Language and the Joys of Genre." *Wired*, May 3, 2012. https://www.wired.com/2012/05/joss-whedon/.

Romano, Aja. 2012. "*Fifty Shades of Grey* and the *Twilight* Pro-Fic Phenomenon." *The Mary Sue*, March 3, 2012. https://www.themarysue.com/50-shades-of-grey-and-the-twilight-pro-fic-phenomenon/.

Romano, Aja. 2016. "The Harry Potter Universe Still Can't Translate Its Gay Subtext to Text. It's a Problem." *Vox*, September 4, 2016. https://www.vox.com/2016/9/4/12534818/harry-potter-cursed-child-rowling-queerbaiting.

Romano, Nick. 2019. "How Eric Kripke's Superhero Satire 'The Boys' Riffs on DC and Marvel." ew.com, July 17, 2019. https://ew.com/comic-con/2019/07/17/the-boys-dc-marvel/.

Romei, Stephen. 2018. "African Marvel Full of Surprises." *The Australian*, February 10, 2018, Review edition, sec. Review.

Romney, Jonathan. 2007. "Triumph of the Thrill." *ABC Magazine*, March 25, 2007, first edition, sec. ABC.

Rosa, Christopher. 2017. "Gal Gadot Confirms Brett Ratner Isn't a Part of 'Wonder Woman 2.'" *Glamour*, November 5, 2017. https://www.glamour.com/story/gal-gadot-confirms-brett-ratner-isnt-a-part-of-wonder-woman-2.

Rose, Steve. 2016. "From *Suicide Squad* to *Batman v Superman*, Why Are DC's Films so Bad?" *The Guardian*, August 3, 2016, sec. Film. http://www.theguardian.com/film/shortcuts/2016/aug/03/from-suicide-squad-to-batman-v-superman-why-dc-films-so-bad-zack-snyder.

Rosenberg, Adam. 2018. "'Sucker Punch,' Zack Snyder's Hated 2011 Movie, Is Actually Good. Fight Me." Mashable, November 24, 2018. https://mashable.com/article/sucker-punch-is-actually-good-zack-snyder/.

Rowling, J. K. 2001. *Harry Potter and the Prisoner of Azkaban*. New York: Scholastic Paperbacks.

Rowling, J. K. 2009. "I Am Told That People Have Been Twittering on My Behalf, so I Thought a Brief Visit Was in Order Just to Prevent Any More Confusion!" Twitter, September 17, 2009. https://twitter.com/jk_rowling/status/4057585855.

Rowling, J. K. 2015. "I'm in Edinburgh, so Could Somebody at King's Cross Wish James S Potter Good Luck for Me? He's Starting at Hogwarts Today. #BackToHogwarts." Tweet. *@jk_rowling*, September 1, 2015. https://twitter.com/jk_rowling/status/638641255094853632?lang=en.

Rowling, J. K. 2016. "I'll Use My Influence Whatever Way I Want. This Country Needs to Be Freed of Fascists on Both Right and Left." June 27, 2016. https://twitter.com/jk_rowling/status/747527349525176321.

Rowling, J. K. 2017a. "OK, Here It Is. Please Don't Start Flame Wars over It, but This Year I'd like to Apologise for Killing (Whispers) . . . Snape. *runs for Cover*." Tweet. *@jk_rowling*, May 2, 2017. https://twitter.com/jk_rowling/status/859364426088108032?lang=en.

Rowling, J. K. 2017b. "Robert Galbraith Wrote a Chapter of the next #Strike Book in a Trailer on the Set of the next #FantasticBeasts Movie Today 🎬 🎥." September 19, 2017. https://twitter.com/jk_rowling/status/910241120961093634.

Rowling, J. K. 2017c. "Grindelwald Casting." J. K. Rowling, December 7, 2017. https://www.jkrowling.com/opinions/grindelwald-casting/.

Rowling, J. K. 2018a. "hahahahahahahahahahahahahahahahahahahahahahahahahahahahahahahahahahahahahahahahahahahahahahahahahahahahahahahahahahaha someone told him how to spell 'pore' hahahahahahahahahahahahahahahahahahahahahahahahahahahahahahahahahahahahahahahahahahahahahahahahahahahahahahaha pic.twitter.com/Gf2xxKyFlp." Tweet. *@jk_rowling*, July 3, 2018. https://twitter.com/jk_rowling/status/1014290773934792704?lang=en.

Rowling, J. K. 2018b. "Only for around Twenty Years.Https://Twitter.Com/Mortaldistricts/Status/1044576631132753920. . . ." Tweet. *@jk_rowling*, September 25, 2018. https://twitter.com/jk_rowling/status/1044579634581401600?ref_src=twsrc%5Etfw%7Ctwcamp%5Etweetembed%7Ctwterm%5E1044579634581401600&ref_url=https%3A%2F%2Fwww

.independent.ie%2Fentertainment%2Fmovies%2Fjk-rowling-defends-casting-asian-actress-as-nagini-in-fantastic-beasts-sequel-37359741.html.

Rowling, J. K. 2018c. "The Naga Are Snake-like Mythical Creatures of Indonesian Mythology, Hence the Name 'Nagini.' They Are Sometimes Depicted as Winged, Sometimes as Half-Human, Half-Snake. Indonesia Comprises a Few Hundred Ethnic Groups, Including Javanese, Chinese and Betawi. Have a Lovely Day." Tweet. @jk_rowling, September 26, 2018. https://twitter.com/jk_rowling/status/1044907311058358273?lang=en.

Rowling, J. K. 2018d. "Being Sent Abuse about an Interview That Didn't Involve Me, about a Screenplay I Wrote but Which None of the Angry People Have Read, Which Is Part of a Five-Movie Series That's Only One Instalment in, Is Obviously Tons of Fun, but You Know What's Even *more* Fun." January 31, 2018. https://twitter.com/jk_rowling/status/958812726964424704.

Rubinoff, Joel. 2017. "*Wonder Woman*'s Biggest Enemy? Hollywood Inertia." *Toronto Star*, June 14, 2017, sec. Entertainment.

Russo, Donovan. 2018. "Marvel's Most Powerful Character Ever Is Coming Soon, and It's a Woman." CNBC, September 23, 2018. https://www.cnbc.com/2018/09/23/marvels-most-powerful-character-ever-is-coming-soon-and-its-a-woman.html.

"R/Voltron—Please Send Positivity to Lauren Montgomery." 2018. Reddit, July 18, 2018. https://www.reddit.com/r/Voltron/comments/8zwqge/please_send_positivity_to_lauren_montgomery/.

Ryan, Erin Gloria. 2015. "This Is Your Brain on the *Fifty Shades of Grey* Trilogy." Jezebel, February 12, 2015. https://jezebel.com/this-is-your-brain-on-the-fifty-shades-of-grey-trilogy-1685260335.

Ryan, Marie-Laure. 2015. "Transmedia Storytelling: Industry Buzzword or New Narrative Experience?" *StoryWorlds: A Journal of Narrative Studies* 7 (2): 1–19.

Ryzik, Melena. 2018. "Ava DuVernay's Fiercely Feminine Vision for 'A Wrinkle in Time.'" *New York Times*, March 1, 2018, sec. Movies. https://www.nytimes.com/2018/03/01/movies/a-wrinkle-in-time-ava-duvernay-disney.html.

Sahani, Alaka. 2015. "Hollywood Wants Me to Make a Certain Kind of Movie: Ava DuVernay." *Indian Express*, November 9, 2015.

Sakoui, Anousha. 2017. "'Wonder Woman' Debut Delivers Box-Office Punch for Warner." *Las Cruces Sun-News*, June 4, 2017, sec. Business.

Sales, Bethany. 2013. "*Fifty Shades of Grey*: The New Publishing Paradigm." *Huffington Post*, April 18, 2013. https://www.huffingtonpost.com/bethany-sales/fifty-shades-of-grey-publishing_b_3109547.html.

Salmon, Caspar. 2018. "*Fantastic Beasts 2*: Why Can't They Just Let Dumbledore Be Gay?" *The Guardian*, February 1, 2018, sec. Film. https://www.theguardian.com/film/filmblog/2018/feb/01/fantastic-beasts-2-why-cant-they-just-let-dumbledore-be-gay.

Salter, Anastasia, and Bridget Blodgett. 2017. *Toxic Geek Masculinity in Media: Sexism, Trolling, and Identity Policing*. Cham, CH: Palgrave Macmillan.

Sandifer, Elizabeth. 2014. "The Definitive Moffat and Feminism Post | Eruditorum Press." Eruditorum Press. http://www.eruditorumpress.com/blog/the-definitive-moffat-and-feminism-post/.

Satellite, The. 2017a. "*Wonder Woman* Is Amazing!" June 14, 2017.

Satellite, The. 2017b. "Sequel for *Wonder Woman* under Way." July 5, 2017.

Sblendorio, Peter, Nicole Bitette, and Katie Honan. 2017. "Taking 'Shape': Fantasy Gets Most Nominations in Early Oscar Hint." *New York Daily News*, December 12, 2017, sports final edition, sec. News.

Schaub, Michael. 2015. "'Fifty Shades' Author E.L. James Worth $58 Million, despite Being Spanked by Critics." *Los Angeles Times*, June 29, 2015. http://www.latimes.com/books/jacketcopy/la-et-jc-el-james-worth-58-million-20150629-story.html.

Schedeen, Jesse. 2008. "Batman: Cacophony #1 Review." *IGN*, November 12, 2008. http://www.ign.com/articles/2008/11/13/batman-cacophony-1-review.

Schwalbach, Jennifer. 1998. "'Clerks' Creator Is No Slacker When Spreading Good Will." *USA Today*, March 30, 1998, final edition, sec. Life.

Schwartz, Dana. 2016. "In Defense of 'The Cursed Child.'" *New York Observer*, August 5, 2016.

Scott, Ryan. 2018. "*Black Panther* Becomes King of the MCU: Journey to Infinity War Part 18." MovieWeb, April 27, 2018. https://movieweb.com/black-panther-infinity-war-marvel-cinematic-universe-retrospective/.

Scott, Suzanne. 2007. "Authorized Resistance: Is Fan Production Frakked?" In *Cylons in America: Critical Studies in Battlestar Galactica*, edited by Tiffany Potter and C. W. Marshall, 210–23. New York: Continuum.

Scott, Suzanne. 2011a. "Revenge of the Fanboy: Convergence Culture and the Politics of Incorporation." Dissertation, Los Angeles: University of Southern California. http://digitallibrary.usc.edu/assetserver/controller/item/etd-Scott-4277.pdf.

Scott, Suzanne. 2011b. "Revenge of the Fanboy: Convergence Culture and the Politics of Incorporation." University of Southern California. https://search.proquest.com/openview/ee043f852459475823d3d65db9f78524/1?pq-origsite=gscholar&cbl=18750&diss=y.

Scott, Suzanne. 2012. "Who's Steering the Mothership? The Role of the Fanboy Auteur in Transmedia Storytelling." In *The Participatory Cultures Handbook*, edited by Aaron Delwiche and Jennifer Jacobs Henderson, first edition, 43–52. New York: Routledge.

Scott, Suzanne. 2013. "Dawn of the Undead Author: Fanboy Auteurism and Zack Snyder's 'Vision.'" In *A Companion to Media Authorship*, edited by Jonathan Gray and Derek Johnson, 440–62. New York: John Wiley & Sons.

Scott, Suzanne. 2015. "The Moral Economy of Crowdfunding and the Transformative Capacity of Fan-Ancing." *New Media & Society* 17 (2): 167–82. https://doi.org/10.1177/1461444814558908.

Scott, Suzanne. 2018a. "Of All the Things Making People Nervous and/or Unhappy Here, I Feel like We Should All Be Focusing on the Fact That This Is a VICTORIAN PERIOD PIECE Which Feels by Design to Be a Get out of Jail Free Card for Bad Representational Decisions.Https://Twitter.Com/Ew/Status/1017823761230389249. . . ." Tweet. *@iheartfatapollo*, July 14, 2018. https://twitter.com/iheartfatapollo/status/1018114010502385664.

Scott, Suzanne. 2018b. "This Is a Clear Moment to Reclaim and Recuperate the Brand. The Victorian Context Will Structurally Heighten the Trademark Feminist Ethos, but Also Conveniently Give Him an out on His Longstanding Issues around Race. Joss May Be Many Things, but He's Not Dumb." Tweet. *@iheartfatapollo*, July 14, 2018. https://twitter.com/iheartfatapollo/status/1018119303420399617.

Scott, Suzanne. 2019. *Fake Geek Girls: Fandom, Gender, and the Convergence Culture Industry*. New York: NYU Press.

Seabrook, George. 2015. "Patty Jenkins to Direct *Wonder Woman*." *The Edge*, April 16, 2015. https://www.theedgesusu.co.uk/news/2015/04/16/patty-jenkins-to-direct-wonder-woman/.

Sedgman, Kirsty. 2018. "When Theatre Meets Fandom: Audience Reviews of *Harry Potter and the Cursed Child*." March 1, 2018. https://doi.org/info:doi/10.1386/jfs.6.1.81_1.

Seiler, Andy. 2001. "Kevin Smith Is Seldom 'Silent.'" *USA Today*, August 24, 2001, final edition, sec. Life.

Setoodeh, Ramin. 2017. "Patty Jenkins on 'Wonder Woman 2,' Hollywood Sexism and James Cameron—Variety." *Variety*, October 10, 2017. https://variety.com/2017/film/features/patty-jenkins-wonder-woman-hollywood-sexism-equal-pay-james-cameron-1202583237/.

Seymour, Jessica. 2018. "Racebending and Prosumer Fanart Practices in Harry Potter Fandom." In *A Companion to Fandom and Fan Studies*, edited by Paul Booth, 333–48. Oxford, UK: Wiley-Blackwell.

Shapiro, Rebecca. 2018. "J. K. Rowling Can't Stop Laughing At Trump's Boast About His Expert Writing Skills." *Huffington Post*, July 4, 2018, sec. Culture & Arts. https://www.huffingtonpost.com/entry/jk-rowling-trolls-donald-trump-with-perfect-response-to-his-latest-tweet_us_5b3bf42de4b05127cced6695.

Sherlock, Ben. 2019. "Thor: Love And Thunder—10 Characters Valkyrie Might Choose As Her Queen." Screen Rant, August 11, 2019. https://screenrant.com/thor-love-thunder-characters-valkyrie-choose-queen/.

Shick, Michal. 2016. "*The Cursed Child* as Fanfiction, and Where the Problem Really Lies." *Hypable*, August 2, 2016. https://www.hypable.com/the-cursed-child-fanfiction-or-canon/.

Siddique, Haroon. 2013. "JK Rowling Publishes Crime Novel under False Name." *The Guardian*, July 14, 2013, sec. Books. https://www.theguardian.com/books/2013/jul/14/jk-rowling-crime-novel-cuckoos-calling.

Siegel, Tatiana. 2016. "'Batman v. Superman': Married Creative Duo on That R-Rated DVD, Plans for DC Superhero Universe." *Hollywood Reporter*, March 17, 2016. https://www.hollywoodreporter.com/news/batman-v-superman-married-creative-874799.

Siegel, Tatiana. 2017. "The Complex Gender Politics of the 'Wonder Woman' Movie." *Hollywood Reporter*, May 31, 2017, sec. News.

Silberg, Jon. 2000. "Community Access." *Variety*, December 18, 2000.

Singh, Anita. 2011. "JK Rowling Launches Pottermore Website." June 16, 2011, sec. Culture. https://www.telegraph.co.uk/culture/harry-potter/8579560/JK-Rowling-launches-Pottermore-website.html.

Sinnreich, Aram. 2010. *Mashed Up: Music, Technology, and the Rise of Configurable Culture*. Amherst: University of Massachusetts Press.

Slattery, Denis, and Chauncey Alcorn. 2016. "'Wiz' Kids! Potter Fans Scoop up New 'Book,' U.K. Play Opens." *New York Daily News*, July 31, 2016, sports final replate edition, sec. News.

Smith, C. Molly. 2017. "'Wonder Woman' Director Patty Jenkins Just Wanted to Direct a Hero Trying to Be a Hero, and We Love Her for That." HelloGiggles, June 2, 2017. https://hellogiggles.com/reviews-coverage/movies/wonder-woman-patty-jenkins-directing-hero/.

Smith, Kevin. 1999. "Kevin Protests 'Dogma.'" View Askew Productions, November 13, 1999. http://www.viewaskew.com/press/dogma.html.

Smith, Kevin. 2004. "Closing Time." View Askew Board, May 10, 2004. https://web.archive.org/web/20100716182143/http://www.viewaskew.com/newboard/messages571/3329.html.

Smith, Kevin. 2006a. "The View Askew WWWBoard—Welcome." View Askew, 2006. http://www.viewaskew.com/newboard/.

Smith, Kevin. 2006b. "My Boring Ass Life » The Red Bank Stash Signing: A Day That Will Live in Infamy." *Silent Bob Speaks*, August 8, 2006. http://silentbobspeaks.com/?p=272.

Smith, Kevin. 2010. "My Boring Ass Life » Thoughts Provoked by Reading the COP OUT Thread on the View Askew Message Board." *Silent Bob Speaks*, February 1, 2010. http://silentbobspeaks.com/?p=390.

Smith, Kevin. 2013a. *Tough Sh*t: Life Advice from a Fat, Lazy Slob Who Did Good*. New York: Penguin Publishing Group.
Smith, Kevin. 2013b. "My Boring Ass Life » IF YOU LIKE MY STUFF, THEN YOU LIKE WOMEN." *Silent Bob Speaks*, December 28, 2013. http://silentbobspeaks.com/?p=1016.
Smith, Kevin. 2014. "My Boring Ass Life » Of Bats and Walruses. . . ." *Silent Bob Speaks*, July 8, 2014. http://silentbobspeaks.com/?p=1087.
Smith, Russell. 2012. "S&M Sells." *Globe and Mail*, April 5, 2012, sec. the Globe Review Column; Books.
Snyder, Zack. 2017. "The World Has Lost a Master. Thank You for the Inspiration. You Changed My Life with Your Art. You Will Be Missed. #georgeromero #dotd." Tweet. @zacksnyder, July 16, 2017. https://twitter.com/zacksnyder/status/886740874918469633?lang=en.
Sobolewski, Samantha. 2014. "Batmobile Is Back in Black: Director Zach Snyder Tweeted a Picture of Bat-Man's Car after Unofficial Photos Surfaced Online." *The Gazette*, September 15, 2014, early edition, sec. Arts.
Sorrentino, Mike. 2019. "Disney Plus: A $13 Bundle with ESPN Plus and Hulu Takes on Netflix." CNET, August 8, 2019. https://www.cnet.com/news/disney-plus-streaming-service-release-date-price-shows-and-movies-to-expect-hulu-espn-plus-d23/.
South Burnett Times and Rural Weekly. 2013. "Does Comics Justice." July 5, 2013.
South China Morning Post. 2017. May 25, 2017, sec. Editorial/Content/Features/Life/Arts & Entertainment.
South Wales Echo. 2008. "*Doctor Who* Will Get Scary Says New Writer." *South Wales Echo*, August 4, 2008, first edition, sec. News.
Souza, Alison de. 2018. "*Black Panther* Raises the Bar." *Straits Times*, February 19, 2018, sec. Life.
Spiegel, Josh. 2018. "The Ascent of 'Black Panther' Director Ryan Coogler." *Hollywood Reporter*, February 15, 2018. https://www.hollywoodreporter.com/heat-vision/black-panther-ascent-director-ryan-coogler-1084901.
Staff, CBR. 2006. "Talking '300' The Movie with Frank Miller | CBR." CBR.com, October 26, 2006. https://www.cbr.com/talking-300-the-movie-with-frank-miller/.
Stanfill, Mel. 2017. "Where the Femslashers Are: Media on the Lesbian Continuum." *Transformative Works and Cultures* 24. http://journal.transformativeworks.org/index.php/twc/article/view/959.
Stanfill, Mel. 2019. *Exploiting Fandom: How the Media Industry Seeks to Manipulate Fans*. Iowa City: University of Iowa Press.
Star, The. 2017. "The Flash's Rough Ride to Go Solo." April 8, 2017, E1 edition, sec. Entertainment.
Steele, Anne. 2014. "J. K. Rowling's Mysterious Tweets: What Is She Hinting At?" *Christian Science Monitor*, October 7, 2014, sec. Books.
Stefansky, Emma. 2017. "Ava DuVernay Is Prepared to Surprise People With *A Wrinkle In Time*." *Vanity Fair*, October 8, 2017. https://www.vanityfair.com/hollywood/2017/10/ava-duvernay-unsure-audience-response-a-wrinkle-in-time.
Steger, Jason. 2012. "Bookmarks: HarperCollins Looks to the Future; the Lives of Publishing Phenomena; Banville Back in the Black; Fair's Fair in Melbourne; Amis and the Booker." *The Age*, July 7, 2012, sec. Life & Style; Books.
Stein, Louisa Ellen, and Kristina Busse. 2014. "Introduction: The Literary, Televisual and Digital Adventures of the Beloved Detective." In *Sherlock and Transmedia Fandom: Essays on the BBC Series*, 9–24. Jefferson, NC: McFarland.

Sternbergh, Adam. 2003. "Selling Your Sex Life." *New York Times*, September 7, 2003, sec. Magazine. https://www.nytimes.com/2003/09/07/magazine/selling-your-sex-life.html.

Stevens, Christopher. 2013. "After All the Hype, Mr Potty Mouth Had Better Be Good." *Daily Mail*, August 5, 2013.

Strachan, Alex. 2012. "Comic Book Men Is 'a Guy Thing'; New AMC Docu-Reality Series Follows Lives of Secret Stash's Clerks, Geeks." *Vancouver Sun*, February 11, 2012, final edition, sec. Arts & Life.

Straits Times. 2003. "Who Says They're Just for Kids?" November 7, 2003.

Strauss, Bob. 2001. "The Fat Guy Everyone Identifies With: As a Movie Director and as the Character Silent Bob, Kevin Smith Speaks for a Generation of Filmgoers." *Globe and Mail*, August 18, 2001, sec. Weekend Review.

Strauss, Bob. 2011. "Live Podcasts Inspire Filmmaker Kevin Smith." *Daily News of Los Angeles*, April 8, 2011, Valley edition, sec. L.A. Life.

Strauss, Bob. 2017. "Female Power." *San Gabriel Valley Tribune*, June 18, 2017, sec. S.

Streeter, Leslie Gray. 2018. *Palm Beach Post*, February 22, 2018, final edition, sec. Accent.

Stuever, Hank. 2012. "Kevin Smith Reality Show a Missed Opportunity, Reviewer Says." *Daily Gleaner*, February 11, 2012, sec. Business.

Sun, The. 2011. "Sherlocks Like a Nice Girl, Holmes." December 9, 2011, 1, national edition, sec. TV Biz; Features.

Sun, The. 2015. "*Sherlock* 'Upheaval.'" March 29, 2015, Northern Ireland edition, sec. News.

Sunday Tribune. 2011. "Sucker Punch Sucks." April 17, 2011, E1 edition, sec. Life.

Sunday Tribune. 2018. "Hot New Hero on the Prowl." February 11, 2018, E1 edition, sec. Life.

Swenson, Sarah O. 2017. "Representation in Film Matters." *Wetaskiwin Times Advertiser*, June 7, 2017, final edition, sec. Opinion; Making Swens of Things.

Taipua, Dan. 2017. "Thor and His Magic Patu: Notes on a Very Māori Marvel Movie." *The Spinoff*, October 31, 2017. https://thespinoff.co.nz/atea/31-10-2017/thor-and-his-magic-patu-notes-on-a-very-maori-marvel-movie/.

Terror, Jude. 2018. "Zack Snyder Is Releasing the Snyder Cut of *Justice League* as a Webcomic." Bleeding Cool, October 23, 2018. https://www.bleedingcool.com/2018/10/23/zack-snyder-cut-justice-league-vero-webcomic/.

thespec.com. 2016. "J. K. Rowling Announces 8th Harry Potter Book." February 10, 2016, sec. What's On.

Thomson, Desson. 2006. "What Makes the Director Click?; 'Clerks' Filmmaker Nurtures His Fans, and Himself, Online." *Washington Post*, July 13, 2006, final edition, sec. Style.

Tillet, Salamishah. 2018. "'Black Panther' Brings Hope, Hype and Pride: Movie Has Broken Sales Records before Opening." *Dayton Daily News*, February 16, 2018.

Times & Transcript. 2017. "*Wonder Woman*'s Gal Gadot Generates National Pride in Israel." June 8, 2017.

Todd, Ben. 2011. "Now *Doctor Who* Scares off Another 1 Million Viewers." *Daily Mail*, May 3, 2011.

Toronto Star. 2006. "The Pounding Patter of Silent Bob." July 23, 2006, sec. Entertainment.

Toronto Star. 2015. "Mitchell Suffered Brain Aneurysm." June 30, 2015, sec. TV.

Tosenberger, Catherine. 2008. "'Oh My God, the Fanfiction!': Dumbledore's Outing and the Online Harry Potter Fandom." *Children's Literature Association Quarterly* 33 (2): 200–206. https://doi.org/10.1353/chq.0.0015.

Townsend, Bob. 2006. "Slackers Do Grow Up—Don't They?" *Atlanta Journal-Constitution*, July 21, 2006, main edition, sec. Movies & More.

Travers, Peter. 1997. "*Chasing Amy*." *Rolling Stone*, April 4, 1997. https://www.rollingstone.com/movies/reviews/chasing-amy-19970404.

Truitt, Brian. 2012. "Kevin Smith Unleashes His Powers for 'Comic Book Men'; AMC Series Puts Pals on Camera." *USA Today*, February 10, 2012, final edition, sec. Life.

Truitt, Brian. 2018a. "'Black Panther' Could Be the Next Social 'Touchstone.'" *Dayton Daily News*, January 31, 2018.

Truitt, Brian. 2018b. "We Can Learn a Lot from 'Black Panther.'" *Dayton Daily News*, March 27, 2018, sec. Z.

Trumbore, Dave. 2019. "Zack Snyder Reveals Behind-the-Scenes Shot of 'Army of the Dead' as Filming Continues." *Collider*, August 12, 2019. http://collider.com/zack-snyder-army-of-the-dead-image/.

Tucker, Reed. 2010. "Silent Bob Strikes Back: When Kevin Smith's Got a Film to Hype, He Never Met a Feud He Didn't Like." *New York Post*, February 21, 2010.

Tucker, Reed. 2014. "Gone to Pot: His Standards Used to Be So Much Higher. Is Weed Killing Kevin Smith's Career?" *New York Post*, September 19, 2014.

Turk, Tisha, and Joshua Johnson. 2011. "Toward an Ecology of Vidding." *Transformative Works and Cultures* 9: n.p. https://doi.org/10.3983/twc.v9i0.326.

Tushnet, Rebecca. 2007. "Payment in Credit: Copyright Law and Subcultural Creativity." *Law and Contemporary Problems* 70 (2): 135–74. https://doi.org/10.2307/27592184.

Ugwu, Reggie. 2018. "The Stars of 'Black Panther' Waited a Lifetime for This Moment." *New York Times*, February 12, 2018, international edition, sec. Movies.

USA Today. 2017. "No Glass Ceiling Holds Back These Films We Can't Wait to See." *USA Today*, February 6, 2017, first edition, sec. Life.

Valenti, Jessica. 2017. "Did You Weep Watching *Wonder Woman*? You Weren't Alone: When so Many of Us Feel Powerless, Seeing the Extraordinary Power of One Woman Feels like a Cathartic Release." *The Guardian*, June 8, 2017, sec. Opinion.

Vary, Adam B. 2015a. "The Wachowskis Refuse to Take No for an Answer." *BuzzFeed*, February 5, 2015. https://www.buzzfeed.com/adambvary/the-wachowskis-jupiter-ascending-the-matrix-cloud-atlas.

Vary, Adam B. 2015b. "Joss Whedon Calls 'Horsesh*t' on Reports He Left Twitter Because Of Militant Feminists." *BuzzFeed News*, May 6, 2015. https://www.buzzfeednews.com/article/adambvary/joss-whedon-on-leaving-twitter.

Vermeulen, Caroline van Oosten de Boer, Milo. n.d. "About Whedonesque." Whedonesque. Accessed February 18, 2019. http://whedonesque.com/?read=about.

Vogue. 2019. "The Mister: E. L. James, Author of *Fifty Shades of Grey*, Has a New Book, and It's Probably Exactly What You Expect." January 24, 2019. https://www.vogue.com/article/the-mister-el-james-new-book-fifty-shades-of-grey.

walesonline Administrator. 2013. "Who's a New World Record Holder Then!" *Wales Online*, November 24, 2013, sec. What's On.

Walsh, Henry. 2018. "Have Disney Strike *Star Wars Episode VIII* from the Official Canon." change.org, 2018. https://www.change.org/p/the-walt-disney-company-have-disney-strike-star-wars-episode-viii-from-the-official-canon.

Walter, Stephen. 2017. "Steven Moffat Defends His Casting of Male Doctor Who as He Says: 'This Isn't a Show Exclusively for Progressive Liberals.'" *The Telegraph*, December 4, 2017. https://www.telegraph.co.uk/news/2017/12/04/steven-moffat-defends-casting-male-doctor-says-isnt-show-exclusively/.

Walters, Ben. 2005. "Simon Pegg Interviews George A. Romero." *The TOMB—Time Out Film*, September 8, 2005. https://web.archive.org/web/20070217113705/http://www.timeout.com/film/news/631.html.

Warner, Kristen J. 2015a. *The Cultural Politics of Colorblind TV Casting*, first edition. New York and London: Routledge.

Warner, Kristen J. 2015b. "ABC's Scandal and Black Women's Fandom." In *Cupcakes, Pinterest, and Ladyporn: Feminized Popular Culture in the Early Twenty-First Century*, edited by Elana Levine, 32–50. Urbana: University of Illinois Press.

Washington Post. 2018. "An Oscar Nod for 'Wonder Woman'?" January 15, 2018, Web edition, sec. News.

Waters, Darren. 2004. "Rowling Backs Potter Fan Fiction." BBC News, May 27, 2004. http://news.bbc.co.uk/2/hi/entertainment/3753001.stm.

Weintraub, Steve "Frosty." 2015. "The Wachowskis Talk JUPITER ASCENDING, Creating the Chicago Sequence, SENSE8, and More." *Collider*, February 4, 2015. http://collider.com/wachowskis-jupiter-ascending-interview/.

Weiss, Josh. 2017. "How Ryan Coogler Took a Deep Dive into African Culture to Make *Black Panther*." SYFY WIRE, December 28, 2017. https://www.syfy.com/syfywire/how-ryan-coogler-took-a-deep-dive-into-african-culture-to-make-black-panther.

Weiss, Sabrina Rojas. 2017. "Here's Why Ava DuVernay Wanted to Direct 'A Wrinkle In Time.'" Refinery29, July 12, 2017. https://www.refinery29.com/en-us/2017/07/163066/ava-duvernay-reasons-a-wrinkle-in-time.

Weist, Ellen Fagg. 2015. "Review: If Only There Were Shades of Nuance in 'Fifty Shades of Grey.'" *Salt Lake Tribune*, February 12, 2015, sec. News; Features.

Wells Journal. 2015. October 1, 2015, sec. News: Others.

Wendig, Chuck. 2018. "To Conclude: This Is Really Quite Chilling. And It Breaks My Heart. I Am Very Sad, and Worried for the Country I Live in, and the World, and for Creative People All around. Courage to You All. I Have a Dire Fear This Is Going to Get a Whole Lot Worse before It Gets Better." Tweet. @*ChuckWendig*, October 12, 2018. https://twitter.com/ChuckWendig/status/1050826821766393857.

Wenzel, John. 2018. "'Black Panther' Is Groundbreaking." *Denver Post*, February 16, 2018, Friday Scene edition, sec. Features.

Westbrook, Caroline. 2015. "Mallrats." *Empire*, October 14, 2015. https://www.empireonline.com/movies/mallrats/review/.

Western Mail. 2010. "Fans' Chance to Go on an Adventure with the Doctor." November 1, 2010, First edition, sec. News.

Western Mail. 2013. "The Doctor Can Never Be Bond or Bourne." March 23, 2013, 1; National edition, sec. Weekend; News.

Whedon, Joss. 2005a. "Joss Luvs Veronica." Whedonesque, August 11, 2005. http://whedonesque.com/comments/7502.

Whedon, Joss. 2005b. "No. 1 Fan Joss Whedon on "Veronica Mars."" ew.com, October 11, 2005. https://ew.com/article/2005/10/11/no-1-fan-joss-whedon-veronica-mars/.

Whedon, Joss. 2006. "Wonder Woman." Script. https://indiegroundfilms.files.wordpress.com/2014/01/wonder-woman-aug7-07-joss-whedon.pdf.

Whedon, Joss. 2007. "Let's Watch a Girl Get Beaten to Death." Whedonesque, May 19, 2007. http://whedonesque.com/comments/13271.

Whedon, Joss. 2018. "Well I Was Put in Twitter Suspension but Luckily There Was Also a Jock, a Weird Girl, a Socialite and a Rebel and It Turns out We're All the Same or

Something (?) Anyway They All Hooked up and I Had to Write This Tweet so I'm Not Sure, Trump Still Killing the Country Tho Lol." Tweet. *@joss*, April 6, 2018. https://twitter.com/joss/status/982411016997752832?lang=en.

Whedon, Joss. 2019. "We Have a Racist, Fascist President Who's Using Armed Thugs in Law Enforcement & Illegal Militias to Keep Us Cowed & Hopeless & He'll Take the 2020 Election by Armed Force & Blatant, Treasonous Criminality & That's Us Now, We're the Country with Concentration Camps so Happy 4th." Twitter, July 4, 2019. https://twitter.com/joss/status/1146904868185092097?ref_url=https%3a%2f%2fboundingintocomics.com%2f2019%2f07%2f09%2favengers-and-justice-league-director-joss-whedon-we-have-a-racist-fascist-president%2f.

Whedon, Joss. n.d. "Frequently (Soon to Be) Asked Questions." DrHorrible.com. Accessed June 13, 2012.

Whitehead, Deborah. 2013. "When Religious 'Mommy Bloggers' Met 'Mommy Porn': Evangelical Christian and Mormon Women's Responses to *Fifty Shades*." *Sexualities* 16 (8): 915–31. https://doi.org/10.1177/1363460713508904.

Williams, Joe. 2001. "Do-It-Yourselfer Kevin Smith Fills out His Jersey Universe." *St. Louis Post-Dispatch*, August 24, 2001.

Wilson, Adam. 2012. "Movie Review: *Cabin in the Woods*." *Barrie Advance*, May 8, 2012, final edition, sec. News.

Woerner, Meredith. 2017. "Director Wants to Let a Hero Be Herself: Patty Jenkins Keeps It Simple, Leaving Wonder Woman as Goddess, Protector of Love." *Toronto Star*, June 3, 2017, sec. Entertainment.

Woerner, Meredith, and Katharine Trendacosta. 2015. "*Black Widow*: This Is Why We Can't Have Nice Things." I09, May 5, 2015. https://i09.gizmodo.com/black-widow-this-is-why-we-can-t-have-nice-things-1702333037.

Woodmansee, Martha. 1984. "The Genius and the Copyright: Economic and Legal Conditions of the Emergence of the 'Author.'" *Eighteenth-Century Studies* 17 (4): 425–48. https://doi.org/10.2307/2738129.

Wu, Tim. 2008. "Fan Feud." *New Yorker*, May 5, 2008. https://www.newyorker.com/magazine/2008/05/12/fan-feud.

Yam, Kimberly. 2018. "New 'Fantastic Beasts' Trailer Spurs Debate Over Asian Character." *Huffington Post*, September 28, 2018, sec. Asian Voices. https://www.huffingtonpost.com/entry/new-fantastic-beasts-trailer-spurs-debate-over-asian-character_us_5bad1f92e4b09d41eb9f7c5a.

Yamato, Jen. 2017. "Making a Charge for Oscar Gold: 'Wonder Woman' Tries to Buck the Odds for Superhero Movies at the Academy Awards." *Los Angeles Times*, November 12, 2017, home edition, sec. Sunday Calendar; Calendar Desk.

Yang, Ling, and Hongwei Bao. 2012. "Queerly Intimate: Friends, Fans and Affective Communication in a Super Girl Fan Fiction Community." *Cultural Studies* 26 (6): 842–71. https://doi.org/10.1080/09502386.2012.679286.

"Zack Snyder." n.d. Urban Dictionary. Accessed September 29, 2019. https://www.urbandictionary.com/define.php?term=Zack%20Snyder.

"Zack Snyder Movies Profile." n.d. Metacritic. Accessed January 12, 2019. https://www.metacritic.com/person/zack-snyder.

Zanottie, Emily. 2018. "Joss Whedon Wants President Trump to 'Die, Don. Just Quietly Die.'" *Daily Wire*, April 4, 2018. https://www.dailywire.com/news/29075/joss-whedon-wants-president-trump-die-don-just-emily-zanotti.

Zax, David. 2014. "How Did Computers Uncover J. K. Rowling's Pseudonym?" *Smithsonian Magazine*, March 2014. https://www.smithsonianmag.com/science-nature/how-did-computers-uncover-jk-rowlings-pseudonym-180949824/.

תרצה. 2017. "Wow Can't Believe the Woman Who Wrote a Children's Book with Hook Nosed Banking Goblins Is Bad at Recognizing Fascism in Real Life." Tweet. *@kateljacobson*, August 18, 2017. https://twitter.com/kateljacobson/status/898729319324762112?lang=en.

Index

Abbington, Amanda, 16
Abrams, J. J., 157, 161
Academy of Motion Picture Arts and
  Sciences, 79, 147–48, 157, 159
Affleck, Ben, 65–68, 82
African American Film Festival Releasing
  Movement (AFFRM), 159
Agyeman, Freema, 17
Akerman, Malin, 117
Alexander, Julia, 44
Allen, Jeff, 70
AMC, 74, 81
American Foundation for Suicide Prevention,
  121
American Splendor (2003), 129
Anderson, Jeff, 85
Anelli, Melissa, 47
Angel (television series), 88, 89
Ant-Man and the Wasp (2018), 145
Aquaman (2018), 123, 155
Army of the Dead (film), 123–24
Arrow (television series), 78
Astonishing X-Men (comic), 87
Avatar (2009), 154
Avengers, The (2012), 87, 92, 98, 132, 148, 154
Avengers: Age of Ultron (2015), 87, 106, 132,
  148, 154
Avengers: Endgame (2019), 132, 148
Avengers: Infinity War (2018), 132, 148

Barker, Meg, 35, 36
Barnes, Henry, 98
Barrucci, Nick, 77
Barthes, Roland, xiv, xvi, 50
Batgirl (2021), 95
Batman (comics), 83–84
Batman (franchise), 111
Batman: Cacophony (comic), 75
Batman Begins (2005), 111
Batman v Superman (2016), 77, 108, 110,
  111–12, 115, 119, 121, 123, 138, 154
Beachler, Hannah, 138
Berlanti, Greg, 78
Berman, Shari Springer, 129
Berry, Halle, 129
Bigelow, Kathryn, 130–31, 157
Birds of Prey (2020), 146
Bitten by Twilight (Click/Aubrey/Behm-
  Morawitz), 19
Black Cat (comic), 134
Black Panther (2018), 126, 128–39, 142–44, 146,
  147–48, 154
Black Widow (2020), 146
Blade (franchise), 130, 137
Blodgett, Bridget, 112, 119
Boden, Anna, 145
Book Club (2018), 35
Borgia, Danielle, 36
Boseman, Chadwick, 138
boyd, danah, 102

Boys, The (television series), 123
Breakfast Club, The (1985), 102
Brummitt, Cassie, 43, 46, 49
Buffy the Vampire Slayer (1992), 95
Buffy the Vampire Slayer (television series), 88, 89, 91, 94, 96, 100, 104
Bunch, Sonny, 130
Burton, Tim, 75
Busse, Kristina, xii, xviii, 4

Cabin in the Woods (2011), 34, 98
Cage, Nicolas, 75
Cameron, James, 139, 154
canon, xi, xvii, xix, 12, 40, 43, 44–47, 50–51, 53–54, 62, 69, 105, 108–10, 118, 148–49, 151, 161
Capaldi, Peter, 6–7, 14, 17
Captain America: Civil War (2016), 138
Captain Marvel (2019), 127, 145–46, 161–62
Captivity (2007), 90
Carlin, George, 76
Carter, Lynda, 127–28
Casual Vacancy, A (Rowling), 58
Catwoman (2004), 129
Cavill, Henry, 109
Chasing Amy (1997), 62, 64, 65–66, 75, 84
Chen, Ming, 70–71, 81
Chernin, Peter, 92
Chibnall, Chris, 15
Chin, Bertha, 73
Christopher Robin (2018), 138
Clerks (1994), 62–64, 68, 70, 75, 82, 84, 97
Clerks: The Animated Series, 62, 63, 68
Clerks II (2006), 62, 68–69, 72
Clerks III (film), 85
Cloak and Dagger (television series), 160
Clockwork Orange, A (1971), 116
Cochran, Tanya, 91
Cole, Kai, 97, 105
Comic Book Men (television series), xx, 74–75, 80–81, 84
comic books, xx, 62, 75, 83, 87, 98, 107, 110, 113, 118, 125–26, 128, 132, 136–37, 144, 157, 160. *See also individual comics franchises*
Coogler, Ryan, x, xvi, xxi, 11, 24, 126–29, 131–39, 142–46, 147, 149, 154, 157; politics, 139, 143, 146
Cop Out (2010), 76

Cosby, Bill, 116
Coupling (television series), 7–8, 13, 16
Coyle, Richard, 8
Creed (2015), 128, 136, 138
Cruel & Unusual Films, 109, 124
Cumberbatch, Benedict, 15–16
Curry, Arthur, 123
Cuthbert, Elisha, 90

Damon, Matt, 67
Daredevil (comic), 75
Dark Knight, The (2008), 111, 130, 160
Dark Knight Rises, The (2012), 111
Davies, Russell T., 4
Dawn of the Dead (2004), 113
Day, Felicia, 104–5
DC Comics, 62, 75, 79, 113, 133, 140
DC Extended Universe (DCEU), xii, 79, 95, 111–12, 119–24, 127, 129–33, 137, 149, 155, 157, 160
DC television universe, 78–79
Degrassi (television series), 61
Depp, Johnny, 55
Devil's Rejects, The (2005), 90
Diary of a Teenage Girl, The (2015), 129
Disney, 138, 142, 152, 157, 160
Divergent (2014), 141
Doctor Who (television series), xix, 3–18
Dogma (1999), 62, 66–68, 74–75, 79
Dollhouse (television series), 88, 92–94
Downey, Robert, Jr., 128
Doyle, Arthur Conan, xix, 4–6, 12
Dracula (2020 television series), 18
Dr. Horrible's Singalong Blog (2008), 88, 98, 103–5
Dumezweni, Noma, 50–51, 54
Dushku, Eliza, 94
DuVernay, Ava, x, xxi, 24, 32, 128, 133–34, 138, 145, 150, 156–60; political approach, xxi, 150, 158–60

Ebert, Roger, 64–66
Edelstein, David, 90
Edwards, Chandler, 152
Ellis, Warren, 83–84
Evey, Kim, 104
Ewell, Dwight, 65

fan auteur axis, xvi–xvii, 3, 21, 39–40, 47, 61, 108, 127–28, 148–49
fanboys, ix–xi, xiii–xx, 8, 21, 23, 34, 62–69, 74, 76–83, 87–88, 93, 95–100, 106, 107–8, 112–19, 124, 125–27, 147–62; curatorial, xix, 4–5, 11, 70, 98; toxic, 108, 112–13, 116–17; transformative, 70, 98, 148
fandom, x–xix, xxi, 4, 6, 8–9, 22, 32–34, 37, 40–42, 61, 67, 70–76, 83–85, 89, 98, 100–106, 108, 111–12, 124, 125, 128, 145, 148–51, 154; affirmational, xi, xvi, 108, 148–49; transformational, xi, xvi, 148–49, 154, 158
fan fiction, xix, 5, 8, 19–20, 22, 26–29, 31, 33–34, 40, 41–42, 46, 47, 52–54, 98–99, 148, 154–55
fangirls, x, xix, 20–25, 30–34, 38, 39, 41, 98, 104, 149–51, 154, 156–57, 161
Fantastic Beasts and Where to Find Them (2016), xx, 41, 44, 46, 54–57, 154
Fantastic Four: Rise of the Silver Surfer (2007), 157
Fate of the Furious, The (2017), 157
Feige, Kevin, 145
feminism, xx, 79, 89, 91–98, 105–6, 119–20, 140–41, 149
Fifty Shades of Grey (film franchise), 23–24, 131
Fifty Shades of Grey (novels), xix, 13, 19–20, 25–37
Fiorentino, Linda, 67
Firefly (television series), 88
Fisher, Ray, 120
Flanagan, Walt, 74
Flash, The (television series), 61
Fleck, Ryan, 145
Ford, Rebecca, 125
Foucault, Michel, xiii
Fountainhead, The (Rand), 108–10, 117, 118–19, 122
Freeform, 160
Freeman, Martin, 16
Frozen (2013), 132
Fruitvale Station (2013), 136, 138
Furious 7 (2015), 131

Gadot, Gal, 123, 129, 138, 140
Gaiman, Neil, 17
Game of Thrones (television series), 124
Gatiss, Mark, 5–6, 11, 16, 18

geek culture, x, xiii, xvi, xxi, 27, 69, 100, 107, 112, 117, 119, 150
gender, x–xii, xvi, 6, 14–17, 22, 24, 25–32, 34–37, 39, 55, 64, 79–82, 88, 91–94, 96–97, 105, 114, 116–17, 120, 126–36, 139–46, 147, 151, 155–61; misogyny, xx, 16, 18, 66, 79–82, 89–91, 93, 96, 108, 116–17; politics, 14, 16–17, 25, 88, 141–42
Get Out (2017), 134
Ghostbusters (2016), 26, 120
Gibbons, Dave, 111
Gillan, Karen, 14
Goyer, David, 115
graphic novels, 107, 114, 121
Gray, F. Gary, 157
Gray, Jonathan, xiv–xv
Green Arrow (comic), 75, 78
Green Book (2018), 148
Green Hornet, The (2011), 77
Grint, Rupert, 50
Guardians of the Galaxy (franchise), 57, 152–53
Guggenheim, Marc, 78
Guild, The (web series), 104
Guinness Book of World Records, The, 84
Gulliksen, Zoë A., 81
Gunn, James, 57, 152–53, 159

Hall, Anthony Michael, 102
Hamill, Mark, 68
Hancock (2008), 129–30
Hanshaw, Billy, 9
Harrington, Ellen, 5
Harris, Neil Patrick, 104
Harry Potter (franchise), xvi, xix, 31, 39–45, 99–100, 151, 154; fan websites and podcasts, 41–42, 45–47, 54; politics, 56, 58
Harry Potter and the Cursed Child (Rowling/Thorne/Tiffany), xx, 40–41, 44, 50–54, 55
Harry Potter and the Deathly Hallows (Rowling), 41
Harry Potter and the Deathly Hallows Part 2 (2011), 148
Harry Potter and the Goblet of Fire (Rowling), 44
Harry Potter and the Philosopher's Stone (Rowling), 41
Hartley, John, xiv

Hartnell, William, 5
Hawking, Stephen, 14–15
Hayward, Amanda, 31
HBO, 106
Hellekson, Karen, 22
Heller, Marielle, 129
Hemsworth, Chris, 138
Hills, Matt, 3–6, 12, 73
Hitchcock, Alfred, 94
Hodson, Christina, 146
Holland, Travis, 40, 50
Holy Terror (Miller), 113
Howell, Charlotte, 93
How I Met Your Mother (television series), 101
Hudson, Tim, 104
Hulu, 160
Hunger Games, The (2012), 141

Inside Man (2006), 18
Iron Man (2008), 129
I Will Follow (2010), 156

James, E. L., ix, xvi, xix, 13, 19–38, 127, 149, 151; engagement with fans, 22, 32; politics, 25
Jamison, Anne, 27, 30–31, 34
Jane Got a Gun (2015), 137
Jay and Silent Bob Reboot (2019), 84–85
Jay and Silent Bob Strike Back (2001), 62, 68–69, 79–80
Jenkins, Henry, xii, 42, 70
Jenkins, Patty, ix–x, xxi, 10, 24, 93, 113, 125–42, 145–46, 149, 157–59
Jessica Jones (television series), 160–61
JKRowling.com, xix, 40, 42–43
Johansson, Scarlett, 98–99
Johnson, Bryan, 74, 80–81
Johnson, Derek, xii–xv, 95
Johnson, Rian, 161
Jones, Bethan, 25, 33, 72
Jones, Leslie, 26
Jordan, Michael B., 136
Josie and the Pussycats (2001), 129
Juola, Patrick, 49
Jupiter Ascending (2015), 154–56
Jurassic World (2015), 132
Justice League (2017), 106, 108, 111, 115, 117, 120–21, 123–24, 133, 151

Kalil, Dua, 89–90, 92
Kaplan, Deborah, 129
Kavanaugh, Brett, 153
Kennedy, Kathleen, 161
Khosla, Proma, 43
Kim, Claudia, 55–56
Kim Jong-un, 141
King, Martin Luther, Jr., 157
King, Stephen, 58
Kingsman: The Secret Service (2014), 24
Kingston, Alex, 16
K-19: The Widowmaker (2002), 131, 157
Kreisberg, Andrew, 78
Kripke, Eric, ix, 123
Kubrick, Stanley, 116
Kurtz, Benjamin Derhy, xiii

Last Photograph, The (2017), 123
Leaver, Tama, 103
Lee, Jennifer, 132
Lee, Spike, 133
Lee, Stan, 61, 64, 76
Legend of the Guardians: The Owls of Ga'Hoole (2010), 114–15
Legends of Tomorrow (television series), 78
L'Engle, Madeline, 157
Lin, Justin, 157
Linklater, Richard, 76
Lolita (Nabokov), 27
Lord of the Rings, The (franchise), 61, 62, 69
Lowery, David, 138
Lucas, George, 61, 76
Luke Cage (television series), 130

Mackie, Pearl, 17
MacLaren, Michelle, 130, 137
Mallrats (1995), 62, 63–64, 69, 74–75, 83, 84
Man of Steel (2013), 108–9, 115, 118, 121, 123
Marr, Barnard, 18
Marston, William Moulton, 140
Martin, George R. R., 24, 150
Marvel Cinematic Universe (MCU), xii, 61, 63, 87, 119, 123, 128–32, 134, 136–38, 142–43, 146, 149, 160–62
Marvel Comics, 62, 75, 153
Marwick, Alice, 30, 102
masculinity, 108–9, 118–19, 155; toxic, xx, 13, 113, 116, 118–19, 126, 155

Master of the Universe (fan fiction), 19–20, 33–34
Masters of the Universe: Revelation (television series), 79
Matrix, The (franchise), 153–56
Matrix Reloaded, The (2003), 154
Mayer-Schonberger, Viktor, 47
McCloud, Scott, 114
McDormand, Frances, 159
McLeod, Dion, 40, 50
Mendelson, Scott, 57
Meteor Man, The (1993), 130
Mewes, Jason, 79, 84
Meyer, Stephenie, 20, 28, 31–32, 34
Middle of Nowhere (2014), 156
Miller, Frank, 109, 113, 115
Miramax, 63, 68, 77, 82
Mirren, Helen, 14
Mister, The (James), 37–38, 149
Moffat, Steven, ix, xvi, xviii–xix, 3–18, 22–23, 26, 127, 149; politics, 13; relationship with fans and fandom, 4–9, 11–13
Momoa, Jason, 123–24
Monster (2003), 125, 133, 134, 137, 159
Montgomery, Lauren, 129
Moore, Alan, 111, 116
Moore, Nate, 142
Moore, Ronald D., ix, 40
Morissette, Alanis, 66
Morrison, Grant, 111
Morrison, Rachel, 138
Mosier, Scott, 74
Much Ado About Nothing (2012), 98, 101
Muntean, Nick, 101

Nagenda, Tendo, 142
Nakagawa, Chiho, 36
Nelson, Diane, 119–20
Netflix, 79, 106, 123, 124, 130, 160
Nevers, The (television series), 106
New Gods (film), 133, 157
Newsies (1992), 101
Nolan, Christopher, 111, 115, 118, 119, 160

O'Neal, Shaquille, 130
100, The (television series), 150

Pack, Scott, 29–30
Pebler, Luke, 72

Pedowitz, Mark, xii
Peele, Jordan, 134
Perry, Alex Ross, 138
Peterson, Anne Helen, 101
Pete's Dragon (2016), 138
Phillips, Tom, 70
Phillips, Whitney, 12
Portman, Natalie, 145, 162
Pottermore, xix, 40, 41, 43, 44–47, 49
Prince-Bythewood, Gina, 133–34
Producers Guild of America, 141

race and ethnicity, x–xii, xvi, xx, 17, 26, 41, 45–46, 50–51, 54, 55–56, 64–65, 79–80, 88, 91, 106, 113, 128–31, 133–34, 137–46, 148, 151, 157–60
Radcliffe, Daniel, 50
Raiders of the Lost Ark (1981), 76
Raimi, Sam, 118
RAINN, 71, 82
Rand, Ayn, 108–9
Random House, 20, 31–32
Ratner, Brett, 140
Red State (2011), 72–73
representation, 15, 17–18, 51, 54–55, 66, 68–69, 92, 106, 127, 139, 142–45, 158, 161
Rhimes, Shonda, 151–52
Rickman, Alan, 67
Riefenstahl, Leni, 110
Road Warrior, The (1981), 116
Roberts, Nora, 37–38
Rocky (franchise), 128, 136
Roddenberry, Gene, xiii–xv, xvii, 61
Rodriguez, Gina, 151
Romance Writers Association, 27–28
Romano, Aja, 29
Romero, George, 107, 113
Rosenberg, Melissa, 160
Rowling, J. K., x, xvi, xix–xx, 24, 39–59, 103, 122, 145, 149, 151; relationship with fans, xix–xx, 41–43, 49, 52, 57
Runaways (television series), 160

Salter, Anastasia, 112, 119
San Diego ComicCon, xi, 10, 19, 22, 65, 85, 100, 120, 123, 146, 162
Saturday Night Live (television series), 145
Saw (2004), 90

Scorsese, Martin, 109
Scott, Suzanne, ix–xi, xv, 40, 72–73, 106
Searchers, The (1956), 116
Sedgman, Kristy, 52
Selma (2014), 157, 159
Serenity (2005), 88
sex, xix, 7, 13–15, 17–18, 21, 26–30, 35–38, 42, 65, 75, 79–80, 88, 97, 107–8, 122, 140–41
sexual orientation, xii, xx, 15, 45–46, 54, 56–58, 66, 79–81, 93, 95, 144–45, 150, 152, 160; asexuality, 15; homophobia, xx, 15, 41, 54, 80; transphobia, 58
Shawver, Michael, 138
Sherlock (television series), 4–8, 10–11, 15–16, 18
Shick, Michal, 53
Silver & Black (unproduced film), 133–34
Silverman, Greg, 135
Silver Sable (comic), 134
Simpsons, The (television series), 100
Smith, Kevin, ix, xx, 22, 34, 61–85, 87, 97, 98–99, 103, 111, 122, 149, 151; politics, 79–80, 82; relationship with fans, xx, 7, 33, 70–71, 73; writing comics, 75–78
Smith, Matt, 14
Smith, Will, 129–30
SModcast podcast, xx, 74–75, 85
Snipes, Wesley, 130
Snow Steam Iron (2017), 122
Snyder, Deborah, 16, 109, 112–13, 124
Snyder, Zack, ix–x, xvi, xx–xxi, 13, 23, 61, 76–77, 79, 107–24, 126–27, 133, 137, 138, 149, 151, 153, 154, 155, 160; engagement with fans, xx–xxi, 108; politics, 122
social media, xvii–xxi, 7–9, 18, 25–26, 37, 39–41, 43–44, 50–52, 55, 56, 57–59, 62, 69, 80, 84, 88, 89, 94–96, 101–2, 104–6, 108, 113, 118–24, 136, 138, 139, 140, 148–53, 157, 159–61; Comicsgate, 125–26, 133; #Gamergate, 25, 120, 150; Instagram, 122; #MeToo movement, 37, 55, 97, 141; trolls and trolling, 11–13, 25, 47, 67–68, 71–72, 149, 152; Twitter, xix–xxi, 7–8, 25–26, 37, 40–41, 43–44, 50–52, 56, 57–59, 80, 84, 88, 89, 94–96, 101–2, 104–6, 108, 113, 118–22, 124, 136, 138, 139, 140, 150, 152–53, 157, 159; Vero, 121–22, 124, 151; YouTube, 9, 104
Solo: A Star Wars Story (2018), 131
Sony, 134

Southwest Airlines, 72, 82
Spiderman (comic), 64
Spielberg, Steven, 4, 76
spoilers, 11, 41, 52
Stanfill, Mel, xi, xiii, 15, 40, 46
Stargate (franchise), 154
Star Trek (franchise), xii, xiii, xv, 80
Star Trek Beyond (2016), 157
Star Wars (franchise), xii, 57, 61, 62, 63, 65, 69, 76, 116, 120, 131, 132, 148, 157, 161
Star Wars: A New Hope (1977), 63
Star Wars: Return of the Jedi (1983), 63
Star Wars: The Empire Strikes Back (1980), 63
Star Wars: The Force Awakens (2015), 148
Star Wars: The Last Jedi (2017), 161
Steel (1997), 130
Stein, Louisa, 4
stereotypes, 18, 29, 35, 56, 94, 108, 113, 116, 130, 143, 149
Stern, Howard, 76
Story, Tim, 157
Sucker Punch (2011), 108, 112, 115, 116–17
Suicide Squad (2016), 108, 117, 153
Supergirl (television series), 61, 78
superheroes, 21, 57, 62, 77, 83, 98, 103, 109, 111, 115–16, 118, 123, 125–36, 141, 145–46
Superman (franchise), 125, 153–54
Superman Lives (Smith script), 75

Talalay, Rachel, 129
Tank Girl (1995), 129
Tarantino, Quentin, 70, 109
Taylor-Johnson, Sam, 23–24
technology, 28–32, 49
television, 3, 61, 97, 135, 137, 150. *See also* individual television shows
Tennant, David, 14
Theron, Charlize, 137
This Is the Life (2006), 157
Thomas, Rob, 100
Thompson, Tessa, 145
Thor (comics), 128
Thor (2011), 144
Thor: Love and Thunder (2022), 145, 162
Thorne, Jack, 40, 51–53
Thor: Ragnarok (2017), 126, 128, 134–35, 143–44, 154
Thor: The Dark World (2013), 137

300 (2006), 109–10, 113–14
Through the Looking Glass (Carroll), 58
Tiffany, John, 40, 51, 53
Titans (2018), 160
Townsend, Robert, 130
toxic masculinity, xx, 13, 113, 116, 118–19, 126, 155
transmedia franchises, x–xviii, xx, 39, 41, 62, 69, 70, 74, 76–79, 85, 87, 89, 104, 147, 149–50, 154, 161
Trooperclerks (2000), 70
Trump, Donald, 58–59, 102, 141, 143, 152, 159
Tushnet, Rebecca, 53
Twilight (franchise), 19–21, 25, 27, 29, 31, 34, 35–36, 91

Valenti, Jessica, 140
Vander Ark, Steve, 47
Varley, Lynn, 113
Veronica Mars (television series), 72–73, 99–100
Vertue, Beryl, 16
Vertue, Sue, 16–17
View Askewniverse, xx, 62–69, 70–71, 74–76, 80–82, 84, 99, 151
violence, xx, 26, 90–91, 108, 113–17, 124, 126, 139

Wachowski, Lana, 153–56
Wachowski, Lilly, 155–56
Wachowski sisters, xxi, 127, 150, 153–56, 160
Waithe, Lena, 159
Waititi, Taika, x, xvi, xxi, 126–29, 134, 137–39, 143–46, 149, 162; politics, 139, 144, 146
Wan, James, 124
Warner Brothers, 46–47, 56, 110, 119, 121, 123, 125, 131, 133, 135–36, 138
Watchmen (2009), 107, 111, 114, 115, 117, 121
Watson, Emma, 50, 51
Wayne, John, 116
Weinstein, Harvey, 77, 81–82, 116
Wendig, Chuck, 120, 153
Whedon, Joss, ix, xx, 3, 13, 34, 55, 61, 62, 75, 76, 78, 79, 87–106, 110, 115, 119, 120, 122, 126, 149, 151, 154; engagement with fans, xx, 7, 88, 100–105; politics, 88, 96, 101–2
Whedonesque weblog, xx, 88–92, 94, 99, 100–103, 105–6, 151
Whitehead, Deborah, 35

Whittaker, Jodie, 15
Wolf Creek (2005), 90
Wonder Woman (2009), 129–30
Wonder Woman (2017), 108, 111, 117, 125–42, 144–46, 154, 157–59
Wonder Woman (Whedon script), 88, 93, 94–95, 103
Wonder Woman 1984 (2020), 131, 140, 141, 146
Wong, Lena, 47
Wrinkle in Time, A (L'Engle), 157
Wrinkle in Time, A (2018), 138, 157–58
Writers Guild of America, 103
Wuornos, Aileen, 137

Xena: Warrior Princess (television series), 89

Yates, David, 56

About the Authors

Anastasia Salter is an associate professor of Games and Interactive Media at the University of Central Florida. They are the author of *Toxic Geek Masculinity in Media* (Palgrave Macmillan, 2017, coauthored with Bridget Blodgett), *Jane Jensen: Gabriel Knight, Adventure Games, Hidden Objects* (Bloomsbury, 2017), *What is Your Quest? From Adventure Games to Interactive Books* (University of Iowa Press, 2014), and *Flash: Building the Interactive Web* (MIT Press, 2014, coauthored with John Murray).

Mel Stanfill is an assistant professor with a joint appointment in the programs of Texts & Technology and Games and Interactive Media at the University of Central Florida. Mel's research has been published in venues such as *New Media and Society*, *Critical Studies in Media Communication*, and *Cinema Journal*, and a book, *Exploiting Fandom: How the Media Industry Seeks to Manipulate Fans*, published by the University of Iowa Press.

www.ingramcontent.com/pod-product-compliance
Lightning Source LLC
Chambersburg PA
CBHW030621230426
43661CB00053B/2094